THE ONLY SOLUTION FOR INDIA

THE ONLY SOLUTION FOR INDIA

Bharatiya Lok–Jan Tantric Government

Pandit Om

KALPAZ

ISBN: 978-81-7835-973-1

Price : ₹ 715

First Published 2013

Published by

Kalpaz Publications
C-30, Satyawati Nagar,
Delhi - 110052
E-mail: kalpaz@hotmail.com Ph.: 9212142040

Laser Typesetting : Rajender Vashist, Delhi
Printed at : G. Print Process, Delhi

Cataloging in Publication Data--DK
Courtesy: D.K. Agencies (P) Ltd. <docinfo@dkagencies.com>

Pandit Om.
The only solution for India : Bharatiya lok-jan tantric government / Pandit Om.
p. cm.
Includes index.
ISBN 9788178359731

1. Representative government and representation--India.
2. India--Politics and government. I. Title.

DDC 320.954 23

Dedicated to
My late Parents

'Even if *108 Annas, 558 Kejariwals* and *1008 Ramdevs are born* in all corners of India simultaneously, there could be no system change much less transformation of governance until baffled populace, concerned intelligentsia, involved elites and young generation as an 'Article of Faith' read this book, *presenting a whole structured integrated systems approach to governance* - not only for India but the world at large'.

Contents

Preface

As it is the product or produce
but the marker and producer,
So is the man greater and powerful not the Laptop,
mobile or computer.
Similarly by using the terms supreme or fundamental
under the Constitution
No one becomes so, not even the Constitution,
Which was encted and adopted by
Fundamentally Supreme Sovereign People of India,
Who can still make, unmake or replace it.

India has never, after coming into force of the Constitution in 1950, been in such a flux economically, politically, socially, morally, ethically, administratively, judicially as it is today; not even during Chinese and Pakistani aggressions. This book for the first time and for all times to come provides an integrated solution, a whole panacea the only remedy to such pessimistically sunken state and chaotically anarchic disintegrative misrule. Author believes that it is neither the volume nor the numbers but the issues and the quality of a work that matter with the readers and for the society. Poet Valmiki composed only one Epic '*Ramayan*' and Gandhi ji only wrote 'The story of my Experiments with Truth' also known as 'My Biography' in short '*My Experiments with Truth*'.

This book would come as ultimate saviour to Indian polity when Anna Hazares would have failed, Ramdevs fallen, Kejarivals isolated and all experiments of governance - absolute majority, two third majority, limited party coalitions, huge multi party coalitions, mixed economy, capitalistic economic system, free economy, technocracy, bureaucracy and professionalism had shattered all hopes, expectations and dispositions of the people. There are no piecemeal solutions for India now as that would make boil cancerous. The model of governance and draft of the Constitution presented in this book only could rescue the nation and bring the people of India out of their miseries, misfortunes, sorrows, wretchedness of misrule, afflictions of bad governance and distresses of system for ever. Not only for the people of India but with the new awakening, for the people of corrupt democracies or autocracies of the world budding and bidding for democracy, the book presents a perennially inbuilt model of government and governing system that they may call their own, assuring the world at the same time clear of autocratic dictatorships and bloodshed.

The book, based on the shaking experience and working of present Constitution and Parliamentary form of Govt. in India, the torments, agonies, curses, anguishes of and excesses on the people since 1950, endeavors to present a structured module, a wholesome holistic model of governance, a unified egalitarian entity of the people for the people by the people. The proposed form and system of governance is the only solution for all problems of India and many other countries may it be corruption, crimes, injustice – excesses - unfairness, suppression - repression, poverty, starvation, hunger, depression – recession, exploitation, atrocities, immorality, unethicality, depravity, plundering, looting, instability, stagnation, unemployment, dilapidation, chaos – anarchy – indiscipline, deception –dishonesty - disloyalty to people and the country including rebellion, cession, treason, treachery whatever.

Unlike other books so far written giving piecemeal solutions to problems, this book presents the whole solution, a systems approach to all the problems of the people and the country which is 'Bhartiya Lok - Jan Tantric System of Governance' (Bhartiya Loka Jana Tantric Shasan Vyavastha / Paddhati), the only solution for India that is moving towards lawlessness state of no – return. Under the system there shall be elected Prime Minister and Deputy PM for the country and Chief and Deputy Chief Ministers for the States. There shall also be an Appellate Court of India and time bound justice delivery system with vicarious liability of Govt servants including Referendum on national or general issues, cumulative punishment, summary trials for corruption – rape etc., unicameral legislatures for the states and unemployment allowance or insurance and so many others. Thus, the book not only attempts to bell the cat which everybody else was hesitant or pondering-who first and how, but is also an invitation to legal community for debate.

At first the author thought it futile to write a book of this nature and present such alternatives before the people of a country where blood has become water. But propelled by inner conscience and impelled by some invisible power to realize the pity of the very people and at least put before them a concrete, ideally viable alternative, a model, a proposal, an option which they have been waiting for long for salvaging their destiny and laying down the impregnable foundation of governmental system for the country but for ignorance and want of vision could not visualise or conceptualise the form and give it a shape. This book is therefore a unique effort to exhort the conscience of the general masses, intellect of the wise, energies of the educated youth and drive of young generation to pause, ponder and rediscover India of their dreams i.e., of Suraaj, Paradise or 'Jannat' meaning a perennial panacea for all their sufferings, sorrows, torments, miseries, distresses, tortures and agonies.

As the book reflects *Vox Populi* and is therefore *Vox Dei* expressed as 'Janata Janardan' in Hindi' it needs no certificate, testimonial or forwarding for authenticity and validation. It presents 'Bhartiya Lok — Jan Tantric form of government' and with a modified Constitution before the people of the country, otherwise known as the Presidential Form of Government in the politico – Constitutional world, that visualises India of everybody's dream fulfilling the cherished desires, long awaited hopes and meeting heartfelt cravings. This book in fact manifests people's inner imaginations of good governance i.e. Suraj and Su – Shasan, called 'Good Governance' their only Vision.

The greatest thing about this model is that although it forms only part of the whole still would constitute the Soul the 'Aatman' of the whole Constitution and hopefully be simulated by the countries of the world in due course for checks and balances of governmental power, built - in mechanism for restoration of systems together with a participative democracy, a republic in action, a polity with effective and strong federal functioning.

This book may be a store house for brainstorming - for any people, any country. If however, that intellectual debate springs from US, UK or Canada it would go wild in India within days bringing the change within couple of years that would otherwise have come in or after more than ten years.

The book is in simple language to be intelligible to all throughout the length and breadth of the country, amongst the general masses of India not so conversant with English, easy for a person in the streets to understand from Malada (Bengal) to Khagaria (Bihar), Phek (Nagaland) to Tura (Meghalaya), Lathi (Guj) to Parui (Ker), Hinkara (TN) to Deval (Uttarakhand), Leh (J&K) to Puh (HP) apart from cosmopolitans of Delhi, Chennai, Kolkata, Mumbai, Bangalore, Hyderabad - without going into grammatics, dictionaries and linguistics. The readers; author expects, would only draw the essence, tenor, meaning, and intent of the work written for transformation of their lot along with the country. The book is least concerned with style or literature but only with the loftiness of the purpose to be achieved, something great for the people and the country.

This is entirely a new dimension of thinking on people's frustrations, depressions, anxieties, vexations, distresses and corrupt politics of bad governance of the country. Radical problems require radical remedies. Therefore, there is only one perennial solution for India and her people - to change the present form of government and go for the new system of governance called 'Bhartiya Lok — Jan Tantric Paddhati' rather than Presidential Form with a modified Constitution as suggested here in.

The author on July 2010, a week before the Parliament session, sent a write up through the Chairman RS (Rajya Sabha) and the Speaker LS (Lok Sabha) addressed to all members supposed to represent peoples 'General Will', on the unconstitutionality of perpetuation of 'Reservations' but in vain. Earlier in June he had sent it to various Newspapers representing the 'will' of the vested interests, therefore, naturally fell in deaf ears. The shock greatest, the thunderbolt was, when Uttarakhand High Court also did not hear the Writ Petition (filed in the nature of Public Interest Litigation) in June 2012 after spending so much money, making humble requests with complete communicating Mobile numbers apart from address. Five copies were sent to HC wherein Union of India and State of UK were made parties. In addition the copies of WP were sent to three Judges of HC separately. They had no courtesy even to inform the petitioner on such an important constitutional issue of general public import and national importance raised for the first time after 1950. Disappointed, the author could not dare file two more WPs - one against 'Ramdev' involving the question of interpretation of limit and extent of fundamental right to freedom of religion. Whether Constitution give freedom of destroying the established philosophies, norms, notions, concepts and ethos forming part of a religious entity since time immemorial and replacing it / them by one's own under the veil of teaching and preaching religion to ignorant people and followers of that religion while in fact the same amounts to destroying the very fundamentals of that religion as recognised under the Constitution. Second, against State of Uttarakhand, whether civil right of any caste or castes could exist in any primordially deontological religious place or places of cardinal epistemological existence for usurping the income of such places in contravention and derogation of the fundamental right of other citizens to equality of opportunity, employment and livelihood particularly when such places have been declared national heritage by the State therefore constituting societal ownership and common assets.

After reading this book government employees hopefully, would realize true meaning of the term Public Servant and government service. This is for the first time since independence that a book is so crisply reminding the masses, the wise, the intelligentsia and the youth of their sovereign power not only of routinely throwing a political party or parties out of governmental power but the power of transforming the very systems of governance and the Constitution. This is something like Jamvant - the monkey venerable - reminding Hanuman of his strength, capacity, capability and power of crossing the ocean.

Hindi Version of the book is also at the offing, possibly to make the system change and *jnan* (gyan) of Constitution, a movement throughout the country. It has been written in English in the first instance only to make aware that class which matters in shaping public opinion as well as the class which frames policies, interprets laws – Constitution, executes and administers but is convalescing under the misconception that they could befool all people all the time. Let them all understand and very clearly, that they are there till people desire them to be there for their own governance and no more. People have collectively delegated their power to different wings and organs of state to make it good governance for their welfare, people friendly, smooth, corruption - crimes free and work for general well being and not for managing by mismanagement, chaos, anarchy, *'gundagardi'*, *'Dadagiri'* and bad governance.

The question however remains why this state of chaos, anarchy, injustice, immorality, unethicality, exploitation, trafficking, arbitrariness, whims, loot, violence, plundering – laundering, Mafiosi highhandedness, corruption, indiscipline, lawlessness, favouritism, nepotism, disrespect, inhumanity, and crime? The answer is inherent in the question. How many out of 125 crore and odd people of India, heard the word 'Samvidhan' or Constitution, not even 25%, and how many have seen it, is perhaps less than 5% and the percentage of those who read is not even 1%. How big again a paradox it is that 50% Netas in India could not write or spell Constitution and 50% could not even 'Samvidhan'.

After the proposed change even ordinary people would know Constitution, at least 'Samvidhan' as they know

Ramayan, *Mahabharat*, *Gita*, *Koran*, *Bible – Testaments*, *Avesta* or *Guru Granth Sahib*, *Tripittak* or *Purvas* and *Angas*. The biggest maddening question would however remain - 'How many people know what the Constitution is, how much have they read it, how many understand it, how many could interpret it and how many discover it ?

With the proposed change not only would people know Constitution but also their absolute collective constitutional supremacy that Constitution is enacted and adopted by them for their own good governance not vice versa. Present Constitution was neither enacted nor adopted by the people nor even ratified by their elected representatives, hence this ignorance and apathy amongst them.

'A servant would remain a servant and could never be the master', would be realised by the government employees including Legislature, Judiciary, and Executive once people get awakened of their power.

Constitution is not law is one thing but it is not even Supreme law as taught by western jurists and not at all a set of rules as being taught by CBSC to class IV students in India. Constitution in one word is the 'SHASTRA' - the Scripture codified by the people through 'Sovereign General Will' for their good governance, materially exhilarating well being and exalted blissful earthly life through a systematic disciplined National Government. In this view Constitution could never be interpreted against the interests of the general public who founded it on the principle that individual interests will surrender to general interests and group interests will subjugate to common will while collective national interests will supersede both. Being the source of all laws and source of power of all Wings and Organs of government it must in the event of conflict or dubious meaning be interpreted in favour of public and the people and not in favour of government or government machinery.

Now, therefore, there is only one option before the people - dying as animals whole life or living like dignified humans and valued citizens forever. With this change certainly people will have to not go to administration for societal service or personal work, instead administration would come running to their doorsteps begging, which would be real constitutional 'Suraaj', equal and just society in action, government of the people for themselves in fulfillment therefore by the people.

We may do whatever, debate twenty four hours, put everything on fire, destroy all property, trains, planes, ships, buildings, buses, bridges, kill and loot all, go to courts, appoint Commissions, form Committees, resort to Naxalism, Maoism, throw out party in power, vote others or combination of parties, commit suicide, demonstrate, strike or even sabotage or take recourse to chaos, rebellion, terrorism, media pretensions or subversions, channel - cinema hypocrisy nothing would change in the country, no improvement at all, unless the system of governance and the Constitution are changed, changed by the people in a democratic manner, consciously and quickly.

Thirst, hunger, want and disease of masses, shrieks and screams of poor, pain and sorrows of common people, nudity of deprived, porn of big, incest of rich, vanity of moneyed, ostentations of wealthy and dilapidation of general public could never be removed with this form of governance and lego-judicial system.

Dissatisfaction amongst MPs even after three fold salary increases, Commonwealth games loot, 2G scandal, Coalgate plundering, land loot, food scams and spoilages, floods, inundations, sex exposition and consequent rapes and crimes, nude display of riches and naked conspicuous consumption exposes bankruptcy of governance more than anything else. Bhopal gas scandal, fodder – food grain scandals, wheat – sugar – land scams, cricket gyps, corrupt – easy - cheap black money, the reign of terror and Mafiosi are only drops in the ocean. The Ocean of malignancy, evil vileness of sins and base avarice is unfathomable, the height of dissipated dissoluteness and depth of loot of people's money and plundering of wealth of the country has no limits.

Present organised governing gangs in India have reversed the 'Sky is the Limit Theory' of western management. Here they see cosmos as the limit forgetting that it is heading towards a 'Big Crunch' making only the earth as the bottom and upper limit. Time awaiting to hit without any warning and without making a hiss even.

Under present lego – judicial functioning in India good has surrendered to bad in the name of law and justice while virtues have given up to evil in the name of fairness and constitutionality, both in turn creating a lego - Constitutional anarchy in the name of Constitutional functioning. As bad money drives away good money so have bad people driven away good people from political governance scenario of India. State has become madly despotic; Governance dumb, administration deaf, justice lame, governments irresponsibly blind, Netas cruelly corrupt and businesses basely exploitative. It all appears a free for all Mafiosi Raj, a return to primitive 'Jungle Rule'- the survival of the fittest - "The Killing Instinct" that westerners taught us. Therefore, no change much less any improvement could be brought under present Constitutional system, what of 'Transformation'. Therefore, the need without any loss of time is for brainstorming at all levels and national debate for system transformation and enacting and adopting a modified Constitution as proposed in this book.

If not today, after 5 - 10 years, India will have to go for such Constitutional model. After all it took Gandhi ji 1915 to 1947 transforming India and roughly 47 years if the period spent in South Africa is included. With that will come to an end the evils of governance, ills of system, sins of human follies and weakness of Constitution together with caste - class feuds, communal strifes, belligerency, rebellion, violence, rage, inland terrorism, separatist tendencies, Maoism and Naxalism.

However, with this, knowledge the cognition of one's true and correct history emits the fragrance and touching emotionality. Such blend would inspire the sense of dignity infusing morale and self respect making this land a Paradise – the '*Swarga - Zannat*' in real sense.

Finally the author is obliged to his son Prabhakar who arduously helped in the completion of the book by typing, comparing and correcting including suggesting improvements particularly training the author in Computer applications.

Author finds this the opportune time for publishing the book iron being hot and country mentally prepared for yet another change, people awaiting transformation and an alternative model. Author left no stone unturned to find a Publisher in India, disappointed he tried in USA and when the process was at final stages with couple of publishers, author still continued looking desperately for publisher in India and was fortunate to have come in contact with Gyan Book Publishers who in their magnanimity recognised the potential, promise and importance of the subject and deriving essence thereof agreed to publish the book encouraging the author against all odds and disappointments in fulfilling the cherished social and national objectives, in fact inviting people of India achieve their treasured wishes never to repent again. Author has no words to thank the Entrepreneurs of Kalpaz Publications and the team of specialists, experts and intellectuals they have, but expresses heart sprung gratitudes, real and genuine in giving marvellous standard to the book. Author hopes to have stood to the expectations of general masses of India and treads to thank the fellow countrymen in advance guessing he may have succeeded in putting an alternative genuine model of governance before the countries and people of the world as well.

Pandit Om

1

Why India Needs Change

Need for Change

India has, just within a period of sixty six years reached such an incorrigibly impermeable state of ravaged politico - economic and moral – ethical depravity that has cynically perplexed common man more than the intelligentsia and mugwumps, former being the largest contributors to the prosperity of the country. But instead of having biggest share in the growth, wealth, affluence and fortunes they are the greater sufferers of this depravity, decadence, degeneration and turpitude. This is because as they are instead being exploited as a resource inanimate and inert. This really is a baffling state, unintelligible, incomprehensible and irreconcilable to all except the corrupt, criminals, fallen, pseudo rich, neo elites, debased politicians and power wielding money hungry, wealth laundering - dude governing clique. These manipulators of people's convictions and looters of national wealth have, unfortunately been dominating the political scene. They have done it not by compassion, wisdom, vision, statesmanship and governing acumen, morality and ethics, but by the dint of same corrupt money power – politics, caste rigmarole. This is coupled with muscle power and crimes backed by superstitions of Bhartiya psyche blended with absolute ignorance, illiteracy, meekness and tolerating nobility of Indian polity.

We never perhaps had a situation of the type where even God fears to tread, leaving it entirely on the people to find their own remedy for their problems and sorrows and invent panacea for own miseries and plights of misfortunes once for all. HE has already during the last 1000 years given us so many chances to learn and mend but we have neither learnt nor are perhaps ready to learn any lesson from history. Therefore HE also is no more inclined to incarnate, hence, the greater need for reading forgotten history once again to equip and prepare ourselves for yet another change, not simply a change but Transformation'.

भूल गये तो फिर पढ़ो भारत का इतिहास
क्यों सदियों सदियों रहे भारतवासी दास

(If forgotten - read again the history of India, why Indians were slaved for centuries)

Though God is great and will always be merciful still HE would not even according to 'Shastras' incarnate for next couple of lacs years. Therefore people of India will have to find their own perennial remedy out of this nauseated predicament by "Changing the Constitution and the form of governance" in a democratic way, that is perhaps what God also desires.

Anybody who thinks, there could be one single solution for all the ailments and problems of India under the present anarchical chaotic situation may be living in a 'fool's paradise'. There is nonetheless, one single solution, for all the problems of people and ailments of the country and that is 'Changing the form of government and the Constitution'. Transforming present system of governance to either 'Bhartiya Lok – Jan Tantric' or Presidential form but with a new Constitution. The only way to save the people and the country of the present incorrigible imbroglio. This seems to be perhaps the last opportunity to redeem. More so, when in flagrant contravention of the Constitution the government has under the pretext of Liberalisation and free economy brought in the western '*laissez faire*'. The 'Directive Principles of State Policy' have been shelved to enable this. These constitute the vision of the people of India for their future. In other words the State has destroyed the basic structure of the Constitution second time by stealing the very dream of the people of India. First time it was by

42nd Constitutional Amendment in 1976 when the 'Preamble' of the Constitution (The Kashi) constituting the Mission Statement of the people of India, was amended incorporating 'socialist secular' there in. (Kashi according to Bharatiya Pauranic mythology is said to be on the Trident of Lord Shiv – beyond the limits of this earth. So is the 'Preamble' beyond the provisions of the Constitution therefore beyond the amending power of Legislature and State). The Preamble could only be amended or changed by the people of India through referendum and by none else.

With the experience of the last more than sixty six years, it could, very well be said that only the proposed Constitutional transformation to 'Bhartiya Lok Jan Tantric' or Presidential form of governance with a new Constitution could bring the long awaited qualitative change in the life of the people and polity of the country. The proposed model would prove not only a panacea, but an idealistic answer to existing stinking and sinking system of governance, a living misery for more than 70 per cent of citizens of the country. The Parliamentary form of Govt. having utterly failed to deliver and is rather now proving a dead weight on the half fed, hungry, starving populace.

Enough of talking; now is the time for acting. Legal, judicial, legislative and administrative systems have completely been desecrated and vilified. There is no way out to absolve people of the shackles of hunger, poverty, exploitation, loot, plunder, launder, oppression and liberate the country of the load of crimes, corruption, social chaos, administrative despotism, judicial anarchy and injustice. Above all is the complete system failure and mismanagement of governance overshadowed by heartless Netas and insensitive judiciary. This is in fact openly raping the people in unison and kidnapping the future of India.

Unless, therefore, the system of Governance and the Constitution are changed and changed radically there could never be liberation from present atrocious yoke of terror, brutality, injustice, hunger, poverty, squalor, disease, unemployment, despotism of governance, colossally vicious administration, monstrous cruelty of Netas, blindness of law and mercilessness of judicial administration.

Frustrated with present conditions of the country many people seriously concerned with, cry out of emotions mixed with anger and anxiety asking for hanging the corrupts, black marketers, adulterators, criminals and terrorists or demand enacting strictest laws and severest punishment to culprits including looters, abductors, rapists, plunderers of national wealth and in that rashness at times plead for dictatorship or army take over. But 'Easier said than done'.

By the way no such person or for that matter any person, has ever come with tangible, plausible and concrete proposals for good governance of the country, as how to radically ameliorate the situation much less transform. India has maximum number of laws in the world, at every step we have one, now numbering over perhaps 15000. Every action of ours is under legal lense, still we are one of the most corrupt, dishonest, and fraudulent, badly governed criminalised countries of the world where laws are made more for contravention just to shut the mouth of people rather than for compliance. Therefore India has today become a haven for all monsters and paradise for all demons exploiting the weaknesses of our lego – judicial system combined with 'Netagiri' oriented parliamentary form of vote politics, not of good governance, that has failed and utterly failing to deliver. Judiciary has distorted the constitution and the laws. She is in their activism encroaching upon the jurisdiction of other wings and has practically brought the system at the verge of a parallel constitution and governance therefore to collapse, without any results much less fruitful, visible gains to masses not at all. If the situation continues, the governance would very soon come to a practical stand still with all sufferings only to the people again. The country is in fact moving towards a legal anarchy courtesy - Judiciary.

Punishing even by capital punishment as many people suggest, for every offence, is neither possible nor a lasting solution unless we transform the system as a whole. After all there are sizeable numbers in every society, equally in communism that are not afraid of any punishment including capital. The fact of the matter remains that under the pretext of all pervasiveness Judiciary has usurped the power creating a parallel constitution through the cobweb of case laws that has resulted in utter confusion, mist and obscurity in functioning of the system itself. In the pretence of interpretation of laws and inferring intention of the Legislature, courts have played and playing the role of super Legislature undermining the elected representative body of the people that represents their Sovereign General Will. This is a different matter that the body has over the period lost its credibility being dumped by scoundrels. These Netas not only brought bad name to the temple of 'Vidhayika' but to the country and the people who elected them and who such representatives represented. Therefore the system as it stands today has brought the whole governance at its nadir.

People of the country are too naive to understand all this. If judiciary herself violates the constitution and exceeds her constitutional limits, only God could save the country. Nothing fruitful whatsoever is likely to come out of present system whatever we may do. There is no possibility of any good to the people as nothing radical is likely to happen in a conservatively modeled administrative and judicial system based only on Westernized Bhogvad called Hedonism in other words.

In the first place, politicians themselves are now hardly interested in doing something concrete to their masters the sovereign people of the country. They are so engaged in game playing and playing politics or otherwise busy in other pursuits that they have little time to think of the people who voted them to power, what of country; not at all for human development index. Otherwise, the Directive Principles of State Policy, even the 'Preamble', the Vision and the Mission of the people i.e. the constitutional obligations of the state, constituting basic structure thereof, would have not been discarded and bumped in the oblivion so easily under the impact of Western Bhogvad. Whatever politicians do today, they do, keeping their political ends in mind. If by chance anything good for the people is attempted or acted the same stands interfered with by Judiciary. Such interference has not in any way proved beneficial to the masses resulting neither in to apparent good governance nor tangible amelioration of condition of the people or the nation. Otherwise so much of interference and activism would have established Ram Rajya long ago or brought Suraj by now. Things have rather worsened badly. Painfully, Judiciary has failed as much, as politicians in discharging her duties to the people of India who made this constitution for themselves for their wellbeing and service by state functionaries. Judiciary in the fulfillment of her egoistic displays and other interests including flaunting protection of Fundamental Rights served the interests of big businesses, elites and criminal, corrupt classes. Unfortunately, all functionaries of state think themselves as the bosses of people and people as their servants. They least realise that collectively and constitutionally people were their masters and they all servants to serve the very people in whom vests the sovereign power even to change this constitution and snatch or limit or circumscribe all such powers and authority these functionaries boast of.

People, otherwise, also collectively represent the voice of God as says a Latin proverb rightly 'Vox Populi Vox Dei' and therefore could make or mar theirs as well as country's future the same way as gods and nature could, but people have not yet unfortunately realised their that power which they now need to realise as within them rests the inherent power of transforming the face of the country and their own fate. The day people realise their powers, their sovereign power of changing the form of Government and Constitution, all the functionaries of government, organs of state and wings of administration would start realising their real places in the hierarchy. The people need to know that any constitution democratically made including this constitution is made by them for their own good through good governance including welfare and humanistic living and have appointed all functionaries for their service not for bossism.

The public is none else but the people of India, the real bosses, the repository of all powers, who have but for their ignorance, superstitions and illiteracy been reduced to the status of slavery, exploitation, suppression and excesses.

Therefore, unless people are ready for a paradigm shift in governance, there is no possibility of any change in their condition, life, well being and fate and they would continue to curse themselves, their fate and gods for their sufferings while in fact they would be suffering for their sins of not realizing their power and need for change. Present constitution has become a mockery and our laws puppets in the hands of corrupt, criminals, rich moneyed and rascal bureaucrats as well as politicians including Judiciary and we the people of India are suffering for our sins as well as theirs i.e. suffering doubly.

In fact, all Constitutions in a democracy are meant for people for themselves, therefore whenever there are two opinions or interpretations possible or there is any ambiguity in the meaning of the provisions the one in favour of the people collectively or masses in general or as citizens of the country shall be accepted and not that in favour of government or any wing, organ of the state or functionary of government including government servants.

Under the present circumstances the way things have worsened, there is one and only one solution, a permanent solution for all ailments of India and problems of people for all time to come and that is replacing the present Parliamentary form by Presidential form or Bhartiya Lok Jan Tantric form with a new Constitution. This is the only one democratic weapon left in the hands of people now to save the country and save them for perpetuity.

The present parliamentary system, aped primarily from our erstwhile masters the British, has defiled the governance as the government 'of power brokers and scoundrels for' corrupts and criminals though in both the cases authenticated by the people, thus unfortunately making democracy a 'Mobocracy', a situation incredibly appalling and awfully filled with dangers. Experience has shown us in no uncertain terms that merely a right to vote would not make a democracy - government of the people and for the people or Swaraj with Suraj of their dreams. Had voting changed anything politicians would have abolished it also long ago. Had voting changed anything the system would have not worsened worse than erstwhile foreign despotic rule.

The conditions as they now exist in India could make it easier for people to act than think, which only needs somebody - a Leader - to come forward or otherwise a collective leadership will emerge. Transformation would be possible only by action rather than by mere contemplation, day dreaming or 'Bhashanas' (speeches). If the people of India particularly the youth apply not these remedies as proposed in this book, they will have to be ready to face more evils worse than the present ones, waiting ahead, and by the time the time teaches, everything would have been lost and that would be the calamity.

Let all of us now be sure that just as a panther would not change its spots, cobra venom and crow colour, the Netas, administration and the system would not change its modus operandi, colours and nature of functioning , therefore, more the need for immediate, radical changes. Generally, a change even though, from worst to best, appears inconvenient initially, but the youth having ability of understanding could act as a catalyst in bringing this change for betterment. After all, the wind of change is blowing throughout the world and so within the people of India. We find along with the economic order of the world economics of India has been changed to the starvation of people and pauperising of masses let same people and masses change politics and political order to make that economics easier. Ultimately, it is the happiness of society, human development, and well being of masses and prosperity of the country, which is the end of all governances. We have been taught that in modern Bhogvad (materialistically economic) world there could be no other happiness and development greater than 'economic', let people therefore act to achieve the same democratically in time rather than atone later. People today have only the right to vote but not it's counting, which is equally important for good governance to succeed. People have presently no right to judge the performance of their Netas and government or recall their elected representatives and elect new ones, except once in five years unless there is midterm poll. In political landscaped genre of India Netas have taken people as crowd (*bheed*) the same way as Babas - Gurus –Swamis – Sanyasinis have taken them simply as sheep (*bhed*). Netas and government functionaries busy exploiting the crowd and bloody Dharmic Karmkandis bullying the sheep. Politicians systematically robbing Peter to pay Paul, plundering the nation, the masses and siphoning it off those on whose support they remain captured to and retain power i.e. the criminals, capitalists, marauders, corrupt and Mafiosi. Once the kings and queens built their palaces and paradise on the ruins of people the present day government butchers on the bones of same people. If however, things continue, as at present people will find no more their bones for butchering.

Countries of the world had two or at the most three cheers for democracy we already had four in 1947–1950 and 1952 and 1977 and fifth the last is awaiting which would be complete the moment People of Bharat opt for 'Bhartiya Lok - Jan Tantric Vyavastha' or Presidential form of governance with a new Constitution. Let the youth of India therefore, sagaciously awaken, apprise and back the masses against the classes before the sinking middle and lower middle classes sink further along with already sunk poor class and with that sinks the democratic system.

The floods of money gushed into the politics today have become the biggest pollutants and pollutions of democracy in India as well as the world. It is therefore time for us; when bad men combine, good must unite else they would fall one by one. We all have therefore either to bang together or we shall all be hanged separately.

Politics has now become too serious a matter to be, left to the politicians alone. In India, it is a marathon not a sprint as here political language is designed to make the lies sound truthful, murder respectable and even dirty lies appear pure truth. Everything morally, ethically, and humanly evil and wrong has been made politically right. Therefore, sooner the political parties break up, the better. There has in fact been something radically wrong with us right in the beginning immediately after freedom, when we collectively left undone those things which we ought to have done, and done those things we ought not had done. There could be no place now, in 21st century democracy for the people with medieval exploitative mindset, corrupt culture, caste orientations, feudal psyche, snob behaviour, unprincipled practices, whimsical dispensation of justice and archaic laws with unconstitutional inequality galore.

The New Constitution would not only open the opportunity for the masses to move towards a new, rich, powerful, great humanitarian society but make them recognise their sovereign power of not simply electing the governments but changing even the constitution and the system of governance. The reflection of that power itself would change entire administrative spectrum making the Sahibs of present day India the real servants of the people. The failure of Parliamentary form of governance has clearly demonstrated that we are accustomed either to the dictatorial Kingships or to despotic imperial rule which has somewhere blended in our blood over the years.

However, we have now either to choose Bharatiy or Presidential form of governance or perish because freedom and slavery could be mental states but not equality, justice, prosperity and welfare; which are physical states and could only be assured and ensured under a radically new system of government. Even a slave, when resolves not to remain a slave, his chains fall to show the way to others. Such liberty then accompanied by equality would not simply mean the freedom of denouncing the system of governance but the freedom of governing the system itself. Present parliamentary form takes care neither of law and the system nor allows people to take care of them. People had for the first time, though partly, realised their power of changing the government in 1969 yet fully only in 1977. Thereafter, changing governments became normal for them. Now what remains is changing the form of governance and the constitution. The moment they realise this power, the country would need no more laws for governance, as everything would be so smooth, systematic, complete, and accurate flowing automatically as flow of water. The impact of mere realization of that power itself would be as great on present system of governance as unimaginable.

Under new Constitutional system freedom would not be liberty for the perverted, debouched, depraved and erotically vulgar. It would be but really precious respecting others more than the self, sharing and enjoying discipline not an indisciplined encroaching nuisance. Under the proposed system of governance politics, power, authority, and money could not be used for committing crimes, fraud or exploiting people. In it law will govern as King of Kings in its true spirit. Today criminality, corruption, Dadagiri, and injustice are better organised in India than morality, ethics, justice, and law. Freedom would mean duty to others, accountability to society and responsibility to nation and dignity to oneself - as the British even when alone formed an orderly 'Q' of one.

We are perhaps the only people in the world who have not learnt from the history, not at all from the history of past 1000 years therefore the question of drawing lessons for future has also not arisen. In fact, happy would be the people of America, West and Europe whose historical annals have been blank. Let us now learn to live for a short period like a tiger than 100 years as a sheep. We the people have inherent sovereign power as well as constitutional authority to have the form of government and constitution we want and have a government for our fulfillment, accomplishment, and actualisation and for getting what we want and wanting to be. Much of our political – economic – legal - administrative and social confusions come from the fact that we know neither what happiness is nor how to obtain it, what the Constitution is and how to change it and have a form of government and constitution we want to have. Neither Dharma nor science could find the remedy for this apathy of human beings towards themselves or of human beings to human beings. Time has now come for us to decide and decide firmly our future and future course of action. Neutrality only helps the oppressor never the victim. Silence encourages the tormentor never the tormented. Let us therefore decide and decide finally to go for Presidential Form with a new constitution else we may call it 'Bharatiy Paddhati', if we really want to live magnificently, live like human beings a dignified life as equal citizens of a free country.

People of India otherwise have two other options also Dictatorship or Gandhism. Possibility of Gandhi to be born under present Bhogvad culture of Epicureanism is impossibility for next one thousand years. Dictatorship is neither possible in India nor could ever be thought of as that would be the last straw. Otherwise also the experiences of dictatorships in the world have been precariously deadly resulting ultimately in the establishment of democracies. Asia and Africa are its best examples, of late Arabian Peninsula. But the example of new president Musari elected after such bloodshed is abhoring as against his sweeping usurpation of power the judiciary of the country had to call national wide strike. Such person deserves only hanging. India had the painful tortuous experience of hundreds of cruel, brute, barbarous dictatorial Rajas and Ranis for thousands of years, which also we have forgotten so soon. Perhaps the present Bhogvad culture of competitive cut throat and killing instinct is leading us to the same direction of individualism where there is only disintegration whether of families, society even the country.

Ultimately the aim, object and purpose is establishment of Suraaj, which would come only by changing the present parliamentary system to Presidential with a new Peoples Constitution that we may also name 'Bhartiya Lok Jan Tantric form'.

Four Main Problems and the Root Cause

India has four main problems (1) Population Explosion - the root cause of all other problems (2) Rampant Corruption – the rootage of unbridled crimes, chaos and indisciplined anarchy (3) Failure of Legal and Judicial system - the primary etymon of all crimes, injustice, inequality, misrule, corruption, exploitation, evils and (4) Black Money that has resulted in system failure.

Therefore as deep rooted the ailments of governance and systematic the evils of corruption, crimes, misrule, bad governance etc as deep and systematic need to be the remedy, not piecemeal but holistic reforms to curb the evils of governance. This would rekindle the convictions of the young and destroy the cynicism of old for which the only solution is to change the form of Govt and appreciably modify the Constitution on the lines suggested in this book.

Population

Population has, over the period unnecessarily become a politico - religious issue. Unfortunately, communalism and casteism rather than becoming the causes for economic growth and strength for the country have reactively become the main cause for population growth which has now crossed 120 crores. Communalism and casteism have so complicated the already complicated problem that there seems no possible escape much less a solution for controlling it except restoration of people's confidence, faith, and trust in the system of governance. Legal – illegal immigrations from other countries have added fuel to the fire. Until population remains a problem, no permanent solution to other problems could ever be possible with present corruption levels. Netas have already lost the sight of and are not in a position, in fact have no guts, morale, or moral force addressing people of the gravity of darkness before and the need for controlling it without any more waiting. Any solution to any problem with such vast and ever increasing population would only be adhoc as all the solutions after a period would become ineffective and almost equal to zero. This would not however mean that if we have to die one day we should swallow poison right now. We have to find solutions collectively and the lasting one would come only with the changing of system of governance and the constitution under which citizens would become entrepreneurs to own the problems of the country as theirs and accept social accountability to ensure real democracy in action.

Corruption, Crime, Black Money

Corruption has become such an explosive problem that has surpassed even the problem of population explosion. It is as big a problem perhaps bigger than the environmental pollution or global warming that has polluted the entire body politic of the countries as pollution has life. Population despite being the biggest problem could be made into strength but corruption remains a threat always and could never become strength as it swallows even the biggest national assets and wealth inside without a belch. There is corruption not because we are poor but we are poor because of corruption. The reasons for and behind corruption include our greed, avarice, self centeredness, fallenness, covetous acquisitiveness, mean narrowness, western life style born false display and reprehensible cupidity. But for corruption India has the capacity to sustain just double of the present population at the existing levels of life standards, living style and general well being. Corruption has within such a short period eaten up the very vitals of the country and impoverished the people to such an extent that given the chance everyone would prefer leaving the country and go outside and perhaps with them those corrupts also to corrupt the same people once again. Corruption has made people forget 'Janani Janm bhumi', patriotism, Seva, commitment to society and love for mother land i.e. Desh Bhakti as it was called once upon a time.

Corruption has hollowed the country and the general masses from within, weakened their morale and moral, zeroed them ethically and would kill if they do not awaken now as there could be no time as right as the present one. Given the resources at the present level, Land, capital, human power, wealth, assets, means and strengths the country has the capacity to sustain just double i.e. 250 crore population at the same level of life style but for corruption. We have come to a situation of worse than that of British Raj. British looted us, exploited us because they were our foreign masters and we their subjects but our own governing system has proved worse making and taking our own people our worst enemies.

The people who are supposed to be the masters dejure and rulers defacto in a democracy have been, reduced to indigence by their servants under the dint of governmental authority and power. What a pity - servants looting the master and master is helpless. What a paradoxical dilemma? Are not these servants terrorists? Are not such Netas traitors? Are not they in combination killers? Terrorists assault with their weapons directly and sever the head or shoot people dead while these empowered corrupt – criminal terrorists hit the stomach of the hoi polloi (populace) every day, play with their livelihood every time and snatch their morsel depriving their children of bread, medicine, clothing, education, shelter, safety – security thus killing the populace by slow poisoning now - a situation worse than that of terrorist attack. These looters hit indirectly from the back as an enemy using the economic weapon, the weapon meant for the wellbeing of the people and development of the country. Where had India been today had there been no corruption is an imagination beyond imagination?

This single system failure of governance and the constitution is the biggest amongst all and sufficient for changing the system preferably to Bharatiya Lok Jan Tantric or Presidential form with a new constitution. This is also the biggest mockery of judicial - legal system, administration and governance that all of them have become not only burden on the people but counterproductive as well. This is the example how servants could reduce their masters to penury and country to paupery. This we also find in everyday life at micro levels in one or the other family throughout the country. There is unfortunately no remedy for under the present constitutional, administrative, legal system. Whatever we had has been messed up by judicial system leaving absolutely no chance even for slightest betterment and improvement. If it has not happened until today, it would not happen at all in future because it is multiplying in so many folds every moment. Neither legislature would dare bring nor would judiciary allow any reform in judicial-lego system, the root cause of all corruptions. Netas have become as corrupt as never tired of chanting "Jai ho Judiciary ki" and this is what Judiciary exactly wanted – to prove her supremacy, none interference in its alleged absolutism under the pretext of all pervasive power of justice next to gods. But this sycophancy has neither left justice nor just - judges any more. Meanwhile the sovereign Janata, the masters of the Constitution and creator of all these institutions for their wellbeing and good of the nation has become sandwiched in between.

The most unfortunate has been the tendency of usurping the Executive - Legislative power by Judiciary and even going into the constitutionality of the constitution resulting indirectly again in to a parallel Constitution undermining the power of the legislature the repository of people's faith in democracy thus amounting to an indirect challenge to the sovereignty of the People. If Netas are bad and corrupt or criminals and the Parliament is not the temple of democracy but is bad and corrupt, it is only an institution.

Under present constitutional system aped on the lines of Westminster Parliamentary governance, even prior to the age of so called coalitions, one corrupt to dislodge another from corridors of power. They compromised and conspired with so many corrupts and conspirators making it a never ending process that has now reached an incorrigible ebb. This is what ultimately even Ramdev the self styled Yog god man did to save his skin in the name of the people and the country the same way as political scoundrels have done and doing whether belonging to Treasury or opposition whosever beginning historically with Nazi Hitlerian Germany that was on top. So rightly says Arvind Kejariwal they are all one from inside.

While corruption has hollowed India from within, crimes have corroded her from without and population appears a burden only because of these two. Finding solution to all the problems including above ailments at one time might appear a joke to some, mockery to others, and impossibility to many while ridiculous absurdity to common man. However, if something could be a joke it could also be magic. All absurdities of yester years have become realities of today. Similarly the absurdity of today could also be a reality of tomorrow. Impossible could become and has in fact become possible in this word itself. In fact the word 'possible' also finds place in dictionary only after 'impossible'.

All these problems have cumulatively made India chaotic, anarchic, indisciplined, exploitative, unsafe, criminalised, and corrupt. Governance and justice remaining silent, Netas and police became accomplices resulting into a situation of things being decided on the roads, by force or violence. If people take law in their hands they are accused, if they ask for justice, they are refused. The better course for the people therefore would be to have a system change where law would come at their doorsteps without asking for, and the system would take care of everything in a just manner. Situation in India worsened more because government and judiciary were engaged in bouts with each other, abdicating their duties and shifting blame on each other. People got entangled in between. The uncalled for interference and blame game resulted in fear psychosis of punishment demolishing the principles of separation of power and bringing passivity in governance. None having time realize the plight of the people. Inordinate delays in judicial decision making and justice delivery resulted in grave injustice compelling people to lose faith in the system and more on the governance that ultimately shook the credibility of legal – judicial system and judges as well.

In a country like India, with an uncontrolled population of over 120 crores, increasing faster than in any other country, to increase faster in future. It ranks but around 100th in human development index or human economic wellbeing, having 80 % corruption, even internationally estimated around 70 %, such state of affairs, amounts to judicial cruelty, governmental villainy, administrative deafness and above all legislative blindness, put concisely the Jungle Raaj, the "Matsya Nyaya' i.e. the bigger fish or the snake eating the smaller ones, the barbarian rule of "Survival of the Fittest", the absurd Darwinism has as if come to stay in India, an evidence of complete failure of Parliamentary form of government.

The present chaotic growth by no index of human development or well being could be called progress much less development. A paradoxical situation indeed of individuals becoming richer and society pauper. Individual wealth and accumulations brought at the cost of society, and personal prosperity at the expense of the country. Both proving a curse to the tearing masses of India being an evil baby of Western Bhogvad and individualistic capitalism, a reversal of situation and falsification of all claims and canons of sustainable integrated humanistic and holistic growth made by government and its propaganda machinery. This in fact is the open loot in the name of economic liberalisation that has added more to the agonies, woos, and miseries of already shattered masses not only in India but the world at large. People broken with hopes tattered, situation at the verge of explosion everywhere came came on roads as French in 1789 and Russians in 1917 or Eastern Europe in 1990–91. The tolerance and pardoning psyche, philosophically imbibed, restrains the people of India from coming on the roads the way people of foreign countries. This is true however, that the fatalistic superstitious impact of Hindu Theological Mythology is also contributing towards this attitude.

People apart; the Government, Judiciary and Netas have also lost the vision. None has time to look into and find ways to control corruption because they themselves are so engrossed in it. That is the reason for government taking the issue of black money so casually. Black money has reached such awful dimensions, crossing according to some even the levels of our national income estimated around 85–95 lac crores. A rough estimate of corrupt black money given below is appallingly revealing;

Category	*Amount (in lac crores)*
Jogi Babas, Gurus, Mahants, Swamis, Sanyasinis, Mandirs etc	5 - 6
Netas	12 - 15
Govt. employees and public sector employees	20 – 22
Private sector employees	6 -7
Capitalists and Big Businesses	45 - 50
Don, Mafia, criminals, terrorists	6 -7
Others petty – sundry	4 - 5

From the latest estimates black money has reached new dimensions at $450 billion dollars while according to other estimates it has reached as horrifying a height as one trillion to 1.5 trillion dollars. If it is so, it is maddening. Thus, our poverty is not the reason for present corruption, rather corruption, is the reason for our poverty. In other words, we are corrupt not because we are poor but we are poor because we are corrupt. It could, therefore be imagined, where had, we been had there been no corruption and where had all that prosperity, riches and wealth gone.

Appendix to the book gives the pattern for proposed utilisation/investment of black money recovered

Not spiritually but fundamentally the material reason for corruption, crime and accumulating wealth and riches is, people believing themselves to be immortal despite seeing others dying in front irrespective of age and time when in reality all leave the earth empty handed. Therefore even saving beyond fair and reasonable limits particularly accumulating by usurping and plundering for the sake of progeny also is as big a sin as the offence of corruption and crime. People never realised, exceptions apart, that disasters come without warning, making no difference between rich and poor, men and women, King or destitute, both leave everything behind. Therefore, sharing as advocated by Sanatan philosophy is the only way for eliminating corruption and abolition of crimes from body politic; not Western 'Bhogvad' that only is aggravating.

Casteism: The Rogue (Rog) Factor

Casteism is yet another problem of Indian polity as big as above problems but is different and independent of others. It has not only eaten up the very vitals of Indian democratic polity but having deviled into the most powerful vote catching device has over the period degenerated into regionalism, provincialism 'language – ism' and 'dialect – ism'. Casteim is one single crucial determinant of the course of Indian political elections in most of the states that even overshadows and overtakes honesty, ethics and morality. Hence the solution for India's problems cannot be found under the present rotten parliamentary system and the obsolete Constitution. Casteism has become the biggest rogue of Indian democracy which in Hindi is called 'Rog' meaning disease that has not only percolated down the line and polluted the whole governing system but divided the government machinery worse than the British divided India to rule her for perpetuity.

The number rather than quality based Indian power politics has reduced caste system in to 'caste – ism' which has become as loathsome a factor in increasing the population of the country and reversing the trend of population mix as communalism.

But casteism has in addition bemired in to perpetuation of Reservations in government and public services which is not only unconstitutional under Art 16 (4) and (4A) read with Art 14 and 15 of the Constitution of India but is completely against the intent and overall constitutional philosophy, simultaneously frustrating the vast majority of the country. This is not merely yet another contravention but destruction of the Constitution by the state including Judiciary.

In any case, if reservations in promotion in services are unconstitutional, under the state; its perpetuation is all the more unconstitutional. This is not because the language in both the clauses of Art 16 is the same. But it is because the intention, philosophy and aims and objects of the Constitution are equality, rule of law, non discrimination on the ground of gender, race, caste, birth, religion, etc. and above all, Common Civil Code for all citizens.

Reservations in India rather than being elevating – ameliorating have become the dirty but easy tactics of and for vote catching amongst ignorant, illiterate and traditionally superstitious naive masses. They are the main cause of rampant corruption, indiscipline, inefficiency and over all decadency in the public services, governing ethos and value system which is impossible to be corrected even slightest under present system of governance and Constitution.

This type of casteism has proved more disastrous to Indian polity than sectarian violences and conflicts or bloodshed under other faiths - religions or racial communities of the world. This is even worse than class struggle of Karl Marx which further strengthens the imperativeness of the need for proposed changes as suggested in this book. The proposals that India should have one head of state and government to be elected by the voters of the country along with his deputy called either 'President – Vice President' or 'Prime Minister – Dy. Prime Minister'. In the States / provinces they may be called 'Governor – Dy. Governor' or 'Chief Minister and Deputy' elected by the voters of the respective States / provinces. This, will be the beginning of establishment of Bharatiy Lok Jan Tantric Shasan Vyavastha with proposed Constitutional changes.

The fact of the matter is that the old Varna System stands uprooted long ago in India. Today there is only one Varna in India and that is Vania. Irrespective of caste creed religion everybody has become a Bania bidding goodbye to old Varna system. There are no more Brahman, Kshatriyas, Vaishyas and Shudras by profession or occupation. All are after money. Therefore reservations based on birth and caste has lost its relevance and its continuance has no more justification. OBC (Other Backward Castes) certainly not. How can reservations be upheld constitutionally under a constitutional scheme which is aiming at framing 'Common Civil Code' for all its citizens under its directives.

Discontinuance of unconstitutional reservations is one most effective remedy amongst all others. This will result in renewal of such shattered society and paradoxically not only for establishment of class and casteless society but also for restoration of quality in government and public services besides elimination of corruption. Reservations under the veil of equality are creating more inequalities. A disintegrated society particularly now when they have become privilege over equality. In other words excessive equality in fact exploitation of majority in a democracy by minority to strengthen the 'Vote Bank'.

Hopefully if put to vote more than fifty crore voters out of seventy crores would willingly opt and accept these transformational changes as presented in this book.

Reservations not only in promotion but in the services of the state also on the basis of caste, gender, community and religion are equally unconstitutional. The basis on which these are unconstitutional in promotions under Art 16 (4A), on the same basis reservations are unconstitutional in the services of the state under Art 16 (4) as the language of both is substantially the same. So is the case with Women's Reservation. Women in India put themselves equal to men in all spheres of socio – economic - political life and assert their equality in all walks. Unlike in the whole world also ask for reservations at the same time despite the provision for Common Civil Code in the Constitution though here also caste, community and class have come on the way. Such duple and dichotomous society needs radical steps to be set right.

There are people who despite abuses like "Tilak Taraaju aur Talwaar, Inko Maro Joote Chaar" are licking the feet of such abusers because judiciary takes no action against such disintegrative forces including divisionists likes Shiv Sena, MNS, Khalistanis and the like the veiled LTTEs. Governments of Neta Nagari are already afraid of taking action being obsessed by vote bank mania. Now is the time to allow if anybody wants to become Buddhist, let him; rather than destroying the social fabric, quality of governance and services. We tolerated insult to Tri-Color, to National Anthem, to Mother India and that is how separatist elements raised their heads. They were all excused not even taken to task. There is no fear of law – justice and punishment. Mother DMK Party was the reaction of defeat of Late VK Krishanamenon in Bombay in 60s on Marathi Vs Madrasi parochialism. Somebody asked, what did Justice M. Katju do when Judge of HCs and SC. What's the use of writing such articles now in TOI when things have gone out of hands so badly? This could now only be set right by changing the form of Govt and the Constitution not otherwise. One Mod Gen educated in US rather advocated taking Tri-Color to toilets and stitching an under wear. Overall the main cause of all frustrations of the people is economic that will in times to come multiply in an accelerated way with the ever increasing population.

Constitution has lost its Originality

As chronic the disease as radical will it need the treatment. As serious the ailment as severe will be the remedy. A casteist society, reservation infested governance, greed oriented - self centered psyche and corruption ridden system standing at the verge of population explosion and crime mentality would only need operational structural changes for transformation and recouping, no less. Even if 108 Anna Hazares, 558 Arvind Kejarival are born in all corners of the country at a time and 1008 Ram Devs simultaneously at left right and centre, nothing is going to improve. Nothing would happen and nothing would change even slightest under the present constitutional and judicial – legal system may that be corruption or black money what of governance even by appointing Jan Ayukta or Lok

Ayukta or Jan – Lok Ayukta or otherwise enacting as many laws unless radical structural changes are made in the system of governance itself by changing present constitution and the form of government.

The situation has appallingly reached the point of 'no return' the same way as that of Karmakanda – Jyotish ritualistic cobweb and Baba – Guru – Swami – Sanyasini Dharma trade net work. Present Parliamentary form has not only failed to deliver but failed utterly to meet even the bare expectations of people much less fulfilling their aspirations to live like human beings. The system of governance has failed the same way as the institution of Dharma. The Gurus, Babas, Swamis, Sanyasis who would have liberalized the people of mental slavery, irrationality, conservatism, ignorance including superstitions and the country of the rut, fear and inferiority, have rather sunk in the filth. Same as politicians and soiled the very institutions of Dharma, gods and godesses, that would have helped build a morally ethical and politically strong India. Any more continuance of present "corruption oriented - reservation infested' system of governance, with non-accountable Judicial system, blind legal set up and deaf administrative structure would rather than bettering the fate of the country push people to doom and disaster, remorse and repentance, nothing else. However, that may be too late in the day if action in that direction is not taken right now. This Constitution has in any case lost its originality as the number of amendments is likely to cross 115. Its vulnerability could also be perceived by the fact that Constitution needed amendment the next day of its coming in to force i.e. right on day one and has now lost its originality in the process without any improvement even slightest in the governance or removal of miseries of the masses and sorrows of the people or in changing the fate of the country. The situation has rather gone from bad to worse and further likely to go from worse to worst. Therefore, the only solution for all ailments of the country and problems of people is to change the present form of governance and the Constitution and opt for a new system of governance with a new constitution either called 'Bharatiya Lok Jan Tantric Paddhati or

Presidential System' as proposed and presented in this book.

The prevailing situation as we are living in India has correctly been described by a poet in the following lines but what will be the situation after 2019 and by 2024 is impossible for any 'Kitab', Jyotishi or Guru – Baba to predict.

इस देश में इन्साफ का ये दस्तूर हो गया है
जो जुल्म करायें, वही अब देते हैं सजा भी

(In this country, inflicting of punishment by those who commit offences or get crimes committed, has become a way of dispensing justice)

Oath Broken - Constitution Destroyed

Those who swore by Constitution to protect it have themselves destroyed it time and again and now only the body remains without the soul. The Constitution was destroyed the day its Preamble being the Mission Statement said to be enacted and adopted by the people was amended by 42nd Amendment in 1976 substituting "socialist secular' along with 'Sovereign Democratic Republic. Parliament usurped the power of sovereign people of India that was never given or intended to be given to her but Parliament on the other could not save her Constitutional power and authority when judiciary went in to the Constitutionality of the Constitution by deciding the Constitutionality of the Constitutional amendments made by Peoples Parliament, the greatest ever unconstitutional act. The black day in the Constitutional history was the day when judiciary some time in 1994 held that giving the bribe of four crore rupees each to three JMM (Jharkhand Mukti Morcha) MPs was an issue concerning Parliamentary affairs and arising out of Parliamentary business therefore beyond judicial interference. Subsequently the same Judiciary interfered in the legislative business of UP Vidhan Sabha unconstitutionally. It directed her to elect CM in a particular manner (rather than by the House in its own natural course) and unconstitutionally allowing an extra - constitutional authority Shri Jagadambika Pal to occupy Chair besides Speaker. An equally dangerous unconstitutional assault was the direction to the Union Govt to implement 'Common Civil Code' and framing of 'quota based Reservation Scheme. This perpetuated inequality against all canons of Constitution of India besides laying down the conditions of appointment of CVC in so glaring violation of the constitutional principles of separation of power as this was entirely an Executive function of government.

The whole scheme of Constitution and law was demolished the day judiciary held that prior permission of President or Governor was required for prosecuting Govt or public servants including CMs / Ministers and holders of such public positions even for committing crimes and offences not arising out of their bonafide discharge of official duties in good faith. The final blow was the liberalization of the economy in demolition of 'Directive principles of State Policy the Vision statement of the people for their future that Constitutes the basic structure of the Constitution. Today, Part IV of the Constitution stands shelved and has become almost non-existent. Nobody despite taking oath to do so protected the present and future of the people who are said to have enacted and adopted the Constitution and gave it to themselves. It is a different matter that otherwise the constitution has lost its originality over the period for so many amendments.

Blunders and Omissions of Present Constitution

Alas! Surprisingly not merely the modern western educated or public school - schooled generation but even the people of the earlier period and generation were either ignorant or deliberately spread and created an impression as if the Constitution of India was made by one man. This is how a serious wrong impression was created undermining the contributions of other luminaries. The truth is that the Constitution was drafted by a sub - committee of Constituent Assembly chaired by late learned Dr BR Ambedkar and ultimately after long drawn discussions, alterations, improvements and modifications approved by the Constituent Assembly.

It hardly needs mention that immediately after independence a Constitution was needed for the country and present Constitution was drafted in haste following generally the Westminster Parliamentary model and copying mostly the provisions of Government of India Act 1935 with which India, particularly the leadership of the country was by the way fairly acquainted. The copying was so deliberately selective that copiers took full advantage of poverty, ignorance, and illiteracy of people of India. The Constitution did not incorporate such good things of foreign Constitutions that would have made India in effect a democracy for the people, a real people's democracy, a participative clean democracy in action. However, whatever was there in the Constitution for the masses of India has since 1995 been snatched and people robbed as the Constitution has lost both its public welfare purpose and Welfare State philosophy.

Omissions under the Constitution

The Constitution thus made gravest omissions and serious blunders by not incorporating following provisions which perhaps was done keeping in mind the future elections, pleasure of power and bliss of authority and their flesh - blood relationship with money and corruption;

1. Absence of Fundamental Duties: As much we talk and talked of or claimed Fundamental Rights, we had never the Fundamental Duties. The presence of lawlessness in government services, chaos in Public Sector, anarchy in Private Sector, confusion in legal system, disorder in police, contempt for administration and disrespect for judiciary are because of our asserting coupled with judicial leanings towards Rights and liberty hardly ever balanced by duties and discipline. Mrs. Indira Gandhi brought Constitutional amendment during emergency in 1976 incorporating Fundamental Duties with the intent to perpetuate her despotic rule that ultimately marred the loftiness and sanctity of duty that never therefore saw the light of the day.

2. Absence of Vicarious liability of government servants: Absence of individual or collective vicarious liability of government servants for negligence, deliberate negligence, gross negligence and / or habitual negligence has only resulted in bad governance, very bad governance, inefficient governance and corruption as it made these employees not public servants but government employees with constitutional safeguards reinforced by judiciary making them instead masters of the people. Vicarious liability would have made government employees irrespective of positions held, (not the government), liable to payment of damages and compensation to people – individually or collectively or to a group for the loss caused due to the negligence – gross, deliberate or habitual of such employee or employees.

3. *Absence of Cumulative Punishment:* It means punishing culprit, offender, criminal committing more than one connected / inter linked crime or offence, with the punishment provided for each such offence or crime undergone separately but cumulatively one after the other as it is in USA, UK, Europe and not merely the highest maximum punishment provided for one of such offences as is in India.

4. *Absence of exemplary pecuniary – punishments:* It means high damages, compensation, fines, and costs as is in USA, UK, Europe, while in India it is negligible compensation or cost even pecuniary punishment by way of fines, penalty, damages including for misuse of legal and abuse of judicial processes is scant. Over and above the unwarranted, uncalled for and misplaced sympathy shown by the courts to criminals and offenders not only abets further criminalization of society but shocks public conscience and fuels their anger, frustrations, agony, sorrows and pains still the inhuman sins, evil crimes and wicked offences of criminals and offenders continue. In Europe and America our ideals and idols pecuniary punishment are such that offenders, criminals, evil doers dare not go to courts and make all efforts and settle the cases outside.

5. *Absence of Time bound Justice Delivery System* i.e. time limit on the decisions of the courts at each stage of hearing of cases including finality of hearing and decision.

6. *Absence of summary trials* in corruption and certain other offences in the nature of rape, kidnapping, sexual abuse of children, crime against women, insurance settlements and accidents etc and punishing on the basis of prima facie proof in certain other crimes.

7. *Absence of Right to re-call or Negative Voting:* Voters or the people of the constituency have no right to recall their corrupt, demoralized, unethical, and sleeping representatives nor there is right of negative voting at the time of election and countermanding the election if such votes reach or exceed certain per centage.

8. *Unchecked excessive and discretionary bails:* Absence of checks and limits on un- restricted bails, stay, and injunction jurisdiction of courts.

9. *Excessive discretionary, quota – permit power and monetary relief* – grants and other powers of ministers - officials including PM / CM.

10. *Absence of provision for referendum:* There is no provision for public voting or opinion by way of referendum on any disputed legal provision, Constitutional issues, unnatural or controversial legislative – executive subject affecting morality, ethics and public conscience or point of public importance or of general import including controversial and improper - unfair judicial interpretations.

All the above constitutional or legal provisions collectively or severally exist in the European countries including UK, Switzerland as also in America.

The Biggest Setback: Anna Team vs Baba Ramdev and Kejarival Party

The biggest setback rather a blow to the movement against corruption including black money was the latent 'Havas' (avarice) of Ramdev and Kejarival to become Prime Minister of India.

Ambition coupled with hidden jealousy of Ramdev against Anna's popularity and aspirations of Kejariwal twined with veiled manipulations not to allow Ramdev to snatch the show poured icy water on the zeal and hopes of the people as well as collectivity of the momentum of the movement to fight against the system and bring about system transformation.

However, Ramdev Baba taking advantage of his popularity through his Yoga, impersonating as Patanjali Yoga, was planning to form a political party since 2009 to become PM of India but finding cold response by middle and intellectual classes he sadly and unwillingly continued postponing his plans. While lower middle classes still took Ramdev as good a Prime Minister as anybody of fraternity, intellectuals and higher middle classes considered him castiest despite his preaching Yoga exercises and pretending an ascetic. Many people were disenchanted by his Babagiri mask as he was only Planning to become PM of India. He spoke something and acted differently as an opportunist. His actions and precepts were glaringly in contrast and contradictory that mainly drew daggers between him and Kejarival ji.

He could not digest Anna's popularity and in a conceited mindset launched his own movement under the guise of Black Money as against corruption and Jan - Lok Pal taken up by Anna's so called Civil Society and got the backlash in Ramlila grounds in May 2011. This is as surprising as worthy of noting that while ascetic Ramdev Yadav aspiring to become PM of India has not spoken a single word against reservations he has only taken up the issue of black money deposited in foreign countries and not within the country as he knew most of the Jogis, Gurus, Babas, Sanyasinis and Joginis would be trapped the same way as he has already been. Besides cheap popularity and vote bank catching device this approach of Ramdev suited a section of Netas and political parties who have black money mostly within. This is however not surprising that black money inside the country including that lying idle in religious places and Managed by Guru - Swamis, Babas and saffron or white clad Vyasas, is no less.

Therefore the 'foreign black money' mask of Baba Yadav was to save such corrupts and divert attention of people and the Govt off him and his patrons and sponsors. The tactical division of Anna and Ramdev and then of Aam Aadami Party not only divided the people but has also thrown them behind besides dragging the change by several years until after at least 2019 that too if they unite and become one

In anyway, by 2024 people will realise their blunder. Still those who could read between the lines had no doubt after the joint press conference of Anna ji and Ramdev Baba held on 17 July 2012 that Ramdev would on behalf of both the movements announce future agenda and course of action on 9th August, about which there was no specific indication. The indication if any, impliedly was about formation of a political party and contesting elections for which the committee of both would have met on 25th July at Jantar Mantar, observed token fast and held public meeting. Unfortunately a faction of Anna team apprehending stealing of the show by Ramdev suddenly resorted to indefinite fast on 25th taking Ramdev Yadav aback. But the announcement of formation of political party made Ramdev mad, he felt cheated and hurt and heart in heart decided to teach lesson and take revenge as he did on 9th August. However, while earlier announcement of formation of political party by Anna faction compelled Ramdev to desist from such step for himself, the formation of party brought no advantage to Anna faction either as it was not done in a refined – magnificent way taking the nation or in any case the majority of people in to confidence. The 'Team' appeared in haste and wasted the grand golden opportunity.

People of the nation have by now understood that the country has no dearth of political parties rather these have become a nuisance to them and burden on the country. What the country really needs, is a highly enlightened statesmen with vision and leading, leadership with acumen and political party with philosophy that can bring system change i.e. 'Vyavastha Parivartan'. That can only come by changing the present Parliamentary form of government and the constitution. Nothing would change by simply forming a political party by whatever name or by bringing in Jan Lok Pal or Lok Pal or Jan Pal or Lok or Jan – Ayukt or any Bill or Act or by amending the Constitution in any way as Chief Justice of India has already said in so many words (reported in Media on 15th August 2012) that 'do whatever but don't touch Judiciary'. The indications are clear. Therefore, for bringing in system change or 'Vyavastha Parivartan' people of India in general and educated masses particularly youth will have to read this book, understand it by heart to be convinced to bring not only 'Vyavastha Parivartan' or System Change but transformation. Still such change will come or could be brought or would be possible only after 5 years as it would then come convincingly from the bottom of the heart of the people. This exactly happened during freedom movement that took Gandhi, in a way 47 years (including struggle in S. Africa) but in any case 1915 to 1947.

It shall always remain true however, that under prevailing conditions only Anna ji, Kejariwal Aam Aadmi Party and Baba Ramdev could collectively bring such change despite Baba's weaknesses and hunger for Mike – Manch and Mala. The episode of Nepalese his stooge and suspected spy BK, specially with the IBN – 7 sting episode on sudden missing of their Guru and reported land scandals including the charges of adulterations have in the process reduced the protégé of many political parties and pawn of many politicians – Sri Ramdev ji from a Jogi to simple Ramdev Yadav. Still Ramdev Baba is better than many other Gurus, Jogi - Joginis, Swami – Swaminis. He has at least the guts, caliber and wider following a base. Less his political ambitions he is great having great intentions. He has many strengths of character which many Mahants, Gurus, Aachaaryas, and Mahantanis do not.

After reading this book all agitators and people will be convinced that as by wearing costly clothes outwardly, inner cleanliness and purity do not come so would by simply amending the Constitution or enacting a law or laws transformation, either of the governance or the system or the country would not come. That would be possible only if form of government and the Constitution are changed. A poet has rightly said;

कब तक आखिर ठहर सकता है वो घर
आगया हो बुनियाद ही में जिसकी खलल
बोतल बदल भि जाये तो क्या अगर शराब नहीं बदली
कातिल बदल भि जाये तो क्या अगर तलवार नहीं बदली
कुछ नहीं बदलेगा अगर व्यवस्था नहीं बदली
ये व्यवस्था नहीं बदलेगी अगर संविधान नहीं बदला
वहीं पर खड़े रहेंगे जहाँ पर खड़े हैं हम
अब तो इस तालाब का सड़ा पानी बदल दो
ये कंवल के सभी फूल मुरझाने लगे हैं

(How long could a building stand if the foundation has started cracks. It's no use changing the bottle if wine remains the same and no use getting rid of the assassin if sword remains. Nothing would change without changing the system and system would not change without changing the Constitution. We shall remain where we are. Therefore time has come to change the rotten water of the pond as all the lotuses have started fading out).

If the common masses and middle classes of India still do not understand the truth and come out of the clutches of the caste politics they will have to live with and continue to suffer for their sins. Unfortunately, neither Anna could build on his onetime popularity nor Ramdev on his. Ramdev rather did just opposite of what he used to say and fight for with Kejariwal. Therefore all the three factions now need to forget and forgive and come together to bring the desired system change popularly called 'Vyavastha Parivartan' in fact transformation. All political experiments and 'Siyasi Parties' have failed in India rather proving a necessary evil the same way as the Mahants, Swamis, Gurus - Gurains. A poet has therefore rightly said;

सच कहें तो भयंकर भेड़िये ही अब राम नाम पुकारते

असली भक्त और सेवक कभी कुछ नहीं कहते

(Truly speaking, only the wild canines are now chanting the name of gods, real servants and devotees keep silence)

In any case, non-withdrawal of support by so dear parties of Baba viz BSP and SP to Congress has exposed Baba as much as the 'Kathani and Karani' (words and actions) of these Netas. Voting by JDU, CPM, Shiv Sena and CPI to UPA candidate in Presidential election has exposed not only the Parties but the entire political system of the country. These are the parties who a couple of years back brought 'No Confidence Motion' against UPA government, bent upon to dislodge her and created pandemonium in the country over nuclear power generation treaty issue with US. Renowned poet Niraj says rightly;

जिनके पास शब्द हैं जितने उतना उनसे अर्थ दूर है
शब्द झूठे हैं सभी सत्य कथाओं कि तरह
भाषण निर्लज्ज हैं सभी वैश्या कि अदाओं कि तरह

(Those having as many words are as away from their meaning. Therefore the speeches have become as shameless as the gait and pace of a prostitute and words as false as the rumoring or gossip stories)

The irony, the greatest tragedy with both Anna team and Ramdev Yadav Satsang is that none of them - barring a couple of people who have also detached themselves because of disgruntlement - could associate and co-opt common intelligentsia and integrate judicious public and wise people with, not at all the educated youth the instrumentality of change, which is the biggest failure of both the movements. Both have underlying fights for ego not only inter se but inter group resulting in disintegrating of the movement started by Ramdev. Therefore Ramdev needs more to understand that only a united fight; a collective movement could bring system change which needs great penance following the foot prints of Gandhi. Otherwise it shall prove as much a fiasco as his crusade against junk or packed food other eatables and cold drinks, the production, sale and profits of which have increased three fold since 2006. He will have to abandon the tactics of maneuvering or compromising with one corrupt to bring another corrupt down and widen the scope of black money as well as corruption. The question also is – is not the immense, immeasurable cash–money, valuables and huge wealth stored or lying idle in the coffers of temples or religious trusts or Ashrams or elsewhere also Black money? The god men and women have in fact made not only religious places and religious trusts but also the temples of gods the dumping grounds for black money and corruption, creating a psyche compelling theists to become atheists and mod Gen westernized Bhogvadi being frustrated by such hypocrisy.

Failure of this united movement now at this juncture would perennially make corrupts and criminals the king of kings rather than Law and Constitution. Hence both the fractions have to come with clean hands forgetting the past and forgiving each other abandoning duel faces as also the lust for power, avarice for positions and pelf by burying under the soil the ego and the issue of false prestige whatsoever and work selflessly the way *Gita* says. Ramdev Baba being an ascetic has to take the initiative and understand true essence of scriptures before giving sermons.

It is still the propensity of expectations of the people that is keeping both the movements alive but for how long? If people see no tangible or visible results soon the distant drums will stop sounding well and both the movements will fade away in the very near future.

Despite the foxy wishes of both Arvind Kejariwal and Ramdev to be the Prime Minister of India, Anna ji Hazare has also in the end proved that he could not be the driver of the country. The Anti Corruption – Anti Black Money Movements will also otherwise meet the same fate as everybody in India, top - down and below – above either partially or completely is soiled. Paradoxically the same corrupt people participate and raise slogans in such anti corruption movements who only await an opportunity for grabbing. The biggest disaster with such movements is that it gets no hearty support of higher echelons of society whether intelligentsia, shrewd public or government servants, middle and higher middle classes even the youth or students because everybody is deep down in corruption one or the other way. While Arvind Kejariwal was the stumbling block in the co-option of wise, visionaries, intelligentsia and committed urban elites and enlightened youth, the approach of the movement on the whole - exceptions apart - philosophically did not allow such co-option perhaps intentionally, for so many fears resulting in below than mediocrity level of participation in the movement.

The deception played on Ramdev at the last moment and the perception of the people about absence of unity of command and leadership in the self styled Civil Society itself proved a blow to its success in July 2012. The hasty way the formation of political party was announced without taking masses of the country into confidence made it a fiasco and proved frustrating to all. Even though it was very pious and bona fide and had public good and national purpose behind it. Over and above the approbating - reprobating behaviour of Anna created uncertainty and instability in the movement compelling such a majestically grand movement die its own death. This satisfied many politically, morally, ethically and financially vile elements and known corrupt–criminals. Mostly the Political Parties only shed crocodile tears with press release, like: 'Anna appears tired – fatigued of such political frictions within and without because he basically is a 'Sanyasi' a patriot a rare patriot in India today'.

Ramdev on the other, knowing very well and expecting grand success of any such anti corruption movement in India took up the Black money issue to lame it and hoping magic out of his movement. While it is true that his Black Money movement annoyed only one party politically and only a section of people having maximum or most of their Black money in foreign banks, Ramdev forgot that by abandoning corruption and perusing BM deposited in foreign banks only he was giving health tonic to hungry and starving as says a Shire rightly;

'मुझे उस वैद्य की विद्या पर तरस आता है,
भूखे लोगों को जो सेहत कि दवा देता है'.

Ramdev also failed because of his own involvement in black money and alleged frauds and malpractices. He failed also because he failed to convince educated people, the intelligentsia particularly the enlightened youth about the immeasurable black money with Guru – Babas, Jogi – Joginis, Swami – Sadhvis, Mahants – Jagat Gurus, or cached idle uneconomically in temples and other abodes of gods including religious trusts. He utterly failed to impress upon the masses what black money in fact was. Ramdev, no doubt, because of Yogic charms succeeded in co – optation of the desired strata of people but failed because of his cheapness – vanity, emptiness and lack of 'Gurutva' within as says Kalidas in Meghdoot

"अन्तः ऽसारं भवति हि लघू पूर्णता गौरवाय"

which in Hindi gives the meaning of "अधभर गगरी छलकत जात"

Ramdev lacks delegation, he wants to be the only one as against, Anna delegated excessively and both failed.

The valency expectancy of both has now failed to stimulate people's morale as it has become mere fighting without any results at sight. Earlier thcy were suffering all pains, bearing all sorrows hoping something good will come out soon, but now they are hopelessly hopeless seeing no hope of turning around fortifying Kalidas the great Sanskrit poet who said rightly (Kumarsambhava: Sarg – 5 / 86);

क्लेश: फलेन हि पुनर्नवता विधत्ते

(Pains and difficulties motivate for renewed efforts and spring new vigour only when success is seen at sight or has been attained. A movement would get revitalized the same way only if results are perceived or are at sight)

Anna ji needs to understand the psyche of the people of India and why Nehru did not renounce power and abdicate Premiership. We are the same people who voted the castiest, corrupt, criminals to power and glorified them the same way as erstwhile Raja – Ranis who sided with the British including that of Tehari in Uttarakhand where people lighted lamps at the memorial of great martyr Shridev Suman every year but throughout voted the family of princely estate to power said to be the killers behind. These were the mind boggling worries of Pandit Jawahar ji when all Raja – Ranis revolved around Raja ji forming Swatantra party besides people since 1952 voting the same Rajas - Ranis who sided with British. If the 2012 elections of Uttarakhand were eye openers, the elections of UP, Punjab and TN were no less pace setters and the HP elections have finally set the pace calling upon all the three– Anna team, AAP and Baba to unite and tight as a single force. Though there are hardly any exceptions now such psyche has made honesty, morality, ethics, patriotism, sacrifice and service abusive words still before it becomes the culture and national character as it had in Bihar, the course of time and events needs to be changed - the earlier the better. Therefore people either have to suffer for their Karmas and pay for their sins or in repentance penance by transforming India of their dream in the manner presented and suggested in this book.

Anna must understand - what of honesty without power? Power means and in India particularly – governmental political power. What could he do without power? Nothing. He has failed rather fallen apart and fallen away, while Netas, corruption and crimes are where they were – prospering, flourishing and flowering. Corruption has rather increased 20% since the start of Anna and Ramdev movements, a slur on our denuded mentality. Honesty is one aspect but Anna ji must also understand that without honest governmental political power no change could be brought in the country therefore the decision of actually forming the Political Party was not wrong, only the way it was formed was wrong. Even if political power of governance is gained under present system, Judiciary won't allow such leadership or the government to do anything, rotting the plans, philosophy and things the same way. Therefore anybody who wants to bring 'System Change' in the country must first have a viable convincing alternative Model in mind and must bring and place it before people and at the same time convince them to go with, support and adopt it. This book is the first ever enterprise in that direction, a journey towards realizing that dream of transformation.

True as it is, indefinite hunger strike by Anna at this age played havoc not only with his health but with the movement itself and second hunger strike was his biggest mistake deliberately inviting disaster. The correct step, mode and method for Annaji was making it peoples movement by undertaking 'Yatra' of the whole country, involving honest intelligentsia throughout, taking people into confidence and supporting Aam Aadmi Party, contesting elections on the clear promise of the people of the country to vote 500 members of Lok Sabha and two third majority in Vidhan Sabhas, of the party the only way for system change infact metamorphosis as suggested in this book.

Still the remedy for India at the present juncture, the panacea for all problems of people lies in the unity of Ramdev and Anna ji working in cohesion with team Kejariwal with this book in hand as Guru - guide – philosopher for achieving the mission of the nation and along with the vision of the people and their own Vision. A united Transformational movement with an aim for metamorphosis once for all - as presented in this book - only could now succeed in India- no other.

Law and Justice: Pathetic Scene

Law in this country has become a legal luxury of Vakils and Courts. Luxury the way a boy throws stones at frogs just for fun but the frogs dying not for fun but in sober earnest something like, as says a Shire;

मिलेगा न्याय दादा के मुकद्दमों का
ये उम्मीद पोते को अदालत से

(Grandson expects justice from the court in the cases filed by his grandfather).

Justice, that would have been open to the poorest of poor is not even within the reach of middle classes and with the speed slower than a tortoise would never be seen as done and not at all believed to have been done or being done. Inordinate delays in dispensing justice, unabated adjournments and multiplying pendencies have become as big a threat to justice as injustice itself. Justice would be justice only if it is seen and believed as truth in action. Simply deciding a case after 10 – 15 years is not justice to a party and this is what is exactly happening in this country. Therefore it is not simply doing justice but feeling more than seeing, it as has been done. The way justice is being done in such a vast country like India, and the speed at which it is being delivered, is deplorably low. The law, the courts, and police who have always caught the poor and weak in this country were torn into pieces by rich and powerful. It is in fact rich man's justice in this country and the rich man's law. An average goods train load of bad laws; excessive bails and belated justice have become the worst form of tyranny in this country. It has neither been good of the law nor good of the people or of the system but only of the lawyers, judges, criminals, police, corrupt, rich and the powerful that the system is actually serving. The masses, the poor, the honest, the meek and the good all afraid of law, lawyers, police, law courts and judges. 'We the people of India' (The opening words of Constitutional Preamble have and are suffering because of too much of hearing under the cover of uncalled for 'Due Hearing' over and above the 'Reasonable' but without 'Fair Hearing' as the people of China for too little).

Instead of the good of the people, the law, law courts, Vakils and judges have become worst form of tyranny for the very people to whom they are meant or pretend to serve. People for law not vice versa has over the period, become the worst form of governance in this country. The law is dead but there is said to be the Rule of Law the same way as Dharma is dead but Dharm Pracharak Panths - Sects remain. Law has become a cobweb as complicated rather more than the Karmkandic rituals and superstitions propagated by modern Swamis, Gurus, Mahants, Babas, Jyotishhis and channels more to be broken rather than to be complied with. We all know, no scripture, religious treatise not even Ved Vyas could ever interpret truth - truth about reality, nature, world, heaven - hell, God including creation as the Babas, Gurus, Sanyasinis and Jyotishees have interpreted. The same way as the lawyers, Judges have interpreted the truth about Law, Constitution and Justice including natural and fair Justice. All of them today can predict the unpredictable in this country. Just as the modern Hi-Tech Babas, Swamis, Karmakandies, Gurus, Sanyasinis and Jyotishhis have no business with the business of Dharma and Dharma Shastras or Jyotishh except their business, so have the lawyers no business with the business of law and justice but their professional trade. They are, needed not for what we should do and not do, but to tell us how to do what we want to do. The lawyer and police in connivance could get 100 men with guns freed by judiciary and instead manage to put same number of innocents inside to fill the gap and the stomach of papers to shut the mouth of public. People suppressed to tell the untruth and commit perjury before the courts on oath and outside on affidavit, which is the greatest disrespect for law in fact insult to Judiciary still the system is said to be working. It is not enough that the courts fix the dates of hearing unless people feel and perceive that case is being heard and justice being done which is possible only if litigations are heard and decided speedily, quickly and swiftly.

There could be neither justice nor hope of any fair justice to the poor until this judicial system which would continue until this governance but both until this constitution. No improvement at all could be expected from a system that survives on the tax earnings of drugs, alcohol, *charas*, *ganja*, *bhang*, opium, intoxicants, prostitutes and Bar Balas (bar girls), tobacco, *gutka*, trafficking, exploitation of farmers and agriculture and blood of poor masses.

The judicial system has, in fact at all levels tacitly accepted the 'Chalta Hai' working culture. It presumes the system, the government, its officials and employees as negligent, corrupt, recalcitrant and incompetent but without any remedy to the people. This is yet another visible failure of the working of judicial system. Generally the adjournments and consequent delays in deciding the cases are caused by governments, her counsels and officials. The uncalled for sympathy of the courts to governments, its counsels, and officials has become the cause not only of corruption and inordinate delays and accumulation of cases with expensive financial burden on poor countrymen already sunk under the load of inflation, high cost and corruption. This by analogy amounts to the same type of uncalled for sympathy once bestowed upon workers and their unions resulting in industrial anarchy, chaos and indiscipline that pushed this country in to the lap of American individualistic capitalism and western Bhogvad. The functioning of the system reflects as if it is the primary duty of courts to protect the governments and their officials particularly the police and rich rather than the poor masses, the public and the needy who made the Constitution and put all these functionaries at their respective places to serve the cause of general masses and work for the good of the public rather than in their own good. What fairness would people expect if the whole system of justice delivery and legal setup becomes instrumental in harassing the very public, the poor including the middle class. Thus intending to tire them out, to bow or compromise with the corrupt, criminals, rich and men in authority or be the yes men either of the moneyed or the system.

This naturally raises the question - what is the duty of the government employees? What work are they supposed to perform and what for are they paid if people have to pay them again and again for getting their work done.These employees being appointed and paid by government out of public funds i.e. the money belonging to the same public. How could the employees ask for double payment for the same work. In fact asking for bribe is asking for black money. Therefore, as the bribe forms part of BM a government employee asking for bribe commits double misconduct with one transaction inviting equally serious action – criminal as well as disciplinary.

Unfortunately in this country over the period because of system dichotomy, the law and judicial system have become pro inefficient, pro parasites, pro corrupt, pro criminal, pro rich, pro moneyed, anti honest, anti masses, which is the primary reason throwing people in the hands of Naxals - Maoists and anarchists besides creating a general psyche of dishonesty, immorality, crimes – corruption and indiscipline amongst youth. If the system is not changed democratically now, the radicalism, rebellious tendencies and separatist elements would rise in future in different parts of the country A poet describes present Judicial – Legal System rightly in these words;

जज बने हैं बाज गिद्धों की है पंचायत
अपराधिन सी खड़ी है कोयल
इस सिस्टम ने ये बख्शा

(If hawks are judges, vultures the jury naturally Cuckoo would be on trial – this is the gift of present system of governance)

मुवक्किल तो मर रहे हैं कानूनी लड़ाई में
वकील और जज मस्त हैं 'लीगल लक्षरी' में

(While Clients are dying in legal battles judges and lawyers are crazed in legal luxury)

अंधी न्यायपालिका बहरी है सरकार
लूले लँगड़े शासन में
उजड़ रहे घर बार

(In this blind judicial system and deaf governance with lame and crippled administration people and their families are being uprooted)

In our Judicial system where criminals, corrupts, offenders, got uncalled for sympathy of the judges or unwarranted favours of courts, they got emboldened and committed more heinous offences, had expanded fear psychosis, accumulated more illegal and corrupt money. They became Netas glorified by media – visual as well as print, that contributed towards the elevation of such elements to corridors of power and further upward to higher echelons of political authority resulting into a vicious circle of corruption – crimes – money – politics and power. This created insecurity and fear amongst common people, risk of life amongst masses and sense of threatening psychosis amongst good people who started detaching themselves from any legal – judicial dispute or political affairs even from right, legal, justified fights and correct initiatives. While good and honest people received no protection, no security; culprits even hardened criminals were hardly punished. They roamed free, enjoyed all facilities and privileges through approaches. There was so much delay in decisions and inordinate delays in judgments of the courts that people rather preferred to be goons, hoods and thugs, and take law in their own hands or decide their own way which is likely to become the future culture of the country when everything would be decided on the roads. Over and above this, excessive political interference in police actions, investigations and enquiries together with excessive bails, stays, injunctions and writ interferences of courts compelled even policemen to side with and be a part of booty. They conspire or become accomplice in such activities not only in their own interest but in the interest of their families and children even to save their own lives which was always under threat because of no action much less timely, either by Govt or judiciary. The examples of the fate, whistle blowers met was already before them. Even trade - business oriented, profit greedy, TV serials and channel shows repeatedly presented before youth and children of the country such elements enjoying the fruits of life in real material sense. The conditions and environment therefore worsened and deteriorated to such an extent that the entire body of people thought it safe to play safe and share with ills and evils. This has made whole society poorer but individuals richer.

Till 1990 almost, there was public impression, rightly or wrongly, that 'Kanoon ke Hath Bahut Lambe hote hain' (the arms of law are long) but since 1991 the arms started shortening and after 2001 almost vanished.

Alongwith such an unjust system came the Clintonic human rights bogey an ulcer over a boil with NGOs a flourishing business, a trade protector of crooks and wicked, acting as a pressure group on the government and at times on judicial system.

The system of appointing Judges of High and Higher Judiciary is fundamentally wrong, basically erroneous. None has either guts or time to survey how many judges of Supreme Court since 1980 were from Judicial Services even of High Courts. Finding no avenues for such promotions also contributed in making judges of Lower Judiciary corrupt. Present method of selecting judges of High and Higher judiciary is something like going to pilgrimage after swallowing hundred mice.

The full inside working reality of judiciary shall come to light once people dissect and analyse how many Judges rather than CJs of HCs were elevated to SC and how many Vakils rather than DJs from Judicial Services to HC. Therefore, Judiciary rather than setting things right and enforcing law, order and legal judicial discipline indulged in competitive corruption particularly with Netas. Therefore now but for fear of punishment, if at all, people have scant regard for Judges and respect for law. Criminals, big guns, moneyed Mafiosi, Netas, and corrupts merely bother for Judiciary, judges and law and take them as their handmade servants.

Missing Impact of Punishment

Disrespect for law has reached its nadir in India. The truck - loads of laws have no more importance than garbage for both good and bad citizens. The only reason for such mockery and flagrant disregard for law is absence of such punishment that exists in the countries we are aping as our ideals and idols. Justice Delivery system of the country could not set examples by way of punishment and therefore failed to create an impact on Indian psyche, in general and on corrupt-marauders, criminal - plunderers, kidnapper – traffickers and greedy - vultures, in particular. People have now least respect for law and fear of punishment not at all, which they know is manageable and is otherwise, also a rare case in India. If anybody disputes the truth, the best course is to have a referendum on this point. The human rights bogey has also instead of helping establish good, pro people governance, created more problems than solving them. The way criminals, corrupts even terrorists under the pretext of Human Rights have been treated as 'VIPS or VVIPs' or as special guests, has over the period made India a haven for committing such crimes.

Legal – Judicial system in the process of reforming criminals, murderers, dacoits and corrupts has during the last sixty-six years completely criminalised the country, and made the system corrupt besides being an unsafe environment for citizens of the country. We did not learn anything from Gita where in Lord Krishna also says (chapt -10) 'I am the punishment for wicked – oppressor and justice for virtuous and good';

दण्डो दमयतामऽस्मि नीतिरस्मी जिगीषिताम

A lot has been written on Dand' and 'Danda' or whip and punishment in Sanatan Bharatiya philosophy including *Ramayana* and *Mahabharat*. Had we studied that and framed our justice system rather than aping pseudo theoretical western reformist notions, things would have been entirely different in the country.

West has reversed punishment jurisprudence long ago but we still follow the same failed reformist system though feel proud of aping the west. The principles of law and justice that prevailed in this country since time immemorial that is 'no culprit – guilty – offender – criminal would ever be acquitted' has lost grounds. Acquitting hundreds of evil doers, offenders and criminals for saving an innocent has never been Bhartiya Legal Jurisprudence. Western jurisprudence had colonial interests and was mainly developed by British to protect the European repressors, oppressors and exploiters of crimes and genocide committed against slaves and subjects of Empire. Such philosophy has brought civic disaster to this country over the period which has morally - ethically reached the brinks of collapse. The purpose of punishment is only one - to establish a civil society, a virtuous system, free of crimes so that no horse is stolen. Punishment is unusual only if it inspires horror more than the crime committed. Under present justice delivery system in India, it has become the other way round. Crimes have created more horrors than the punishment. The mockery of the system has reached a horrifying state. Glorification of criminals by so called fourth estate helped aggravate criminal jurisprudence and socio – political scenario. Consequently media itself has now been relegated to seventh, corruption having taken 4th, crime 5th and Sex 6th place in the hierarchy of estates.

The scenario in India has now developed to a level where a criminal is least ashamed of his crimes, instead he is politically glorified and feels lauded by getting media attention and gratified by getting socio – political and economic leverages and moves around with equally egoistic snobbery called 'Dadagiri' raising his head much higher than the honest, virtuous and idealists. Though unfortunate, because of Lego – judicial failure to punish, crime has put new feathers on its cap, criminals getting such political upliftment, even becoming lawmakers. What improvement could people expect in legal – judicial system with such people at the helm of affairs. In addition, excessive bails have ruined criminal justice system in this country. Hearing petitions and granting bails even pre-emptive, injunction or stay to the highly placed and moneyed by sitting at the residences could never be a dream for the poor and downtrodden, yet another black spot on the system, still they say and we the people of India ditto - there is rule of law and the system is working - the same way as they used to say and still say "Mera Desh Mahan".

If the grandson has to wait for the decision of the case or suit filed by his grandfather, that too not for sure, and this is when we are say 'law as the king of kings' and system working, to who should people go. No punishment, least the exemplary, that too not timely and free Bail system have boomeranged in India, corrupting even the honest of the honests. Time has now come for law and judiciary to address the common feelings of citizens lest that would be too late.

All our experiments with governance have failed and failing utterly, may that be single party rule, multi party coalition, limited party alliance or absolute even 2/3 despotic majority. People have suffered alike and consequences have been the same. Even extreme right and left became one but only for grabbing power and acquiring pelf. People changed the parties in power, replaced one with the other even with new ones defeated the individuals, still rather than improving things worsened because people only changed the bottle not the wine, changed the killer not the sword and slept; thinking things have changed or they have made the things change, but nothing changed as the Sword and Wine were the same. So says the Shire and rightly;

ग़ैर मुमकिन है कि हालात की गुत्थी सुलझे
अहले दानिस ने बहुत सोच समझ कर उलझाई है

By changing a political party in power today and putting another in power and tomorrow again electing and putting former in power or even replacing with the third, would make no difference in the state of affairs. It may be possible to put off fire by fire, light up fire by water or clean dirt by dirt but nothing could be remedied in the present criminalised politics and corruption based governance working as 'isms' over the period, unless the form of Governance and the Constitution are changed as the system only needs radical changes for restoration of good governance – Suraj and excellent just human development environment.

Punishment besides losing its impact and fear impingement is also losing sanctity because of continued feud between different organs and wings of Government one pitted against the other at times resulting in show downs to establish superiority - supremacy undermining the real superiors, the king of kings, the makers and unmakers of Constitution and the systems - the people of India. Important decisions include whether: to conduct or not to conduct or withdraw CBI enquiries, provide or not 'Z' or black cat commando security or to whom, bailing out the brute – heinous - corrupts, inflicting or non execution of capital punishment. Instead there is rampant executive despotism, inhumanity towards masses, ego of power and authority and misuse – abuse thereof, interfering in spheres and jurisdiction of other state organs and violation of separation of power.

Disease Deep in to the Body Politic: A Diagnosis

The most unfortunate part, rather dilemma of Indian polity today, because of system functioning, is its state of incorrigibility where laws have become a burden on the society and system a load on the people. The alienation and incredibility psyche has worsened the situation to a stage where treatment is proving worse than the disease; cure riskier than ailment. The road up and the road down are the same in the existing corrupt governing system but the corruption and crimes as we have seen are but the symptoms. The disease is deeper into the body politic and therefore all treatments, remedies, interventions and therapeutics have failed, failing and will continue to fail because we are either deliberately avoiding diagnosis of the disease or are not at all interested in diagnosing it. It is just like treating brain cancer as headache by paracetamol, leprosy as itching by Vaseline and typhoid as cold by black pepper.

The Bhogvad pervasiveness has made us simply economic man - everything at a price and price for everything like (God in everything - everything in God) and this is what public service in India has become. Truth either suppressed or exposed not to protect the country from enemy or the people from terrorism, nation from bad governance and society from crime and corruption but to protect the government and its official against the people. Corruption, crime, politics of power – power politics, money power and authority of governance, on the one and Bhookh (hunger), exploitation, suppression, rampant injustice, gross unfairness, glaring inequality, abject poverty, starvation and suicide even by those who provide us food (the farmers), on the other have reduced India to a mere geographical entity. The individualism of 'Pelf and Self' has made everybody - somebody the same way as the liberated have made even their parents O - Baby. Consequently, nobody has remained anybody.

Under such, paradoxical situation, there is only one way by which people of India could have freedom with equality, justice with humanity and governance with fairness and that is to have Presidential or Bhartiya Lok- Jan Tantric form of governance. We in fact are, now living in a state of competitive corruption where one public servant would not like the other equally corrupts to equal or compete him, as an alcoholic would not like the one who would drink as much as he could.

Corruption has though become 4th Estate, crime 5th, sex 6th and media reduced to 7th in the hierarchy of Estates, nonetheless Sex tending to dominate others to be glorified equal to 4th estate i.e. corruption.

Common Wealth Games, 2G spectrum, CVC, Adarsh housing, wheat – food – sugar, mines, Oil, land, Army, defence, fodder and other scams including the known governmental scandals in Maharashtra, Delhi, Jharkhand, MP, Rajasthan, Punjab, Haryana, TN, Uttarakhand and other states like AP, Karnataka, Bihar are only the tips of the iceberg, the unknown – unexposed are all pervading and much bigger. In fact, the entire system is sunk in it. Unfortunately, the religious leaders who were supposed to transform and liberate people and absolve the country of corruption and crimes, are deeper down and have made religion fail.

Ironically, in this country, more than the seconds, minutes and hours the days, months and years have fouled, blundered, crimed and corrupted still the poor seconds, minutes and days suffered the most and punished for the misdeeds, wrongs, evils, sins and crimes of latters so says a *Shire*;

सदियों ने खता की, लम्हों ने सजा पाई

However, the generation born for the last 30 years particularly during last 20 years has learnt to live in and with corruption and crimes since birth and until death the same way as a worm born in filth lives and dies with it.

In India, the general masses (Aam – Aadami) have always followed the big, the higher ups, and the people above them, superior to them in age, power, authority or knowledge. India and the masses including countries of the world hardly had democracy in the known ancient history except at some point of time for limited period. There was Kingship throughout the world including India. People aped or followed the footprints of their rulers including out of fear. That is the reason behind so famous maxim 'As is the king so are the subjects' (*Jeisa Raja veisi Praja*). History stands witness that no change worth the name much less a revolutionary or even radical, ever took place from below unless started from the above. If kings and rulers were honest people and masses were honest, if they were dishonest subjects were dishonest. Despite democracy general masses of India have not and would not still realise their power unless reminded as Jamavant did to Hanuman and therefore suffered and suffering for the wrongs and evils of others including their Netas the present 'Kshatraps' and the employees manning the governments called the 'Bosses' and 'My Baap' including judiciary addressed as 'Huzur Sarkar'.

The total situation in India has now boiled down to a credibility gap, alienation of the people and loss of faith in governance and rulers. The frustration of the people has reached its acme where they even oppose national strategic projects, their own defence and security oriented enterprises, employment generating schemes like atomic – nuclear or dams, something unthinkable - unimaginable. Our enemies around are also awaiting our disintegration even without their taking any positive initiative.

Therefore, after 'Treta Yug', a 'Jamvant' is reminding not one but crores of Hanumans – the people of India particularly the 'Vanary Sena' the youth of the country to realise their power - strength and the wonders they can do. They also need to understand that the situation as it is, not going to improve even slightest by passing the laws in any numbers whatsoever as it only needs transformational changes i.e. changes radical in nature.

Immoral Unethical Impact of Netas

Netas have for self pelf so heterogeneously divided political spectrum of the country. Politics in India today is completely unprincipled therefore wholly confused and disarrayed. The power hungriness, opportunism and opportunistic alliances for power, compromises amongst unscrupulous elements and corrupt *netas* have baffled politics of the country and made it unprincipled therefore unethical and immoral. Netas have become so self centered that they have no hesitation deceiving their electorate for their self interests. For achieving their political ends they can fall to any extent any level and therefore are engaged in parochial politicking, casteism, communalism, regionalism, communalism and corruption – crimes apart in pelf usurpation and sexism that has soiled – dirtied and bemired entire political scenario. None has time to think of the country, the people and of reforming the system rather all heart in heart want this confusion, mismanagement and cobweb to continue. These are also the reasons giving judiciary chance to make already lame Legislature and deaf Executive handicapped for which people of the country had no repentance instead chanted "Judiciary Ki Jai Ho" - unfortunate dilemmatic a situation for and in a democracy. Also the way *netas* are indulged in protecting their dynastic interests and chair of power, had ¼ of it been devoted to national interests, solving societal problems and difficulties of the people things would have not fallen the level they have today. Morality and ethics in fact repenting for their fate in India as both have become biggest ever deficit in the country. The very *netas* who once accused late Indira ji or for that matter Nehru - Gandhi family for extra – Constitutional authority and Congress then and now, for dynasticism have forgotten and forgetting their own glass houses. They have instead surpassed all the limits of perpetuating dynastic rule, not only in their parties but also in governments when and wherever in power and still shamelessly continue pointing their finger towards others. That is the height of shame. Netas and politics in India have made even shame ashamed of itself. This is the height of dissipation ultimately for money, power, pelf, authority and pretentious living with enjoyment of power and not at all for name, fame, principles, or service to the country or good of the people. Why otherwise people still prefer politics despite politicians being so much abused, mocked and accused and politics so much damned in India.

Unfortunate as it is, in such horrible a situation people could have at least expected the hi-tech Babas, Jogies, mod Mahant Gurus and Sanyasinis, the self styled religio – spiritual flag bearers not to be as deaf, dumb and blind as *netas* but they have paradoxically proved much worse, allegorically a situation of blind leading the blind to fall together. Politics and Dharma, Politicians and Dharmics tending to become one, proving as the species of same genesis because only these two remain the most lucrative avocations in this country today, therefore complementary to each other. Guru – Baba – Sanyasi - Swamis needing sheep (*bhed*) and *netas* crowd (*bheed*), one needs disciples, other followers. Dharma Gurus – saffron clads – white enclothed failed to deliver being down to earth in western Bhog; the same west they accused throughout for 'Raga, Moha, Bhoga and Roga'.

This is however, equally true that so long as people worship and channels glorify persons like Hitlers, Stalins, Maos, Saddams, Idi Amins, Ravanas, Kansas, Mrs. and Mr. Marcos, Mrs. Chesesque or Mr. and Mrs. Mao, Mushraffs and Assads, surely only such people would be born and make life of the people as miserable as hellish perhaps more as we are presently experiencing. Like gangsters and gangsterism the politics and political culture of India has become not to groom and leave behind any other man of conviction, character and vision who had the potential to lead the country but who could protect the dynastic interests of groomers, suppress their rackets, stamp down treachery and build monuments and statues after them for glorification. This has further resulted into an alarmingly deteriorated situation that the country today has no statesmen or leaders but *netas* or politicians. A *neta* or politician expecting the people and the nation to die for him, a Statesman, or leader prepared to die for the country and the people. *Netas*, if at all, dying only for power and pelf or self and family interests, at the most for benefiting their relatives or dear ones, least for the people, let country go to dogs.

The mass disease, the epidemic, or endemic prevalent amongst the people or parts of India today is not cancer, leprosy, obesity, diabetes, TB, asthma, blood pressure, but the frustrations of people remaining uncared for, the sorrow of desertion, agony of gross neglect and the stress and pain of alienation. Such experience of alienation, feeling of isolation, tears of apathy, together with helplessness developed over the period has also embedded into governmental functioning including Executive, administration, Netas, and judiciary. If the *netas* like the ones we have, are managing public distribution, agriculture, industry, economics, electronics, investment, development, HRD, foreign affairs, home, finance, power – electricity, railways, or commerce and people dying of hunger, poverty, unemployment, disease or killing time and compelled to begging; should not be any surprise. It will however, always remain a mystery as to why and how such a nice man as Sri Arun Shourie could be so smart a dis-investor of public sector rather than reforming the system. Perhaps everybody has taken it for granted that with the present politico-judicial system and reservationist constitutional distortions there could be no reforms and changes even for the betterment of the society, the people and the nation.

Blaming Public Sector for all the economic ills of the country just to save own skins without realising that the roots of such sickness lied elsewhere amounted to committing same mistake of treating Aids as ringworm and Epilepsy as heat stroke. Consequences were bound to be what we have seen. The ailment in fact was entirely different to the treatment given. The fault was neither of mixed economy nor of socialistic pattern nor welfare state, least of public sector but mainly of corruption, managing impotency, misuse of law and liberalised functioning of legal system and free for all approach of judiciary that included misplaced sympathy at public - national cost to individuals. Instead of improving upon the working and taking reformative steps to revitalise the system and functioning and find solutions to the problems by removing blunders of governance, they for vested interests made mix economy and public sector a scapegoat for own inefficiencies, incompetencies and a cat's paw for their sins.

All *netas* irrespective of political affiliations formed a cartel to serve the inhuman individualistic western Bhogvad, they called liberalisation and globalisation, that brought disaster not only to this country but to even the European countries many of whom have come at the verge of bankruptcy. All political parties ensured the safety of American and European interests at the cost of our own including the welfare of the people as well as development of the country. Recession, depression - inflation - cost spiral - high prices and unemployment vicious circle made living impossible and brought majority on the road and poor practically at breaking point and begging.

Today there are *netas* having black money somewhere 50 thousand to 100000 crores. The number having between 25 to 50 thousand crores is very large. Government officials having 500 crores to 5000 crores is much larger even the number of common and general employees having five crore to 100 crores is 30 % of total employees. The dilemmatic paradox today is that other things remaining equal (i.e. without the issue of human rights particularly none interference by judiciary etc), people are prepared to work as government employees without pay – salary and the number inclined would be twenty times more than the number of government servants today.

Politics also has in this country taken unimaginatively highly ugly turn during the last 20 years i.e. from the time of so called liberalisation also misnomer globalisation. The worse is bloody and dirty cast politics along with dangerous communal politics resulting in civil commotion for which voters and the people in general are also responsible rather should share the blame. This is the only country in the world where *netas* as a class could befool all the people all the times whatever the excuses, unluckily people are also prepared for. It was very late in the day when general masses realised the tactics of *netas* playing communal card and caste politics conniving to make politics their ancestral empire and playing political games without any advantage or benefit to them. Fed up, people did react ultimately and taught lesson to these *netas* but by then it was really too late as people had already lost everything.

Equally, perhaps bigger dichotomous duality of Indian democratic politics lies in the people electing their representatives having no faith on them. They elect not their leaders (Raaj Netas or Statesmen) but *netas* that too reluctantly. Subsequently the same people blame their selves for electing such representatives when these *neta* prove a burden including on the nation. For this reason also people have been led to believe in an insensitive judiciary that failed to deliver in accordance with the Constitution and law. The Judiciary failed and failed utterly to do economic and legal justice to the sovereign people of the country. The judiciary accommodated lawyers more than the sovereign people the makers of all institutions; constitutionally said to be the enactors of Constitution, the masters who can change the whole system even the constitution and judiciary. The judiciary that hardly took or takes action or prosecute dishonest lawyers who deceive or advise their clients wrongly, illegally, deliberately and malafidely, take adjournments, make money exploit the downtrodden poor masses of the country and therefore oppose entry of foreign lawyers though enjoy, consume, wear, use, eat, drink, and read everything foreign and mad to travel to foreign lands particularly US and UK where from generally the lawyers wanted to argue in Indian courts. Many lawyers are afraid because of language, others because of knowledge, but above all is the fear of blocking trickery handlings, including rarity of chances of adjournments.

It is said and quoted that about sixty four years ago the great Winston Churchill, the war time PM of UK predicted this fall of Indian polity because of immorality of *netas*, unethicality of governance, degradation of values, corrupt administration, erosion of systems and was for those reasons not prepared to liberate India.

Political Dilemma and the People

Politics in India within such a short period became as bloody a war as dangerous as terroristic killings and shameless that ashamed the shame. Under the circumstances, politics has therefore become too serious a matter to be left to politicians alone. Once the people of the country decide to change the Constitution and the form of government it would not then be the language of politics but the language of people having finality in all matters all the time. Under present political scenario, we have otherwise also reached a situation of choosing not simply between the bad and worse but between monstrous and disastrous, between worst and hellish or Satanic and demonic. People may possibly imagine a war without bloodshed but not politics in India.

Amongst political parties, Congress having ruled the longest not only knew but also taught others the art of manipulations including making concessions but reserved to itself the right or the vision of recognising the time when to make them. Consequently, politicians instead of placing themselves in the service of the people and the nation placed the nation and people in their service knowing pretty well that just before elections not actually giving but even announcing a concession will make the dent making people forget the past. Under the situation not only politicians and administration even Judiciary could not feel the pulse of the people. None of the three organs could keep itself above suspicion and that is the biggest dilemmatic wonder.

What is more surprising is that although in our system of constitutional governance, whatever it is, men and women are equal, have equality not merely legal but Constitutional and unqualified equality since day one that surprisingly did not exist in many other countries of the world, still women fighting for supremacy in the name of equality. Unfortunately entire country today is lost in reservations. We all perhaps think that everything that is morally wrong could politically be justified in this country, a trend that is proving deadly to social relationships, cohesiveness, hearty equations, amity, togetherness and service to people, in general and citizens, in common, reasons being simple. There is neither '*seva*' or service motive, nor principled political philosophy for economic upliftment, mental elevation or knowledge betterment behind such bogeys but sheer narrow selfish pelf and political opportunism. Therefore deep down into the dirt they are all one. Of late it all has become worst with western Bhogvad of eat, drink and merriment pervading the politics and political arena and with that the psyche of everybody deep down. A situation that is and will continue to bring disasters to this country and is impossible to be reversed under present conditions where we have been put by politicians, together with Karmkandis and Jyotish. Therefore, the only way to put the system on rail is to change the system itself and put on an auto rail that would function as a system the way nature and creation function.

One good thing however of present political Bhogvad is that nobody is a foe or friend of anybody. If at all foes are more than friends it is because it all is opportunistic, a modern gift of west to this country, no one is true to anyone, which has made entire politics uncertain, governance unstable and future unpredictable. Personal pursuits, political interests, individual opportunism and family accumulation dominate all other interests an extremely individualistic, Bhogavad oriented, capitalistic society having polluted a humanistically spiritual and morally ethical society to its nadir. Not only party cadres even the student and youth wings the future hopes, fighting for sex oriented power, pelf and self in the name of politics, religion, regionalism, casteism, provincialism, language - ism and what not, deviating to any extent to grab whatever they could. Marxists, owing more to Mao than Marx, BJP to Jinnah than SP Mukherjee, DMK to LTTE than to India and Congress to America or Berlusconi way of Italian BANGO – BANGO than to the country, BSP to elephants and parks than to Dalits, SP and RJD more to family than to backwards and some others to separatist and terrorists than to religion. Overall, as most of the parties have ideologically become bankrupt and principally vested, so has their quality, acumen, wisdom and service performance to the country and the people. The working of last 20 years almost since 1990, has shown rather proved that Samajavadis and religionists in this country are worse as regards corruption, Casteism and class divisionists than Nazis, Maoists and Naxals they accuse for so many evils.

How could the government of a country - that has gone mad or going cynic for free for all economy, liberalizing foreign investment for perverted poisonous consumption and pursuits, following and allowing killing instinct economic order together with nude, homo, incest porn culture and life style - ever be expected to ponder over such transformational philosophy much less change existing rotten order - the form of government and Constitutional system? Therefore, only people have now to decide collectively – whether to live or perish, live life as humans or simply spend days as animals, be invaded by Bhog - the criminalised incest corrupt homo porn culture of west for the end of life or own sharing co – existence, humanism and socialistic spirituality the basic cultural philosophy of India.

Administration: The Piteous Failure

Surprisingly within a short period, government services in India became sinecure offices, a culture of doing nothing and getting everything. Over and above government employees boasted of being 'Sarkari' rather than public servants and asked the public to pay them for getting their work done. Courts gave this culture recognition by repeatedly saying these servants have Constitutional status rather than the master public who made the Constitution for own self by creating these very services so that the servant may be put in service. Such culture not only affected the whole system but its quality, efficiency, standards, values and dignity which ultimately affected production and services, economy and prosperity leading to disinvestment of Public Sector, that has to be sold for pennies.

Thanks also to excessive judicial interferences under the veil of judicial activism coupled with degenerating morality and ethics of *netas* together with administrative corruption that befouled whole system to collapse. Masses and the common people who needed constitutional protection and governmental empathy were mostly treated as out castes, as animals and uncounted for, while government servants, public sector servants even private sector employees and unions looted and exploited the country. They squeezed the people got liberal concessions, excessive privileges together with constitutional – legal protections pushing the country at the verge of bankruptcy by 1992 by messing up entire Production - Services Sector and ultimately throwing people into the lap of individualistic exploitative US capitalism and *laissez faire* economic order of Europe, the consequences of which we saw, are seeing and will continue to see.

The whole system of governance forgot that no body's interest could ever be above or supersede the interest of the general people and common masses in a democracy. Maintaining and keeping corrupt employees, taking care of such employees under the legal umbrella at the cost of the citizenry and society amounts to hanging the whole body of people alive. This over protection of laws and over nurturing of the employees by courts including the union pressures led the unions and the employees overpower the governance and the system itself resulting in their dominating the people rather than national productivity and public services dominating them. Top - down – above the line *mantri* to *santri* and vice versa became one in this loot of the nation, plundering public and squeezing society became a peculiar phenomenon of Indian governing system. Caste based politics resulted into caste oriented administration reducing the system much below the Paper frame from so called steel frame leaving no frame today except that of corruption. Whatever left was ruined by caste based reservations the perpetuation of which the constitution so avowedly negates.

In this background of the things now, nothing is left for the people but to rise to the occasion before the occasion rises any more against them and ruins forever. It is high time for recognising their long term, general and perpetual interests rather than short term, caste oriented, community, region, language, and gender based prejudices which only would absolve people of their pains and perpetual sorrows forever.

Alas! Even professionalism has in this country not only failed but proved drudgery on the services, as anti people and corrupt as any other discipline or professional function of the government. All have asked, asking for their pound of flesh from the country – society that ultimately means – We the People of India.

The fashion of not working faithfully even for four out of eight hours and feeling gratified for, but demanding all salary, perks, promotions and 'Upar – ki – Kamai' as a matter of right for all the seven days and twenty – four hours has developed in this country as well for want of 'Constitutional Duties' to serve the people honestly - sincerely and the country faithfully – patriotically. Failure of Constitutional obligations to serve the people and the country has resulted into a 'conduit chemistry' of self – aggrandisement that has over the period developed into such a network that neither the chemistry nor electronics could find a counter formula for. The biggest tragedy is that all alleged Bigs, so called Mods, fashionable scantly clothed, western stylish 'Angreji wallas' were and are involved and equally shared the booty.

It is however intriguing, that how right from the next day of freedom the country found itself amidst a mess more so after it became a Republic in 1950. Reasons not difficult to find and trace. Before freedom, despite the victory of Labour Party in UK, freedom for India perhaps appeared remote and uncertain but then it came so sudden that even the Statesmen, the visionaries of the time could not visualise the model for future governance of the country and SURAAJ for the people except self-governance through parliamentary democracy. They had throughout fought and struggled against imperialists and their 'Ism' and suddenly came freedom along with many problems including division of the country coupled with Time Limit Bondage compelling copying the constitutions of other countries and drafting in haste (in the absence of any other experience) adopting particularly British Parliamentary form with which country and most of them were acquainted.

But despite all that, none incorporation of duties or fundamental duties in the Constitution and inclusion only of fundamental rights played a havoc particularly under the communistic impact of that time which later proved disastrous to the country. Along with it, the none inclusion of vicarious liability of government employees in the Constitution proved catastrophic for good governance, the price of which the people and the country is paying so heavily. People's dreams, their Vision for future though enshrined in the Part IV of the Constitution remained unfulfilled and un-enforceable while looters continued to loot the country, plunderers plunder the people and freebooters raiding the society. Hence, neither the Constitution could own the people nor people the Constitution. Today the situation is that out of 125 crore population, hardly ten crores have heard even the word Samvidhan and less than three crores the Constitution. Therefore, nothing short of changing the system of governance and the Constitution would now come to the rescue of people and the country. Constitution did not address people's needs and core issues in legally enforceable way and not at all the Indian psyche in the manner it had to. That was the reason for amendment of the Constitution the next day of its coming into force. This has by now reached as high as 115 almost like reshaping its originality or re- drafting it.

Besides the rights without duties, the authority without accountability, proved another blow to the system, governance, the country, and the people as the events of last sixty years have established and established beyond all doubts.

Ironically, the country had to rely on the same bureaucracy that sided with British and acted against the people and freedom movement. The vestiges and the legacy continued, though in a different form worsening the situation in free India. While during British rule it was the bureaucracy and British who acted against the people of the country, in free India besides bureaucracy were Netas, capitalists, unions, businesses and others combined. They ruined even the finest of the plans by their littleness and trivialness. Who ought to have carried them out for the good of the nation, welfare of masses, benefit of the people and development of society.

As a matter of fact, nothing is moving in this country - though appears to be moving only because it is moving routinely in its natural course, a dilemma not easy to be explained - partly because of uncalled for judicial interferences, partly because of Capitalists – businesses, most of the times because of politicians - capitalists - 'Netagiri' combined, at others by opposition, in all cases by bureaucracy – government employees all the times - every time; over and above lack of political will. Administrative red tape being rampant abetted by corruption, excessive judicial interference without any beneficial outcome, dominance of system by vested interests has created a governance where people - the masters - have become servants and not the system servant of the people, government employees acting as masters of the people, not people their masters, still the system is said to be working. Working; however, yes, but by the grace of God, the same way as litigations in courts, FIRs in police stations, trains on tracks, patients in Hospitals and files in Govt offices. Those in power political or governmental behave with general public as if engaged in belligerency and function as traitors and high treasonists.

Anna's Jan–Lok Ayukt: No Solution

Jan - Lok Ayukt or any Bill or Act of the type would not at all be the solution of corruption particularly if higher judiciary i.e. Supreme Court / High Courts are brought under it i.e. under such institution of Ayuktas by whatever name called. The biggest tragedy with Indian polity and psyche is that out of 125 crore people hardly five (5) per cent know about their own Constitution i.e. Bharatiya Samvidhan. Unless people know their real history - the true history, and Constitution in general, there could be no possibility of any system change for improvement - transformation not at all. Under present Constitutional system, High Courts in the states and Supreme Court in India have the power of Superintendence over all Judicial, quasi Judicial, and administrative authorities including governments. They have the power of issuing prerogative writs in the nature of Habeas Corpus, Mandamus, Certiorari, Prohibition, and Quo Warranto, orders, stays restraining or directing all authorities to act in accordance with the law and Constitution or not to act the way they are. The two courts could sit in appeal over the orders / decisions of any or all authorities : Administrative, Judicial and / or Quasi Judicial and decide not only the legality, propriety, fairness and constitutionality of their decisions orders judgments but the legality and constitutionality of their composition itself. Supreme / High Courts have the power of judging and deciding even the Constitutionality of law made by Legislatures except the Constitutionality of the Constitution that includes Constitutional amendments made by Parliament that represents the Sovereign People of the country. All petitions, in certain cases appeals against the decisions of all such authorities would lie in HC, sparingly in SC. HC / SC could quash, modify, or remand the decision of any such authority. Therefore, putting SC / HC under such authorities whether called Lok - Jan Ayukt or Jana – Loka Ayukta would not only be an absurdity but constitutional impropriety liable to be quashed. This is though true that Judiciary has - because of incompetency of Netas, political corruption rampant, governmental apathy and gross indifference towards public - usurped in a big chunk of power despite the fact that herself Judiciary is not free from such allegations. But that would not and could not constitutionally justify putting Lok Ayukt or Jana Ayukta over.

Our Constitution provides a specific procedure for enquiring into the misconducts, misbehavior, and incapacity of a judge or judges including their removal and impeachment. The relevant Article 124 of Constitution lays down:

(4) A Judge of the Supreme Court shall not be removed from his office except by an order of the President passed after an address by each House of Parliament supported by a majority of the total membership of that House and by a majority of not less than two thirds of the members of that House present and voting has been presented to the President in the same session for such removal on the ground of proved misbehaviour or incapacity.

(5) Parliament may by law regulate the procedure for the presentation of an address and for the investigation and proof of the misbehaviour or incapacity of a Judge under clause 4. Similar provision exists for HC judges as well.

Above Article has been drafted in highly ambiguous language. It neither explains misconduct of a judge nor defines incapacity of a judge. It has used misbehaviour of a judge rather than misconduct, which further makes it open to many complicated interpretations.

In view of the above, any law or procedure to the contrary would be held unconstitutional by judiciary, which may happen even in those cases where legislature i.e. Parliament and / or Vidhan Sabhas make the law or amend the Constitution as the case may be. That would be taken by Courts as changing the basic structure of the Constitution and unconstitutionally interfering in all pervasive judicial power and people's right to justice. No wing or organ of government, even the people of India (seeing the level of literacy, knowledge, awakening and consciousness we have) would be able to do anything in such matters even if patently a wrong decision. If history is any indication, we saw how judges wanted to keep them and have in fact kept them out of Right to Information Act, tried to keep out of declaration of assets, property, and wealth and so on. Corruption cases of Judges of HCs apart, couple of Judges of SC including former CJI KG Balakrishanan are the examples where the same SC, that rarely does so in corruption cases, declined to interfere, at times even in serious and important matters. Therefore, insisting on such Constitutional changes by Anna team, the self styled civil-society is not only Constitutional absurdity and gross trespass into Constitutional fundamentals but is the limit of ignorance. The Constitutionality of each provision of such a law or Act that would keep judiciary particularly higher judiciary under Lok or Jan Ayukt would be open to challenge. Truly speaking such a law or Act as a layman now understands, would never see the light of the day, and die its own death. It is really surprising why Parliament did not pass this and why it did not strike Congress party to get such law passed, keeping SC / HC under Jana–Loka Pal to save its skin. Since such law concerned the ego - prestige and dignity of Judiciary its constitutionality would have been decided by SC / HC within months and declared ultravires, invalid. Though the decisions in other cases have and would take years. Consequently the so called Civil Society which has nothing civil, would have been finished forever and MPs particularly Congress would have saved its face dignifiedly. It appears that Congress was so confused out of fear of being caught and scanned that it did not dare take risk at all. But heart in heart not only Congress, all the parties barring CPI were afraid more than Congress rather duressed and terrified.

In any case, each decision, order, or final judgment of Jana or Lok Ayukt would be liable to challenge in HC / SC. That power of Judiciary could neither be taken away by any Legislature even by Parliament by Constitutional amendment, nor could such jurisdiction be given to any other authority as that would be construed destroying the basic structure of the Constitution.

Though, Judicial Accountability Act appears a remedy against Judicial corruption and improving justice delivery system, still much would depend on drafting and eliciting public support to save such law from judicial interference as Indira ji used to do.

In view of these imbroglios the only solution to all the ailments and problems of the people lies in changing the present Parliamentary form of governance. At this point we need to know that Presidential form or System of governance prevails in more than 70 % countries of the world including super, developed and big powers viz America, Russia, France, Brazil, Mexico, South Africa including China and our neighbours viz Pakistan, Sri Lanka, Indonesia Philippines and others.

While it is no doubt true that under the present Constitution the people of India are supreme and sovereign but its functioning has made them not merely servants but slaves, bewildered, confused, unable to know what to do.

Therefore, if we really want to make the system a Peoples democracy for the people i.e. a Jan-Lok Tantra in action instead of 'Praja Tantra' as we had heretofore, we need to go for proposed change.

Drafting - Jan - Lok Pal - Ayukt Act

Any Act or Law made against corruption and on appointment of Jana or Lok Ayukt needs to be crisp, short, concise, and free from legal encumbrances, providing for time limit for decisions based on summary trials and prima facie evidence in support with capital punishment in certain cases. For recovering the value or actual loss caused by any Commission or Commission amounting to corruption the Act needs to include attachment, auction of property – moveable or immovable of accused, his family members including successors and heirs and in certain cases of relatives if primafacie found involved in, including planning, abetment or actual commission or appropriation thereof. While Lok Ayukts as such needs to have complete freedom of investigation and use of any agency and power to call and inspect any document and person or authority and non interference of HC / SC at interlocutory stages, he / they also need to be under Parliamentary superintendence as the Judges of HC / SC and made accountable to people. Otherwise, the same problem of watching the watch dog and guarding the guard would arise as is the case with Judges, CVC, Election Commissioners, CBI and others. Nobody in a people's democracy could wield absolute despotic powers. How long HC and SC Judges would keep these Ayuktas free from their interferences is yet to be seen. Still non – interference during interlocutory stage law to some extent could restrict. However, Supreme Court / HC Judges need to learn a lesson now that people have started smelling them also.

More complicated than law, would be procedural law, further been complicated by Vakila Samaj. The laws in our country are rigged more because these are in the language of uncommon man and rarely in the languages of masses. Therefore the Rules called procedural law need to be very simple, uncomplicated under the Jan - Lok Pal Act. Justice in this country that too fair, could only be available if, Criminal and Civil Procedure Codes are simplified. Otherwise also both the Codes require radical changes, which whenever attempted by government was opposed by Vakila Samaj as the entry of foreign Attorneys for the same reasons.

Today, corruption itself feels ashamed in this country as we have corrupted the corruption. What could people do for clandestine deals, Dalal economy, Havala and touts or if an Assistant needs Deputy for supervision, Deputy needs Senior and senior a principal and principal a chief. The same way as CBI would super CBI and one day 'Param CBI, but for how long and for what objective? It reminds us of a story where a King went on keeping seniors over juniors to watch and see that water is not mixed in the milk supplied, and to his utter surprise one day he found only water being supplied to his kingdom and there was no trace of milk. That could also be the case with Lok or Jana Lok Pals despite being a Jury.

Therefore piece meal nothing could be achieved or would be gained. The whole system needs to be corrected by attacking from all four corners, all around which would only be possible by changing the present Constitution and form of government and opting the new as suggested.

If this proposal is put to vote, minimum 75% voters of the country would accept, adopt, and enact the changes while it only requires 50% of the voters plus one for adoption or effecting the proposed changes.

Besides, treating government employees, who in reality are the servants of the people, as a separate class, above masses and the people, putting them at higher pedestal than the common man by giving higher and better facilities, amenities, conveniences, and bounties at the expense of the same common man is mockery of democracy. These are some of the main causes of gross apathy and deliberate negligence of government employees towards the people and the country resulting in lethargy and deterioration of public services and governmental functioning in India leading to frustration, alienation and dilapidation of the people. Our courts, for giving everything to such servants went to the extent of distorting

Constitution, by saying that they had Constitutional status undermining those who made the Constitution.

Coverage and Constitutional Status

For the purposes of corruption all government and public sector employees need to be covered under the Bill / Act irrespective of status and position except some positions specifically mentioned under the Constitution, otherwise there is no point having or not having such law. Despite Anna Hazare and Ramdev movements including Kejariwal's, India has internationally leaped from 73% to 90% corruption levels. Corruption in India is as nude as nudity elsewhere. The Act would simply be an eyewash to befool public if top bureaucratic brass is not covered. This is and would again be a tactical trap of Netas to continue with corruption by not covering themselves and top bureaucrats. Under the present constitutional system any argument for not covering Prime Minister is and would be nonsensical. Such people must read history and learn from the mother of democracy the United Kingdom where PMs including great Harold Wilson resigned on the ground of corruption in the government. Prime Ministers of Japan and Presidents and PMs of South Korea are other examples. Prime Ministers of Spain and Italy are recent examples. All of the above are working democracies better than India except Italy. What instability did it create there? In India it is something like Arabian world – not to leave or relinquish or abdicate until thrown out, humiliated or killed. While India follows Arabian world in the matters of corruption it followed Italy and Libya of Gaddafi for Bongo – Bongo means sex and rave parties by keeping the masters of Constitution – the makers of Constitution hungry and starving. Under declining ethical morality of biggest democracy of world i.e. India where Prime Minister enters the ladder of power through back door (Chor Darwaja), not being accountable to people but to a few or aliens, covering of PM under the Act would be all the more necessary.

Why Congressies who are clever people in such matters did not agree to such an Act keeping SC and HC under 'Jana Lok Pal and got it passed is something not understandable rather a mystery. Such an Act would have never seen the light of the day as it would have never been upheld by higher Judiciary. By doing so Congressies would have slept pleasantly and silenced the people of the country forever. Moreover, as such an Act would have otherwise also been challenged in more than one High Court it would have come or been taken up by SC and decided within six months - where otherwise Yugas are taken for deciding cases - as here it was the prestige of judiciary itself which was involved or would have been rather at stake.

Under our present constitutional system, Constitutional status is the maximum that Parliament can give under the Act for maintaining the independence of the institution of JLP. Protecting enforceability of its decisions as no institution, body, or authority under our Constitutional system could be absolute and immune from challenge in the HC or Supreme Court, as already explained.

The Jan or Lok Pal at center or states, needs to be an institution of not less than three persons. This will help in maintaining its impartiality and fairness with auto powers to order CBI or any other enquiry from any agency of the country. In order to investigate the pending charges / cases without any interference of any authority or court.

However, overall effectiveness and success would depend only on time bound decisions making not exceeding one year at the level of JLP and six months at HC / SC levels each. This includes prima facie evidence and summary trials of cases including none interference by HC / SC at interlocutory stages which Parliament is competent to provide for also.

Despite all legal bondages and constitutional status including protection, there could neither be, nor is any guarantee, as is the case with Supreme Court / High Court Judges and CBI also, that the Lok Ayukt or Jan Ayukt or the investigating agencies or other inspecting officials working under them shall and would not be corrupt. The chances would rather be more. Therefore, the only solution for the problems of India thus made complex and complicated over the period, is to have a one time all pronged attack, not piece meal approach as governments have been doing or Civil Society is proposing and that solution is changing the form of governance and the Constitution, a lasting solution, a panacea for all times.

Impeccability of Capital Punishment

Not only the general masses of India, even the judiciary is under the misconception that capital punishment could be awarded only in case of murder under Section 302 of IPC. But Constitutionally Parliament has the power to provide for Capital punishment for an offence naturally in suitable cases including for the offences of corruption and black money and there is no constitutional bar on Constitutional mandate under Art 21 is very clear. Parliament is constitutionally empowered to provide for capital punishment for corruption and black money or such heinous crimes that deprive the people and society of the wealth, asset and money belonging to them or divests the society of its legal movable or immovable possessions benefiting a foreign country. Article 21 of the Constitution empowers the Parliament for making such law or laws providing for capital punishment to a citizen subject to a procedure. Since Article 21 finds place under Part III of the Constitution that deals with 'Fundamental Rights', no court, authority, person, judge and lawyer could or has the right to debate on abolition of Capital Punishment or talk of even awarding capital punishment in rarest of rare cases. Article 21 though a negative FR (Fundamental Right) under the Constitution of India, is nonetheless an FR that says 'Nobody will be deprived of his life except according to the procedure prescribed under the law'. Parliament could therefore, provide even for summary trial of offences and prima facie hearing with simple observance of Principles of natural justice even for according capital punishment which is beyond interference of any court.

While the judgment in Raj Bala's Case tells the people of India to know their worth, it also paves the way for prescribing and awarding capital punishment for any offence involving corruption of Rs 3.5 lacs, in any case five lacs or more. Raj Bala of Haryana, a devotee of Baba Ramdev succumbed as a consequence of police excesses inflicted in Ramlila grounds - New Delhi during anti black money movement launched by Ramdev Yadav in May 2011. Supreme Court of India had fixed human value at Rs 3.5 lacs directing Delhi Police, which as is said earns around 3.5 crores per month from other sources, to pay said compensation to her, though the Court in its wisdom also directed Ramdev Yadav Baba, who had already spent a huge amount on her treatment, to pay Rs. 1.5 lacs to her. Thus, taking extreme situation in India the human price in terms of money has been fixed at Rs 5. 00 lacs at the most, as against million dollars or more in America and Europe, the policies of the countries India boasts to follow. Even in India in one case very recently for an offence many levels lighter to the one mentioned above the same court awarded Rs. ten lacs. The people's democratic laissez - faire Govt of India has under Atomic disaster scheme fixed this price at 500 / per head that reminds the agony of a Shire in these words;

दूसरे देशों में फिर भी महंगी है जिंदगी
अपने देश में जिंदगी का बहुत बुरा हाल है

मौत का भी कोई इलाज हो शायद
पर यहाँ जिंदगी का ही कोई इलाज नहीं

जिन्दा लाशों की सी भीड़ दिखती है चारों तरफ इस देश में
लगता है जिंदगी मौत से भी बड़ा हादसा है यहाँ

(Meaning - in other countries life has value therefore a cost but in India it is in a very bad condition, in poorest state. Death may have some solution but here even life has none. It is like the crowd of living corpses all around that shows life is greater fatality here than death)

Black Money Vs Corruption: The Main Concern

Corruption was not at all the concern of Governments, Netas, bureaucrats or capitalists as none was afraid of. The main concern the worry was for black money. Corruption they knew how to manage including the ways – means and methods. Black Money they considered and take as more stigmatic socially, dangerous legally and ruinous politically, if caught, in foreign banks. Corruption they also know is a long drawn procedure subject to enquiries, committees and commissions and then to legal procedures of courts and litigations and above all to an extent the handmade servant of money power - purchasable and manageable. Otherwise also there is a world of difference in making the law, implementing the law and honestly acting upon it. Then as in many states including the most populated UP, Lok Ayukts have so nominal staff that many of them even do filing and other work with their own hands. While on the other hand, illiterate corrupt ministers and officials have a retinue of assistants. Many of them have no investigating officers. Thus providing for law and providing for infrastructure to efficiently and speedily act upon the law are quite different aspects of the same coin. Catching one or two persons hither and thither is not going to or would impact this bloody system which has become the 'Rakt Beez' of corruption and made India its breeding ground, nor would it change anything in reality rather things would further worsen if not changed now. In this reservation oriented - caste ridden - corruption infested system and society nothing is going to change even worth the name unless the system itself is changed – 'Vyavastha Parivartan' as they call it. With the present system at work the same corrupt – criminal – scoundrels would be voted to power on caste - community - communal lines.

Notwithstanding, the entire system with the Govt was worried more about the movement against Black Money, which they took their biggest catch including that of Netas, capitalists, Bureaucrats and big goons. Black money in foreign countries was something that would have ruinously exposed them putting not only the political career of Netas but the future of political parties at stake perhaps of many in darkest jeopardy. Unfortunate as it is, they succeeded in torpedoing the movement and in the mean time got sufficient time to shift or otherwise manage that money in their different ways. It is not one party or people of one party alone but people of all parties who would have been trapped in. There could be appreciable number of Netas and Bureaucrats, capitalists apart, each having around 20000 - 30000 crore black money in foreign banks and enough number having even more. It's not only foreign banks, within the country a very large number of private – public sector employees would be having above 100 crores each, big - guns, Mafias, goons, businesses apart. Most of them are the people teaching us Desh Bhakti, ethics and morality including the lesson respecting law and discipline. This does not include Guru, Babas, Swamis, Mahants, and Mahantanis - Joginis as that money would be immense and almost all of them would fall within the ambit.

The Sadhu, Baba, Guru and modern Mahants, Sanyasis and Sanyasinis have immense unaccounted wealth and untaxed money lying in strong rooms or hoarded unused. Satya Sai or Puttaparthi Sai Baba is one such, the trust of which the so called socialist and the Messiah of down trodden and said to be the father of PIL in India a retired CJI was the Chair person. There are number of such Gurus, Sadhus and so called detached Sanyasis the ascetics having stores of such un - invested - idle money in lockers earned in the name of Dharm, gods and goddesses while as is said, around 25 crore people in India sleep every night without a meal. Is not such money Black Money – if not what it is? While reservationists only want privilege over equality these white or saffron clads want a privilege over the prerogative in the name of religion calling it Dharm and god while in truth they have reduced God into god with their sins and evils.

Five Elements and Governing Allegory

The lust of elite class, the avarice of governing class, thirst of capitalists, the greed of pseudo - rich and extravagant display by mod - generation believing in speed and results. This includes neo - westerns believing in overnight richness by earning cheap, corrupt, and easy money evoked acquisitiveness and covetousness of general masses towards western Bhogavad. Just a replica of Epicurean hedonism.

All this collectively played mayhem with the ethical, moral values and spiritual - cultural ethos of the country and in turn made life of poverty stricken people hellish which is not only depriving the present generation of essentials of life but moving to completely deprive the posterity of three essential substances of life – Earth (land or Bhoomi); Water (Ap - jal), Air (Vayu-

Sameer). The other two Fire (Tej - Paavak or Agni) and Ether (Akash) are at the verge of becoming scarce. After usurping and dividing land and water man has started dividing space or sky. These are the substances that no science could ever produce, or deny being not the life sustaining elements or survival substances.

Allegorically the five could be, extended to three organs of governance and two pillars of society meaning Parliament (earth), Bureaucracy or Executive (air), industrialists and agriculturists (water), Judiciary (fire) and the ultimate 'Dharma' the 'Shabd' (ether - Akash).

All the above five collectively are supposed to make good governance and happy society. All of them have unfortunately been so polluted that, if after 20 years from now the posterity, which would then be in the age group of 20-30 years; constituting fifty per cent intellectual group i.e. around 75 crores, felt that the present generation had deprived them of these three life sustaining elements. Just for pelf, avarice, conspicuous consumption and been responsible for their agony, misery, woes, pity and distress. They suffered because of the bankruptcy and incompetence of governance, failure and incapacity of legal - judicial system to punish the hedonist looters, Epicurean plunderers, the launderers and raiders of country's wealth. The system failed to check such unbridled lust of this generation. The consequences of revenge perhaps could not even be imagined by this generation. Who would survive to see those only God knows.

Unfortunate as it is, or was, we have aped all bad things of west but none of their good. We have aped worse of the worst things of Western Bhogvad but none of their valued things i.e. honesty, humanity, fairness, morality, ethics, incorruptible governance, speedy, fast and fair justice, holistic lego - judicial system, impartial investigations and the culture of building institutions. Netas in this country preferred to sink along the chair of power they occupied rather than be the great Nelson Mandela, Julius Nyerere, or Dalai Lama. The Netas have vowed and preferred to remain mean, be abused but not to lead by example, die on and with the chair, knowing very well they could never do that. Thus, they have over the period brought the institutions to decay and collapse setting so bad examples before posterity that it would take years perhaps generation (Unless there is an act of God or Nature) to restore the system.

Now, unless, the country adopts the following: a time bound justice delivery system; pecuniary and exemplary punishment oriented criminal jurisprudence; highly moralistic bureaucracy; honest policing; ethical administration; fair investigations; socially accountable and responsible governmental machinery; impartial summary trials with prima facie proof; payment of Unemployment allowance or unemployment insurance, the masses could never have the fruits of political and economic freedom - economic equality never.

Governments, administration, elite class, police, capitalists, law enforcing authorities, judiciary and the systems including Netas expect compliance and obedience from common man, the hungry starving masses knowing not that hunger allows no choice. Irony and unfortunate, as it would have not been, the governing system in India has become slave of the individual or individuals, any individual or couple of them in power could lord upon the system. It is not the system that governs the country. One individual could just make or mar the system and the governance but people in a democracy just could do nothing. A party in power could make law on any subject though not covered by its election manifesto or election promises, plunder and launder public wealth, the hard earned tax payers money on building Elephants, parks or own statues without taking peoples consent. A Chief Minister or political authority could get a discretionary quota allotted or fund created and distribute alms out of public coffers or state treasury to any favourite or for political vested interests without asking and depriving the very sovereign electorates without medicines, water, electricity food, shelter and what not. This is open cunningness deceiving the sovereign people in the midst of democracy and democracy in the midst of people without any referendum or public opinion. The legal system meanwhuile standing blind folded and judicial system helplessly a silent spectator or at the most undecided and therefore lingering the matters and issues for years.

Abject Economic Failure

World economy failed and failed miserably and with that failed economics. It was and is not only the economies of developing countries like India but of big and developed countries that also failed and failing which in fact is the total failure of collective elite intelligence of the world. How could have India prospered which is dependent on all these countries particularly America. Despite however the failure of US economy the $ (dollar) that was worth Rs. 40 two years ago is about Rs. 55 now. Therefore the failure is apparent on the face of governance in India. This is the situation when American economy has reached the lowest. Had it been the same economy of eighties – early ninety's, a dollar perhaps been worth Rs. 80. Not only economies the countries of the world have become bankrupt. Ireland, Spain, Cyprus, Portugal, Italy, France even UK and Germany are in doldrums apart from others. Ivory Coast and Haiti are other examples and most of the African and Arabic countries are eating the dust. Conditions in India could very well be appreciated by the misfortune of those 25 crore people who sleep daily without a meal. They say economy has developed @ of 10 – 11 % and SENSEX has appreciated by reaching 19000 still per day earning of 50 crore people varies from Rs. 30 to Rs. 64. Dy. Chairman of Planning Commission who constructs a toilet for Rs 25 lacs for himself says Rs. Eighteen per head per day is more than sufficient for a man in India to be called rich and bring him out of BPL. This is the state of affairs when 30 per cent supplies including medicines, milk, ghee, oil, pulses and eatables including drinks and flour are fake, forged, adulterated, and counterfeit and 25 per cent of employable educated are in foreign countries. People are thirsty even for a drop of the polluted water which is available. During summer, even guns are taken out and people even kill each other for a pot of water. Since independence we have only been saying and in every election repeating - 'Roti, Kapada or Makan' that has for some time past included – 'Bijali, Pani and Sadak'. It needs no mention that amongst corruption and Human Development Index, India is amongst the worst. Still they say economy is progressing and India would become number one and in any case after China number two amongst world economies by 2025. The number of people starving, hungry or half fed, eating barks of trees, leaves, herbs, and roots is appallingly pitiable. Fifty per cent population is without shelter and clothes. Government still boasts of economic heights as America continues instigating us of our capabilities. Intellectuals do feel and realise very well how an America could save us if she could not save herself.

The fact remains that globalised liberalisation has failed and not only failed utterly but continues to fail. In reality it played deception clandestining erotic hedonism as consumerism while consumer was nowhere on the scene. Combined intellectualism of the world and collective Harvardian intelligence of India failed to solve people's problems. Such globalised Epicureanism protected individual Capitalism but killed the consumer in the name of Consumerism itself. This Western Bhogvad played with the consumer in the name of consumerism. It protected elite interests by abetting hedonism, incest porn, and vulgar conspicuous consumption in the world. All this under the cover including the name and style of modishness on the ruins of poor, needy and their poverty, squalor, hunger, thirst, disease, unemployment and starvation.

In India, public welfare schemes, public services, general facilities, conveniences and amenities have already failed because of rampant corruption. Whatever remained was taken away by killing instinct based cut throat competitive economy. In many big and developed countries such welfare schemes and facilities were withdrawn or reduced in order to affect economy and solvency or turning around or surviving the competition. However, as a matter of fact all these countries became hollow from within like India where opening up of economy on the behest of West gave the rulers and economists the audacity to flagrantly discard Constitutional Welfare State vision and put the Directive Principles of State Policy in the oblivion at the same time perpetuate 'Reservations' unconstitutionally. All governments and state organs have till date so shamelessly violated the Constitutional obligation towards payment of unemployment allowance or providing employment and decent standard of living, developing agriculture, payment of living wage. It includes discontinuance of earnings through immoral unethical avocation and means, stopping alcohol, liquor and other active intoxicating agents including drugs, and so on. Alas! in sheer contravention of the Constitution mandating abolition of exploitation of humans. These governments have legalized engagement of Contract labour so shamelessly that it has in this liberalised – global culture of India left capitalistic exploitative drift un challenged.

Public facilities, no doubt failed because of misuse, excessive use or abuse by the citizens. This was mainly because of public frustrations against governmental functioning and failure of government servants to discharge their duties honestly. Secondly, because of rampant corruption, on the one hand and increasing populations on the other, these facilities and welfare amenities failed to keep pace with the needs of the people as well as basic requirements of changing times. There was total apathy and gross negligence of government machinery and its employees towards such functioning that proved beyond all doubts that corruption was there in India not because the country and her people were poor but both were poor because of corruption.

Personal opulence but public squalor, individual prosperity but societal paupery is yet another paradoxical predicament of the country called Indian and her politico- economic system. Inflation - recession but demand for luxury goods and items, zero rate of inflation but spiraling prices and high cost of living are other puzzles of Indian economy that has falsified economics. Economists particularly Harvardian are already spoofed. Amongst all this have been the baffles of high productivity and higher economic growth with highest rate of unemployment and acute shortages of essential consumer goods. Harvardian economists for few years took investment oriented growth and Sensex as the indicators of prosperity. When it should be the consumer generated growth and agricultural prosperity which should be the real indexes of growth and development. Still to justify and bring in Retail FDI, Sensex was made to spurt within days. These are all 'Sand Walls', misguiding manipulations. Such boastful economic growth of 21st century economists has collectively taxed peoples miseries, distresses and afflictions without a Tax law.

Farmers suicides apart, collective suicides and killing of their offspring by common people out of sheer hunger accompanied by starvation and poverty was being experienced. At the same time there have been spoilages of immense quantities of grains due to shortages of godowns and non availability of storages, mismanagement of and corruption in procurements. These are the clear reflections about the kind of economic growth and progress they are talking about. Even the free lunch or mid – day meal to small school kids, nutritious food programmes have proved a farce and source of manipulations - malpractices, even Ganga – Jamuna cleaning so pious is not spared. Thus, while earth has become such a hell, efforts to land on the moon, discovering water and making that a heaven are on. Leaving crores hungry – thirsty for food and water, half fed and starving, without shelter and clothes even unemployed on earth and discovering water in other planets and planning human settlements in space could only be termed madness, the bankruptcy of mind. Metaphorically, a situation of blind leading the blind. None still realising, where would this population explosion, crime – corruption, food – water shortages, ever increasing cost of living and resultant public frustration coupled with general anger lead this country to. Criminally open destruction of food grains, absurd excuses of government and its ministers as well as employees top down is not only a pointer of their gross animalistic attitude towards public miseries affliction and misfortune. It is also the mismanagement of food grains procured in the midst of hunger – starvation, suicides as well as exploitation of poor farmers by middlemen and agents. This is an outrageous exposition of governmental functioning.

Unemployment in the country is appallingly high and would certainly aggravate further. This is when lacs of educated and literate people are in foreign countries. Still they say India is shining and economy is beating the records. Perhaps they have taken peoples silence as the indicator of everything green in the desert or as the Hindi proverb goes 'the blind in the rainy season sees all green'. This is what exactly the Arabian governments and Gulf rulers did and thought.

The reasons for this pathetic economic failure have been gross neglect of agriculture and non priority to agriculture over industry. The other equally haplessly silly reason was promoting the investment oriented growth rather than consumer generated development. Western styled economists did not and could not realise that rural and farming sector was the backbone of Indian economy and life line of the nation. Harvardian economics and economists combine not only made agriculture a scapegoat but practically killed it at the altar of industry without realising even for a while that this way they were pulling down the foundation of industry and industrial Sector itself. This is what has ultimately happened. They were happy rather very happy initially with investment oriented growth and miragy Sensex. By throwing farmers behind they hit the consumption oriented growth and the whole airy economic building crashed within no time. Otherwise with this population of India there could be no question of recession or depression and unemployment in the country. India itself is equal to a continental market and only needs purchasing power in the hands of common man which was taken away by government planners and policy makers ridiculing agriculture as rural sector forming part of Bharat and not of India therefore as backward. Had even the fifty per cent of that purchasing power - as stashed by corrupts and snatched by industry - been in the hands of consumer India the country would have remained the 'Golden Bird' even in the midst of world economic recession and chaos.

Sustaining such vast, ever increasing population without a booming and prosperous agriculture and without giving priority to agriculture over industry and leaving the economic fate of the country in the hands of industrialists and people in the industrial sector is living in fool's paradise, very short of day dreaming.

Government, economic planners, bureaucracy and *netas* have played all their jokes with the people - gas - diesel - petrol prices including subsidies. Now it is peoples turn to pay them back. Prime Minister has been assuring the nation and people of price control every six months surprisingly parliamentary assurances but never succeeded. Still no privilege motion was brought against him by any person or party. They all have taken people of the country as fools. Earlier they blamed subsidies for economic mess and abolished them, then they played the joke of coalition governments for economic chaos and ills of the country but continued to form and remain in the coalitions practically bringing the country at the brink of moral – ethical bankruptcy, now they are playing their last joke saying the present economic slowdown was due to not allowing the entry of retail trade in the country which in all probability would be their last on the people and the nation both. The misleading statistics misled the people so far but no more, as there could be no better, bigger and reliable statistics than the people themselves. Hopefully, this mess would not simply set in motion but is likely to speed up the journey towards that desired change now famously called 'Transformation or Vyavastha Parivartan'.

Moon, a gift of creation (as the 'Mama'- maternal uncle of children i.e. brother of earth) has now been made an object for scientists to justify their job upon the hunger of the people, thirst of the masses, shelter and clothing of general public. For America it is to justify assistance in alleged research projects in vindication of India's leanings towards, but at what cost? None of us have actually understood nor prepared to learn from American and world disasters that by our actions we are practically snatching the nature from her, compelling ultimately human race to be snatched by nature. Alas! We are not at all prepared to accept and believe that nature is awaiting to snatch America out of this earth.

All Governments including states have in the name of liberalisation – globalisation - open economy and trance of investment and economic growth looted and allowed this country to be looted as if enemies of the people without any apparent benefit and gain to the country or the masses except inflation, recession, nude *bhog*, immorality, *bhookh* – hunger, depression, social calamity and individual poverty.

On world hunger map India even today ranks 65 out of 79 nations surveyed exactly where she was in 2011 then ranking 67 out of 81 countries. India's hunger index is 23 while above 10 is taken very serious. General undernourishment, children's mal/under nutrition, under weight and mortality is precarious so is health and medicine. On these scores India is last amongst 129 countries while these global liberalizers say they have liberlised India of all ailments, sins, ills, diseases, hunger and made her paradise. In America, France, Greece Presidents win and lose on these indexes or on unemployment doles and insurance issues while in India they make merry on the poverty of the people knowing very well the people here deserve only that.

Despite all what has been described the International Rating Agencies also taking advantage of weak *netagiri*, incompetent – ineffective governance every now and then threaten to down rate the economy to internationally down grade India and thus go on looting the country and paupering the people.

"Desh ki Tarakki ki baat karate - karate Desh ko hi nanga kar diya hai. March men menhagai kam hogi – November men menhagai kam hogi, agale teen mahine men hogi, fir Panch mahine men, June men hogi, fir November men kahate - kahate logon ko hi gart men dal diya". The system presently in India is for the classes not for the masses, twenty crore are enjoying at the cost of 105 crores and 200000 odd families laundering and luxuriating at the cost of all others.

India today is 135 in 167 countries for good business and 65 on global hunger index out of 79 countries studied. If that is so, of which development, change, liberalisation, economic wellbeing, betterment, elevation, and growth they are talking of except economics of befooling all the people all the times the way they have about inflation – cost and good governance.

The Bang - Crunch Killing Dualism

More than any government or legal - judicial system, the present Politico – Economic mess resulted because of the entry of foreign looters in the country and successive insensitive leaderships the height of which has been the back door (*chor darvaja*) entry of top boss of government in the so called biggest democracy of the world that never earlier happened in history. But the ulcer on the boil inherently inbuilt with Indian psyche is looting – hoarding mentality, casteism, communalism, superstitions, illiteracy, ignorance and Karmakandic Jyotish.

If money does not grow on trees the Black – Corrupt - Easy - Cheap money does in India where out of total planned - unplanned budgetary outlays maximum 40 per cent though in certain cases less is spent on such planned / assigned purposes / projects and rest 60 per cent or more goes in pockets. What is this? if, not the money growing on the trees, the free fruitage of money without doing anything. Those in hurry and haste, making people of India pauper not only deserve capital punishment but something beyond which is but would certainly be possible the day people, who have not only been but allowed so long to be befooled and exploited by these classes, change the System of governance and the Constitution.

All and entire government machinery top – down is indiscriminately after land, raping it through sale – purchase or whatever form primarily construction – whatever, wherever at any cost not knowing wherefrom food will come to such growing vast population. If Janata has to pay or is paying the price for own 'Kukrityas' today, the visionless mongrels will have to pay it back with compound interest tomorrow. They all are in haste of doing everything anti people, as much and as early, living in a 'Looto' mentality as if all others will die and they will only remain. They like America and China think money - capital can bring and purchase everything even gods and nature's judgments its fury, disasters, calamities and catastrophe. Buddhist countries including China, Japan, Thailand and others were under the same impression and indulged in same cruelty against animal world - as Indian system against her own countrymen - by indiscriminately killing not only what was on land but emptying even the seas of whales and fishes against the basic Buddhist philosophy of compassion, empathy and non – violence. The results are before them.

This Piggy – Doggy type Bhogvad culture (a culture under which dogs and pigs despite surveying wide grounds spread around filled with immensity of shit allow no others to eat rather fight and kill whosoever wants to share even in that common property) is developing in India professing spiritual enlightenment taking no clues from visible - invisible punishments of nature wherein we have routinely seen even the big so called Kings - Queens closed in the same box with the smallest Pawn (Pyada) when the game (as in chess) is over. Nature's justice however, is like nature's justice. It's also only the question of time or the moment when people would understand and get awakened; understand their Constitution and real – true History as they understand Ramayan – Mahabharat or religious – scriptures.

Similar is the case with realties and realters whether business or shows. Realty Moguls care damn for 60 - 70 crore common people. If people stop viewing cinema and TV Serials - which is remote possibility as it requires high level of intellectual understanding and broad mindedness - all the so called celebrities enjoying on the pockets of general – common people will have either or be compelled to spend 50 per cent of their profits on public welfare including their basic and developmental needs. Generally the cinema – serials in India have negative impact on children and boomeranging on the youth - the hopes of future and the families both. Both have duel faces - talking scientific, modern, and western outwardly but dragging people in effect to medieval psyche, vitiating youth morality and ethics, propping superstitious Karmakandic rituals at the same time. All for narrow selfish, pelfish vested purpose of luxuriating at peoples cost, society's cost. Thus, in reality, they have only realty face – their money, luxury and profits whether people live or don't live or national morality, ethics and character are spoilt or society is profanely marred matter not at all for them. The question therefore, before this liberlised BHOGVAD (Hedonistic) economic system in the country is – how can some have a car of 15 crores or 10 even 5 crores of populace have not even cycle and how can a few be allowed to have houses of 500 or 300 or 100 crores in land measuring 10000 or 5000 or 2000 mts even more than 1000 Mts if 33 per cent populace is compelled to live under the sky and 33 per cent practically have bare roof?

Human Rights Mania – A Curse

Human Rights of Clintonic America or if we say correctly Clintonic HR, to this country proved an ulcer on the boil that practically protected the liberty and freedom of brutes, barbarians, devils, and demons alas! even the terrorists. We had never in free India talked so vehemently of freedom from corruption, black money and crime nor have we ever so seriously talked, much less fought, for the freedom of poor, poorer and poorest seventy crore populace from hunger, want, squalor, starvation, sustenance, bare needs for food, water, clothing, shelter and pursuit for happiness as we have for human rights of bloody criminals, corrupts, marauders, and terrorists. We instead of pressuring for Constitutional right to living wage, human standards of living, right to employment or insurance coverage or Welfare State and development of agriculture are fighting to protect, nourish and nurture the Human Rights of inhumans, dacoits, Dons, looters, rapists, killers, Mafiosi and other evil doers. These pseudo activists to boom their business are fastening and in fact have fastened our neck with their hands with the help and assistance of politicians as well as judiciary. Such politico - judicial protection to alleged Human Rights and rightists is as inhuman as treating humans a resource – politically, economically, socially, legally and managerially that too in a free democratic country. Human Rights and Human resources both are sponsoring the causes of all evils, exploitation, and social ruination including judicial wrecking in India, former forcing to treat a brute, a heartless killer marauder as a man a human and latter compelling to treat humans as animals or inanimate factor. Protection of Human Rights of criminals corrupts and marauders have for so long deprived good people of their rights i.e. right to live,

live fearlessly - free and secure life and live life as humans. If criminal - marauders, cruel- brutes, bloody – terrorists, anti national – anti social corrupt – black money and human traffickers, killer – rapists could have Human Rights, why not good people. Why should then poor die of hunger, want of medicine or live like animals and good be humiliated, deprived of their share, their due? Why not a murderer had thought of the human right to life, to live of the man killed and his family including the children and parents would come on the roads?

How America that has throughout violated, more so suppressed the human rights of others, the developing and underdeveloped world could be the saviour of HR of people overnight. Clinton had an axe to grind by pressurizing India to observe HR or face consequences. He wanted to kill two birds with one stone. One ensure his Indian vote bank that constituted sizeable numbers in America and assure Pakistan and patronize her terrorism against India along with the Indian relatives of vote bank he had in America. Mrs Clinton heart in heart is as nasty towards India as her husband who visited India only at the fag end of his tenure. On becoming Secretary of State she talked of diplomacy not of relationship building with India and was sorry leaving Pakistan alone after the fall of USSR. As Jy Bush was the only President in the history of Republican Party having so excellent relationship with India. Clinton was the only Democratic President having so bad relationship.

The people would therefore like also to ask the question for getting a satisfactory reply from corridors of power, power brokers and those actually wielding the power - if all humans were born free, equal in dignity with equal rights, why poor have remained poor and rich became richer. Why some were born with silver spoon and inherited empires without doing anything and others have not half a loaf even after toiling for 24 hours?

Why have we been so much interested in the human rights of plunderers, offenders, inhuman crooks rather than providing food to hungry, clothing to unclothed, shelter to unsheltered and filling the stomach of the half fed and those who sleep without a meal. We have talked enough about equality and human rights of rich, elite, corrupts, criminals, inhumanly cruel animals and atrocious beasts in this country but hardly have we ever shown our concern for the human rights of vast marginalised majority. We have hardly shown our concern when Harvardians shelved the Preamble and Part IV of the Constitution meant for general vast majority of the country. What and why fault with Naxals - Maoists if they feel convinced of the trap of perpetuating exploitation of the masses in the name of development and liberalisation the same way as did the feudalism of yester years? Where have the fruits of development gone? Poor could not see even the buds much less flowers leave aside the fruits since almost 1995 but not at all after 2001. If human rights are so sacrosanct, why are we punishing Naxals and Maoists who are protecting the HR of so many – tribals, poor, starving and hungry primitives?

Time has now come for the marginalised majority, the poor, the middle classes not to say "Jai Ho" and clap for everybody and everything but be ready to write the next chapter by 'Changing the System of Governance and the Constitution'. Present system of governance would never recognise their human rights to decent human standards of living, right to equality particularly equality of opportunity by incorporating the right to employment or right to unemployment allowance or insurance coverage as is being done by 'Guru' America, or Europe, our ideals and idols in all other matters and from whom, in that mad race of aping, we have aped even recession, depression, and culture of sex action, liberalised incest vibration.

Talking is worth no more. We have talked enough of everything. We have for the last 60 years been only talking. Now has come the time for action, action- whereby justice and service would come at the doorstep of the people and they will have not to go and ask for.

The question is where were these HR protagonists were - the Saviors of Fundamental Rights, when MNCs were experimenting and testing their medicines on poor Bharatiyas killing them in thousands without compensation. The known figures estimate this number as exceeding 1300. The question is where these friends of the poor and the pretenders of humanity were when doctors were playing havoc with human lives, and manufacturers selling a medicine worth Rs 2 for Rs 50 or more (revealed also in '*Satyamev Jayate*' of Amir Khan). Under present liberalised – delicensed corrupt system of governance, human life has factually become a trade, a business as a commodity in the market place, open for sale and purchase irrespective of caste, creed, religion, community, birth and race. It is the trader only minting money in any ways, all the ways and always not the 'commodity'.

Failure of Dharma

Dharma, that gave India might since time immemorial and strength to fight such long drawn battle against British and kept us united as a people irrespective of birth, creed, race or community has failed to deter the sins and sinners, crimes and criminals, corruption and corrupts after the 'Bhogvadic Maya' of West particularly since mid 90s. The American tranced epicurean Gurus and Hedonist Babas, the Hi-tech Swamis - Swaminis, Mahants – Mahantanis have made mockery of Dharma and Dharm Shastras as lawyers have of law and politicians of politics. Dharma of today has everything except Dharm. It is lost in the wilderness of lust, pelf, self and Panthas (Sects). Neither have we Sanyasis nor Sadhoos, Saints the least, only Jogi - Joginis, Babas, and Mahants - Mahantanis. In this, the blind is leading the blind. Those deep in corruption and 'Bhog' are teaching us Yog, at the same time patronized by corrupt politicians, bureaucrats, capitalists who in return patronize them for so many reasons including conversion of black money into white. Consequently corruption has corrupted Dharma also. While general masses have guts to oppose the power centers of corruption, these flag bearers of Dharm, self styled Swami – Sanyasis are mum, seen nowhere in the scene with the public. This is the same way as the Pujaris, Priests and Dharma Gurus of Somnath when Ghazani attacked so many times. Ignorance of masses is proving as real bliss to these Mahants, Babas, Gurus and Jogis as to politicians and caste manipulators. As politicians need crowd (*Bheed*) they need herds of masses – the sheep (*Bhed*). There is thus no difference between the two. Dharma has, because of these pretenders of 'Dharma', failed to ameliorate the general conditions of the society and teach lessons to these looters of national wealth and stashers of black money. Like retail revolution, Dharm Gurus, Swamis, Swaminis and Babas have made Dharm a flourishing trade and business for huge earnings retailing into many Sects, Akharas and Panths. As in consumerism, consumer is nowhere so with these 'Dharmics' Dharm is nowhere. Common people are Dharmic naturally for fear of loss, death and expectations of worldly gains. These Gurus, Swamis and Babas are Dharmic for lust, accumulations, building a congregation of disciples and competitive Empires for sex attractions and have in fact over the period succeeded in trancing, bewitching and illusioning even educated, so-called mod western styled 21st century generation, that finds it a highly attractive pleasure hunting and paying profession. These Vyas Gurus, Swamis and Sanyasinis even Bhaktas are very clever and have understood the erotic psyche and porn sensual mentality of present generation and their leanings to western lifestyle and therefore started and engaged in preaching Krishn Kathas of Gopis and Ras Lilas in modernized western Pop form and Rock style. Even in Rama Kathas, they have introduced western dances and music. They have thus sensualised and sexualized Dharm reduced it to 'Keertans' and 'Sat Sangs' noise polluting to fascinate the youth. This is the travesty of the same Dharma that otherwise preaches not just silence rather silence beyond silence. These keepers of Dharma have thus destroyed Dharm in the same way as the keepers of Constitution (the Shastra of good governance and material well being) have the Constitution by contraventions and bad governance.

For a thousand years in the past there had come no Avatar, to absolve us from the yoke of foreign rule but after the western Bhogavad of 90s, so many Bhagvans, Kalkis and Avatars have been born to loot the same way as Netas. It is difficult however to forget that only a man of few kilos, of scant flesh and blood revolutionized the world empty handed with weapons of course but not of gun material, steel or iron but of truth and non-violence and liberated India and her people of atrocities, excesses, exploitation, authoritarianism and despotism of foreign rule and absolved India of the shackles of slavery, miseries, sorrows, and pains. A truly religious in heart who has throughout been prompted by Dharm and Dharma alone who showed way to other countries and people of the world. One spark of Dharm, a single call of a spiritual leader would be sufficient to bring in peaceful transformation in the country but these self - styled Dharm Gurus have instead put poor Dharma itself in defensive even in danger of extinction.

How could any of these Dharm Gurus, Swamis, Sanyasinis, Babas bring transformation who themselves are so ignorant of culture and religion or Shastra - Puranas as calling Ram as Rama, Krishn as Krishna (means Draupadi), Dharm as Dharma and so on.

But nonetheless, if it is true that a 'Thorn takes the Thorn out' this 'Adharm' will also restore Dharm the same way as immorality - corruption, sins, insensitivity and inhumanity of Tunisia in the whole Arab world. History is replete with including the examples of Afghanistan, Iraq, Iran, Nepal, Sudan, Pakistan and so on.

Similar to scientists who are under the misconception of controlling and subjugating nature these Dharm gurus are fantasizing on having befooled 'Dharm' together with the innocent masses ignorant of the scriptures. But both are forgetting however, that the day Dharma and nature would come to befooling, neither the scientists nor the Dharma gurus would be seen anywhere. Dharma and nature both have given us one after another opportunities to beware awaken and behave. The day both come to revenge, the price humanity will be paying is beyond the collective imagination of whole world. Then the Gen next would be no better than vagabonds, animals, and primitives.

We can never however, forget the contributions of our spiritual leaders during freedom movement. Their selflessness, austerity, ascetics, and abstinence empowered the people to fight authoritarian despots and added values to the life of general masses. Present Guru – Swamis and Babas are not only committing crimes against God and Dharma but as scientists against nature and humanity as well compelling Dharm, God, and nature to abstain from protecting and helping humanity which all of the three have actually started doing. Now, people have either to suffocate with the status quo or rise to the occasion. If not now, then never.

The hedonistically corrupt politicians and hi-tech epicurean Gurus have made politics and Dharma a commodity. Consequently the whole psyche of the country is becoming voyeuristic. Globalisation particularly of 21st century, with its quick fix instant 'Nirvan' mindset is propagating smart looking, smart living, sexy style propellants to fuel adolescents and teenagers to slave themselves also in 'sexy' buzz world.

Similarly, Jyotishis / astrologers, who are no better than beggars, though do not know their own future, future of their children and family yet profess to foretell others even of the country, earth, the world and the universe while the foreign rulers without such 'Bhavishya Vanis' ruled this country for 1000 years and looted everything the way these self styled, are now. Nothing could be expected from such people who themselves are parasites on the society. It is only, the masses who could bring and have to bring peaceful change for changing their destiny. The population of today and more of tomorrow exhorts us for such change.

Generically and genetically, we can have neither communism nor dictatorship. For stabilizing democracy with good governance, equity, and justice reinforced by liberty for such vast population, we can only have Bharatiya Lok – Jan Tantric form or Presidential form of governance with a new Constitution as proposed in this book to institutionalize the institutions besides institutionalizing democracy, governance, systems, morality, ethics, and rule of law, liberty, justice, equality and not simply have elections to elect *netas*.

Our present system of governance as our economic planning is working on the lines of Railways i.e. increasing the trains without the tracks, coaches, facilities, safety, security, accidents, collisions, sabotage, delays, daylight crimes – killings, robberies, loot, fear psychosis, inhuman dumping and overcrowding.

We have paid and are still paying for our sins. We have suffered too much for our sins of casteism, regionalism, parochialism, communalism, dynasticism, nepotism, favouritism, anti-nationalism and so on. But enough is enough. This is also the time for remorse and penance. India now needs a peaceful change, a second evolution (not Revolution) i.e. a peaceful, constitutional, democratic transformation by the people as custodians of sovereignty and Constitution. The country can no longer be left in the hands of blind and one eyed few. It has many a times also worked as a type of mobocracy that completely undermined the quality of governance and services. As says the Shire;

जम्हूरियत इक तर्जे हूकूमत है कि जिसमें
बंदो को गिना जाता है तौला नही जाता

Overall, as history also tells us, revolutions took place more out of economic distresses which, became political issues, whether unemployment, food shortage – starvation - hunger, inflation, and corruption. Religion only added to the speeding up of peaceful revolutions but independently never came to the rescue of people and has rarely been the independent cause of any such politico-economic revolution. History and experience are the testimony that exploitation and excesses even by religion have been the causes of revolution as happened in Europe against Church during medieval times. But this happened only when religion mixed it up with politics or political power or power of politics or degenerated itself either in to communalism, despotism, hedonism or egotism including pelf and vested self.

Distortions and degeneration of religion by and in the hands of religious preachers have failed to purify societal life, imbibe values in the general masses, patriotism in the people and sense of sacrifice in Gen next supposed to inherit the future. The sermons and preachings of these hypocrites are world apart from their practices. Many of them are amongst the biggest hoarders of and converters of black money. Others are possessors of immeasurably immense unaccounted wealth and yet others no less land mafias. They have failed to convince youth and children about the lofty ideals of Sanatan Dharm and secular Vedic Arya principles based on the philosophy of "वसुधैवकुटुम्बकम्" i.e. the (World a family). The height of their ignorance and incapacity is the inability to revise, remove and efface the impression 'Hindu' in the psyche of the people that India has never been. Because of lack of knowledge they are rather busy establishing and propagating Hindu Dharma which is neither deontologically born nor epistemologically scriptural nor even mythologically and theologically Vedic and Pauranic. Hindu mainly because of British but earlier with foreign aggressions became an expression of communalism or sectarianism while Sanatan Vedic Dharm is perennial and universal hence could neither be communal nor has ever been circumscribed. It is rather indivisible whole, the eternal truth, a philosophy of life, a collective entity and absolute humanism believing in unity of mankind, equality of all religions and Godhead.

These religious pseudos, rather than unifying the country are fragmenting it. They are responsible for ritualistically narrowing it down to a sectarian philosophy and innumerable superstitions. Gratified by them the whole system of governance in India is indulged in villainy. They are as responsible for creating pollution as scientists. Science is polluting only the environment. rivers, air, water, nature, and mundane human psyche but these Dharmic hypocrites in addition are polluting Dharma, spirituality, faith, scriptures and human values. Therefore as dirt could not be cleaned by dirt they are least expected to contribute in the renewal of society. Dharma, since the day it was made trade and business and glossed with sectarian divide for material usurpations has failed in its purpose of maintaining unity, peace, brotherhood and harmony and this applies to all the religions of the world.

These religious pseudos wearing saffrons or clad in whites, keep long hair and beards take advantage of people's ignorance, illiteracy and detachment with Sanskrit. They use a few iterated quotes of the language the meaning of which even they do not know, narrate some stories, make females weep and boast to be the trustees of Dharma and knowledge thus amass huge un-accounted, un-taxed wealth dumped and in many cases lying idle in the strong rooms of their religious Seminaries as that of Puttaparthi Sai Baba or many others. All this while 23 crore people sleep without food every day. Could these repositories of Dharm and trustees of Yoga, reply -what would such money be called – is it not black money? Are such accumulations in the name of Dharm or religion justified in a poor country like India? These are the examples of shame these shamed Sadhu Babas have kept and keeping before the people of the country. After the failure of legal - judicial system, the failure of Dharm proved a curse to the nation and society as it kept the abettors of corruption, crimes and villainy grow prosperously in the society. Dharma has lost sanctity also because of deceptions and pretenses that have crept rather deliberately brought in to it by self styled Baba – Gurus – Sanyasinis as traders of Dharma. The Mantras have lost effectiveness because of wrong pronunciations, distorted accent and incorrect chanting and reading by illiterate, knavish scandalous scoundrels who feign scholarly but read Ved as Vad.

These religious bigots teach and preach only about the other world nothing about making life splendour, grand and happy in this world as says a Shire rightly:

हश्र में इन्साफ होगा बस यही सुनते रहो
जैसा यहाँ होता रहा है वैसे वहाँ भी हो जायेगा
इसी गफलत में हैं लुटते रहे हम आज तक
मर गये लाखों इसी अरमान में

(There shall be justice in other world after death. But the Shire asks and replies of his own - as it has been here so shall justice be there. We have throughout life been plundered because of this ignorance and millions died with same cravings)

How unfortunate it is that these supposed Dharm scholarly bigots know nothing about own Constitution, constitution of the country, the great governing Shastra the scripture, knowledge of which would in real sense help people make life really divine in this world, on this land. For this reason they never talked about fearing if life is made divine here their business would be ruined. But in that maneuver they have so politicized religion and made it vestedly narrow that people may one day abandon it.

Lessons from History

In ancient India, we had monarchies, kings – queens and kingdoms much better than Constitutional governments of today. Even they were not absolute despots in so many respects. There were many checks and controls over them. The Mantris, Purohits, Amatyas, and Mantri Parishad controlled the authority of kings to a great extent while in present democracy of India they all are masquerading collectively. In addition to the direct curbs, there were many indirect restraints on the authority of Kings and Queens in ancient India. The biggest virtue of the times was law having sacred character and binding even on the King as much as on his subjects. The duty of the king was defined in the Shastras and was considered inviolable by him. This codification is reflected in *Ramayana, Mahabharata* and Puranas even in Vedas. The status of individuals in society in those days was looked not so much from the point of view of their rights but their duty which had moral, ethical and religious sanctions behind, that we have pooh poohed in today's democracy. It created as much sensation if king failed in his duties as an ordinary people and as channels do today. It is true that despite these checks and balances the Kings in disregard of controls did often establish heir arbitrary rule. However, compared to the working of best constitutional democracy like ours, that was much better. This is the time for people of India to learn from Western Societies where people devised many Constitutional ways in phases to curb the despotism and arbitrariness of rulers and kings until people demonstrated their will and forced all rulers to abdicate in favour of the people.

It is not therefore the letter of the Constitution, but the extent to which people are willing and capable of exercising their inherently divine and Constitutionally Sovereign rights along with Sovereign Power that really determines the character of the governance. In judging of any Constitution therefore, the matter of primary importance is to determine the educational levels and political consciousness of the people – their basic knowledge of their Constitution and their true history.

Kautilya in his *Arthashastra* attached due importance to the power of people. There is a reference where king while addressing his army says, "I am a paid servant of the people like you." Kautilya even recommended same mode of lifestyle to the kings as those for people in general. After all, these wise men were not fools. Gandhiji said exactly the same thing. The uprising of people against corruption, their revolting voices against black money and rebellion against elected governments, the cries of general masses against the dacoity and immorality of their representatives, frustration against the system and history of contemporary world, particularly of Arab world, fortifies the deep insight of the people of India.

Historians agree that people in those days had undoubted right of dethroning a king, or even killing him, if he proved a tyrant. All evidence indicates the high political status enjoyed by the people at large. It is born out of the entire historical evidence and could also be said safely that the ideal form of government in ancient India had three elements - the king, bureaucracy, and the people, which were equally balanced, and served as check against the other.

People must have an unshakable faith and allegiance to their Constitution if made or enacted or accepted or adopted by them in a democratic manner similar to Lichchhavis who retorted to aggressor Ajatshatru - 'Lichchhavis were invincible as long as their Constitution remains'. Lord Buddha therefore modeled the organisation of his Mathas / Monasteries on the constitution of Lichchhavis.

It is therefore the divine right of the people to safeguard their right to govern themselves in real sense and Transform the system if it becomes corrupt, immoral, unethical, incompetent, selfish, anti people and unworkable as in India.

Invitation to and Role of Youth

This is time for youth of this country to pause and ponder and for educated youth to brainstorm

- why it is that all water taps are dry but market places flooded with overflowing water bottles or as many water tankers are available,
- why billions of money spent on sculpturing hundreds of elephants, construction of parks and building of statues, while per day income of 60 crore people in the country is just between Rs. 30 to Rs. 64 and fifty per cent population of the state concerned itself is below poverty line, under which law or statutes much less Constitution in a democracy any party or governments or individual derives such power or right without incorporating such plans and scheme in its election manifesto or obtaining approval of the people in a referendum and how a Judiciary boasting of all pervasive power could sit blind folded on such matters,
- why and how thousands of truckloads of grain meant for PDS is sold in the black market, misappropriated or spoiled while 25 crore people sleep without meal,
- why, lacs of tones of grain is spoilt or rotten in open or at railway stations or godowns without selling to the poor needy people while 50 crore people are either hungry or half fed or starving,
- why and how it is that even a constable, a clerk, inspector or Assistant engineer or accountant in government has crores and wherefrom that money came particularly when their known resources are and were known,
- why it is that out of 70 per cent corrupt and 25 per cent highly corrupt government employees only 0.25 per cent are caught and hardly 0.02 per cent are punished,
- why judiciary otherwise boasting of judicial activism and all pervasive power next to gods has been silent spectator in corruption cases accusing sometimes the governments for inaction but granting bail even anticipatory to all such corrupts including stays even in very serious and highly certain cases?

Even a blind can tell the taste, after all wherefrom that water in the bottles has come if there is such shortage of water as not a drop for poor to drink, how the godowns of businessmen, traders and middlemen are glutted with grains if there is less production or crop failure, and how the money is overflowing not only the pockets of government servants but even their children if it was not earned beyond their known resources? How that power for that matter any power or authority or law if any, permitting construction of elephants, parks, statues for extra constitutional imposters out of state fund could and was held constitutional even legal? How long such criminal deviousness and villainy will be allowed to be played with democracy which is said to be the government of the people and for the people? How long in a democracy the vast majority would be challenged so openly by smaller numbers calling their selves or on the ground of castes or classes? This exposes the working of Constitution, judicial - legal system that needs transformation, earliest the better.

This is also the occasion for youth to recapitulate why and how in the fakeness of liberalised globalisation giving high hopes of employment opportunities, skill development, booming technical education, meeting future potentials and career needs, competing internationally the Ministry of HRD delicensed certification and recognition and allowed mushrooming of third rate - fourth grade Management – Engineering – Medical institutions mostly owned by illiterate 'Netas' having no match with need of the country, employment of progeny and career planning or needs of educated youth. Such institutions opened in the streets without any economic planning and predictions of employment or requirements of economy including prospects of economic development in the earlier stages of opening up of economy, charged whimsical capitation fee besides unbearable under the table amount. The certification and recognition scandal of not only of these institutions but even CBSE affiliations is no less Maayaamay. At every step we have new scandals and scams in this country that accelerated since 1995, multiplied with the beginning of ideal twentieth century global village; beating all records since 2005, the speed impossible to catch now. As we have reached the limit of impossibility such rotten system is impossible to mend now by any means whatever, except changing the form of Government i.e. the system of Governance and the Constitution.

There is water for Poly - Nationals to trade in but not for crores to drink. This is the reason and answer also to why there is Naxalism - Maoism in some states and spreading with the times. Land apart the 'Water' the life-sustaining substance, the free gift of nature has become competitively killing business, a deadly trade in the hands of inhuman governments, cruel traders, and brutal multinationals, in this delicensed free market economy. Tomorrow they may or could do the same with air. Land has already been engulfed. Similar, is the case with food grains and sugar. Sugar has become yet another politico–economic weapon in the hands of a couple of *netas* and the lobby to ask for ransom from the country and pound of flesh from the public same as petrol – diesel – gas, despite sky rocketing leave general people just at a loss. Humanity is lost because humans have become a commodity in this liberalised incest sexy Western economic order and Manpower a resource, under this porn infested individualized free market American Homo economic system.

The so called modern HRD developed by America and Western theorists and aped by us without validation in our circumstances has made man, the grandest creation of god or nature, the worst exploited resource in India. We have reached the end and end of everything because we under pressure unwillingly opted for this liberalised economic order in the name of globalisation at the cost of our agriculture. Pretending protection of consumer interests by advancing capitalistic consumption and selling public sector for pennies without referendum and without educating people and taking their sanction. Nude display of riches and pretentious consumption of some people and conspicuous of a section of society has become the biggest causes of envy as well as jealousy leading to this new culture of brutality, vulgarity, crimes, social and individual evils including corruption, gender violence, sexual nudity and havoc with madness for Bhog having horrible results.

History is replete with the examples and events that falling prey to licentiousness proved a veritable ruin to our predecessors. Sex, wine, dice, debauchery, depravity, dissoluteness, resulted in foul diseases the same way as today signaling to the extremes of such conspicuous consumption. Like those kings, queens, princes, and princesses of earlier times we are also, excessively infatuated by sensuality of all kinds and spending ill-gotten money in willed follies. That evil influence which was drying up here has once again become green in the name of liberalisation and Western modernity. This is the silent cultural invasion of Western Bhogvad without making any noise or using a weapon. Those same incredible infatuations to eroticism, unbelievable sensuality, lust, pelf, and nude display are ruling the lifestyles particularly of youngsters, which had earlier brought untold sufferings to the people. The reckless extravagance and wanton expenditure in the name of organizing sports and deep-rooted corruption have brought untold miseries to the people the way it had in earlier history. Not only the people in power and authority and the moneyed but also their sons, daughters, wives, parents, family and relations are all collectively looting the treasury and the country with both the hands under the umbrella of extra – constitutional authority with legal – judicial system meditating detachedly. The sad lack of moral – ethical character, Bhogvad, new oppressive taxes, economic disasters brought about by ruining agriculture and corruption have led to confused, frustrated, hopelessness and helplessness all around except the traders, business houses, multinationals, government employees, corrupt *Netas* and criminals. Devaluation in commitment and duty and unfaithfulness to nation and people have made patriotism the first casualty.

The number of those having steadfast loyalty, stern morality, deep sense of duty, appreciation of ethics, principles, values, ethos is becoming meager day by day. *Netas* openly baking their political bread by inciting class uprising and caste struggle. Illiteracy, ignorance despite, large number becoming graduates continues the same way in the matters of dogmatism, casteism, regionalism, superstitions, and ritualism. Vote politics has made casteism – communalism – regionalism so deep rooted that redemption from under present political conditions and system of governance appears impossible. Economically they have already brought the country at the verge of collapse.

Now the question is; where has the collective intelligence of the world gone, where has the combined wisdom of elite class of India and vision of Harvardians gone, where have the fruits of liberalisation and flowers of globalisation gone? Is it the same consumerism they talked about initially befooling the masses?

Already the greatest tragedy of free India was the inheritance of a completely British indoctrinated Sahib oriented bureaucracy, a Constitution generally shadowed by all their bad impacts with no inclusion of vicarious liability of government servants and in certain cases of governments that is otherwise present in Britain and Europe in general including of course America. That western styled bureaucracy knowing the British modus operandi, culture as well as value system succeeded in convincing the politicians not to incorporate vicarious liability of government servants for arranging money needed for winning elections. Accumulations of such money would have been impossible without corruption. Vicarious liability of employees for negligence, habitual or gross or deliberate negligence would have made corruption impossible.

Until youth educated or uneducated is provided with work / employment / unemployment insurance or allowance, all other actions whether selling land, building skyscrapers, Multiplexes, Malls, landing on moon and searching for water there including compulsory education are fraud, a deception, a sham and dishonesty on the hunger and starvation of the people and the pretended open liberalised economic development a joke, a deceit, a plunder on the poverty of the masses and rape of compulsions of populace. Therefore, - 'Jago' India; 'Jago - Naujavan'.

Only the purchasing power in the hands of masses would change the fate of India, create demand, generate employment, open economic avenues leading to industrial growth and that is possible only by paying unemployment allowance as suggested in this book, discontinuing 'Sansad - Vidhayak Nidhi' and priority to agriculture over industry.

The 'Manthan' (Churning of Brain)

This would be a state of insanity if people go on enduring the acts of ingratitude of governance and the system. Youth is the first - last and the only hope of the teeming masses. The ugly face of corruption is not limited to this or that or only to as we saw in Commonwealth Games, 2G scandal, elephants and parks, land – mining – coal gate scandals but widespread – all pervasive sparing no corner of public – private - governmental – social – economic- political life, all the 24 hours, all the seven days, everywhere no less by the way in religious places, defence and amongst investigating agencies. Even by international standards, it was once 77 per cent in India but is actually worse than Pakistan, Zimbabwe, Bangladesh, Indonesia, Philippines, and Arab countries over 92 per cent perhaps more in Government, 60 per cent in Public Sector and once 90 per cent in Cooperative Sector.

The only problem with the governments of the day in this country today is to act and decide on the behest of foreigners and draw maximum if possible everything out of the masses and pump into the coffers of rich and elites and fill the stomachs of moneyed. Therefore, the only solution for all ailments of the country and problems of the people is to transform the system of governance and change the Constitution of this country i.e. Vyavastha Parivartan at the earliest.

History has taught us at least one striking lesson that the fate of a country and its people is dependent not on anything but the political consciousness of her people, awakening of the youth and sacrifices of the masses and only that could collectively shape their destiny. Nobody has any answer to the problems of India as there is no parallel of the type either in history or even in fictions. Unconcerned governance, corrupt - unruly government employees, treacherous bureaucracy, criminal *netas* and unscrupulous businesses are collectively plundering the treasury for the last sixty-five years but repeating the same plank of *"Roti, Kapada aur Makan"* election after elections befooling the poor masses who died generations after generation in that hope, awaiting throughout their lives that these dreams would come true to their children. Glaring as inequality is injustice which in a country of over 125 crore populations could be called the gravest evil, sin and crime as corruption.

Truly it is; not our poverty that made us corrupt but corruption that made us poor. We are poor because of corruption not vice versa. 'Janata' the sarcastic 'Aam Aadami' of porn culturist *'Times of India'* is utterly exhausted by continuously struggling to sustain that too in a democracy constitutionally Preamblised as the 'Socialistic' Welfare State. Wanton cruelty of *netas*, despotism of economic system and whims of governance together with the apathy of judicial administration have raised the powers of bureaucracy and police as high as it was under British and feudal lords which is not a good omen for democracy and its future.

In the name of coalitions and sham of alliances 'Chor – Chor have become Mausere Bhais'. They have united not for the good of the country and betterment or well being of the people but for their vested interests, grabbing power, remaining in power and aggrandizing self and pelf of their families. They continue to in this so called 21st century globalised mindset, befool the people the same way as in the earlier years of freedom. This is only because people are getting befool. It is wanton. However it is said, that 'Evils bring their own remedy, their own Destruction' and so says Gita 'यदा यदा हि धर्मस्य----तदात्मानं सृजाम्यहम्'. That stage has now set in. Despite feeling secure in their fortified residences like feudal lords of yester years, none of these would be able to hold and resist the frustration and fury of anger of the people, as masses are so exasperated with the rottenness of the system of governance that they feel it like the evil influences of Harems of those days or of Mrs Mao, Mrs. Marcos or Mrs Chesesque of Romania of modern times.

Even Naxals and Maoists killed, looted, exploited, and suppressed only the poor. They have not touched a single known corrupt, criminal, plunderer, Don or Mafia.

The nation now needs political sagacity and statesmen like wisdom. It needs that national consciousness for bringing the change, the change in the system of governance and

Constitution, which she had against foreign aggressor rulers during freedom movement and many occasions there to fore. Still there is no way other than Gandhian non-violence to bring such a great change as did Egyptians. Non-violence tires violence and all other unethical evil means and ways and ultimately succeeds because it never tires while violence tires itself what of others and therefore fails. This was the reason Gandhiji took to non-violence. This takes long but never fails rather compels all others to surrender and bow.

Despite emotional unity created by freedom movement and eternal esoterics created by religious spirituality since time immemorial, we have never in reminiscent history been a nation, a 'Rashtra' but a conglomeration of states called 'Rajya or Desh', kingdoms, Principalities later the 'Riyasats', ruled by Raja - Maharajas, Rani - Maharanis and later by Sultans, Nababs and Kings. Guru Chanakya, Acharya Shankar and Gandhi made it a 'Rashtra' progressively.

Present voting system giving right to vote to the people to elect their government has not in any way changed the situation and is instead drifting us apart, emotionally besides physically despite being a country. The propose Bhartiya Jan – Lok Tantric Paddhati will make us a nation emotionally, spiritually, psychically, mentally and a country physically, genealogically and constitutionally in which vote and voter will not be exploited but valued, not used as a means for politicking but building a strong united India for the welfare and development of all. In such system the 'Vote Bank' as a politics shall never dare to raise its ugly head again.

Activism for Proposed Change: Not an Offence or Crime

Many people even educated, because of ignorance, may be afraid of and ask the question - Is it not offence talking of such changes? Some may consider it a serious crime to talk of changing Constitution, government apart. But, no, it is neither a crime nor an offence, because it is neither unconstitutional nor illegal to talk of such changes. It is no offence talking of transformation either. Changing any form of governance and the Constitution including dictatorial and martial – military rule is the inherent sovereign right of the people, but in a democracy changing it in a democratic way is also the democratic right of the people. People are sovereign, their own masters, sovereignty rests in them and that cannot be challenged. If people collectively decide to bring in the transformation by changing the form of government and the Constitution even as many times, no power on earth can stop that. This, the people of India generally, and educated particularly should have learnt by now especially from the developments of Arab countries and the Gulf. Theoretically it is the prerogative of the people through their collective 'will' to change as many times they want, the form of government and the Constitution but in a practically working democracy it would happen once in a century.

However, in India, it is not only the sovereignty that by natural corollary vests in the people but our Constitution begins with the declaration "We the People of India". Without people there could neither be any government nor could any governance ever be thought of to function without people. Individuals, dictators, kings and queens, armies at times overthrew the elected governments and took over the reins of states and made their own Constitutions but when people collectively decided to change they changed all such governments even by overthrowing and drafted and adopted their own constitutions throwing away the ones in existence. This is what happened in Nepal and earlier in Pakistan, Bangladesh, African countries, Iran and Russia in 1991 and earlier in 1917, much before in France and hundreds years ago in England. This is what happened when communism took over part of the world particularly Eastern Europe and in turn when it was thrown out in 1991 including in Russia. Every time Constitutions were changed. Each regime had its Constitution and every time and everywhere it was changed either by people or the regime taking over and ultimately again by the people when they collectively decided. Whoever resisted peoples 'General Will' had either to go from the world as Gaddafi or hide or fled away or abdicate or was dethroned as king of Nepal or Shah of Iran, Musharraf of Pakistan, dictators of Bangladesh or Ben Ali of Tunisia, Mubarak, Gaddafi and others of Arab world.

How could people who ultimately elect the governments collectively be anti themselves, anti national, anti social? Though the irony of the present system of governance in India is no less bad to what it is or was in Arab world, Gulf, Indonesia, Bangladesh, Pakistan, Zimbabwe and other countries, still it is like marriage that involves violation of chastity yet legalized. Similarly, here it is democratically elected, in all the above it was usurpation of power. Here despite being an anti-people system of governance, obsolete – outdated form of government, incapable of deliverance and unfulfilling, it is accepted to be constitutionally legalized and validated by the people.

The people have now to brainstorm and decide who in reality is anti national, anti their selves, anti social and treacherous; the functionaries who stabbing the people at the back, indulge in corruption and crime, snatch the share of the people including their progeny by misusing and abusing the authority and office and deceiving the electorate or the citizens who ask for sacking and punishing such functionaries and for reforming the system?

In the end and ultimately only such movements succeed that spring from the bottom of people's heart because it then becomes telepathic, a united action, a synergetic force and that is possible only when people are fully and thoroughly convinced about and that is what this book has attempted.

History of This Historical Issue

The issue regarding 'Presidential Form' of Government (not The Bharatiy Lok Jan Tantric Paddhati as it never struck even the intelligentsia) was, first raised during the Premiership of Mrs. Indira Gandhi in 1970s. Subsequently it was raised by Sri LK Advani in 1990s but both the times it subsided the way it was raised as nobody knew how to bring the change when country already had a Constitution and system of governance called Parliamentary form. Whatever happened then apart, the change has now become a question of survival for the masses and therefore the only way for India. The only way left is to live life as humans and dignified citizens. Indira ji and Advani ji had their own views advocating the system but it has now become an issue in the general interest, the interest of the people of India, the only interest of masses, perhaps the only option for survival of all and everybody.

The experience has also shown us that freedom was no guarantee for good governance or Suraj or for politico-economic equality and general wellbeing. Attaining freedom from foreign rule was by no means a guarantee that the elected *netas* would be better than those despotic foreign rulers. Experience has taught us, how worse the elected government could be and how despotic the power and tyrannic the elected *netas*.

We adopted Westminster (British) Parliamentary system of Government mainly because we were accustomed and acquainted not only with British ways of living and lifestyle but more with their traditions of administration, system of governance and legal - judicial forms. America at that time had adversary relationship with India and was alien to this country, a situation that continued until the beginning of 21st century AD despite Democratic governments coming to power from time to time. But worst was Clintonic term of Presidency. Had the situation in 1947-50 been what it is today, India would have gone, and gone hundred per cent, for Presidential form of government but it is too late to mend. We have in between learnt so much that we would have not, had we gone for Presidential system right in the beginning. We could now remove all loopholes, defects, blunders, anomalies, bottlenecks, ambiguities and above all the imbalances by starting anew and establish Suraj - Lok Raj in true sense incorporating effectively the desired checks and balances.

System Change: Inherent, Natural, Constitutional Right

Only the people of India could collectively bring the proposed change but the youth has a bigger role in bringing this transformation. People of India have not only the inherent natural right but also the sovereign Constitutional power to change the form of government and the Constitution at any time they want. The work is difficult not because of any doubt about the right or powers of the people to bring such change but because of lack of knowledge and ignorance. Even without conducting a survey it could, safely be inferred that out of more than 125 crore population hardly even 20 crore people have ever heard the word Constitution or 'Samvidhan' in Hindi or similar word if any in regional languages. Hardly have even one crores seen it, and twenty five lacs read it. Surprisingly hardly fifty thousand understand it, still we call ourselves a Constitutional Democracy, and the Constitution as the peoples Constitution, made or enacted and adopted by them and given to their selves.

However, if dictators, army caucus groups, communists, kings and sultans could thrust his / their will on the people as the law and Constitution binding on citizens / subjects, why not people collectively for their selves make a Constitution in real and legal sense? Constitutionally, in India Legislature can neither bring nor effect such changes by amending, modifying, or substituting the present Constitution, nor could legislature change the form of government under existing Constitutional system in India. The proposed changes could be brought in and effected only by the people of India and only they can substitute or replace the present Constitution by a new Constitution and form of government whether Bhartiya Lok Tantric or Presidential Form. The People of India while enacting and adopting the present Constitution delegated to Legislature (Parliament - in certain cases of course with the ratification of state Legislatures) only the power of amending, modifying, substituting or deleting the provision of the present constitution and to that extent vested her with the powers of Constituent Assembly (the body that made the Constitution). The powers which otherwise, were their own were delegated by the people to their elected representatives. Unfortunately however, the Parliament could not even protect that power, which Judiciary has snatched in course of time. That was the beginning of disgrace to the sovereign people of India otherwise the makers and masters of Legislature, Executive, and Judiciary under the Constitution.

The Parliament not only represents the people but the 'General Will' of the people and has therefore the absolute jurisdiction and power to amend, modify, delete or / and substitute any provision of "this - present" Constitution of India. The people of India gave this Constitution to themselves by enacting and adopting Parliamentary Form and no power or authority on earth has the jurisdiction to go in to and decide the Constitutionality of the Constitution that would include any Constitutional amendment made by Parliament vested with that "Sovereign power of the People" as Constituent Assembly. This, what Article 368 of the Constitution says unequivocally. Still the people of India could compel Parliament to undo with the amendments and express their will in many ways except 'Referendum' as unfortunately there is no such provision under present Constitution. Judiciary could only look into and decide the Constitutional validity called 'Constitutionality' of laws made by Parliament or state legislatures not the Constitutionality of the Constitution, which she is doing in India. Every Constitutional amendment made by Parliament forms an integral part of the Constitution and beyond challenge.

While, Parliament could amend any provision of the Constitution, she has no power to amend the Preamble, and Directive Principles of State Policy, both of which, not even Fundamental Rights, constitute basic structure of the Constitution. Preamble Legislature cannot amend because it fall outside the provisions of the Constitution and constitutes the mission of the people of India and Directive Principles because these are guidelines for future governance in effect the road map for the state and therefore the Vision of the people for their own as well as future of India and have no exceptions.

The Constitution after independence was drafted by a sub-committee of Constituent Assembly and that drafting sub-committee was presided over by Dr BR Ambedkar. Constituent Assembly consisted of people from different fields of society and national life and was presided over by Dr Rajendra Prasad ji. After deliberations, amendments, additions – deletions the draft of the Constitution was approved by Constituent Assembly. Thereafter Constitution was, deemed to have been, enacted and adopted by the people of India, though not put to their vote ever.

The Constitution as framed then began with the words 'We the people of India having solemnly resolved to constitute India into a Sovereign Democratic Republic and to secure to all its citizens';

Justice—social, political and economic; liberty and equality of status and opportunity; fraternity assuring dignity of individual,

Hereby adopt, enact, and give to ourselves this Constitution.

Article (1) of the Constitution begins with "India i.e. Bharat shall be a union of states".

The Preamble of the Constitution was however, amended in 1976 incorporating the phraseology 'Secular Socialist,' and 'Unity and Integrity of the Nation'.

The Preamble laid down the form of Govt that people of India chose to themselves therefore subsequent additions in 1976 were beyond the competence and jurisdiction of Parliament as the Preamble forms not the part of the provisions of the Constitution but the mission of the people therefore beyond the amending jurisdiction of legislature. The Constitution and the form of Government therefore could only be replaced or substituted by the people of India and not by any Parliamentary or Legislative action or decree or judgment of any court as the sovereignty vests in the people alone. Since the people of India collectively gave the Constitution to themselves therefore they only can, the same way, opt out of it.

2

The Form of Government for India

Phoney Party System

The political party system has over the period proved bastardy because of coalition politics and alliances proving yet another form of *hybridism* where nobody is anybody's and no one is anyone's. It is all selfish; selfish also of lowest level, completely pelf oriented, absolutely unconcerned with the people, their interests and plights; sinisterly oriented solely on power politics or politics of power. It is either for saving one's own skin or managing CBI or other enquiries against or for continuing with the aggrandisement of self or family. All political parties betrayed people and their confidence and have over the period lost credibility and alienated themselves from the main stream despite being elected by the very people. The meanness, baseness is so apparently exposed that one ally accuses and defames the other so abusively and still stays on and pretends to be a partner in the alliance while other party openly debases, denigrates the alliance partners, some other even discredits, maligns the largest alliance partner and still continues in the coalition or alliance as a partner. There is no principle of collectiveness at all and still it is called national alliance for running the government of the country. This is not only the limit of dishonesty but open deception on the people by befooling, duping and stultifying them as sheep.

Not only that alliance partners publicly criticize and humiliate the single largest partner wielding real power but curse and make even politically crucifying statements against. They make such threatening show offs as if quitting the alliance to befool the public and the voters but hang on to the alliance making so many excuses for such hanging on. This has over the period made entire system scoffing, barren of *'Zerf'* i.e. substance and pith. All political alliances in the country are system destitutes, self denying, based on sheer opportunism and seasonality no matter what the cost to the people, nation & the society. They have on the whole brought the country to as much disrepute as some *netas* brought a stage not only of losing self esteem but creating identity crisis to states like Bihar, Jharkhand, Chhattisgarh, Uttarakhand, Delhi, Punjab, HP, TN, Haryana, UP, MP, Maharashtra, Rajasthan. In any case, the voting by JDU, CPM, Shiv Sena and CPI in favour of UPA candidate in Presidential elections has exposed entire political party system in the country. These were the parties who a couple of year back brought 'No Confidence Motion' against UPA government, bent upon to dislodge her and created pandemonium in the country over nuclear power generation treaty with America. CPM in addition had always drawn daggers against Congress. But everything including all their policies and philosophies changed overnight. To quote Kavi Niraj;

जिनके पास शब्द हैं जितने उतना उनसे अर्थ दूर है

शब्द झूठे हैं सभी सत्य कथाओं की तरह

भाषण निर्लज्ज हैं सभी वैश्या की अदाओं की तरह

All our experiments with governance have failed and failing utterly, may that be single party rule, multi party coalition, limited party alliance or absolute even 2/3 despotic majority. People have suffered alike and the results—consequences have been the same. Even extreme right and left became one but only for grabbing power and acquiring pelf. People of India changed the parties in power, replaced one with the other even with new ones, defeated the individuals, still rather than improving, things worsened because people only changed the bottle not the wine, changed the killer not the sword and slept, thinking things have changed or they have made the things change, but nothing changed as the Sword and Wine remained the same. So says the *Shire* and rightly;

गैर मुमकिन है कि हालात की गुत्थी सुलझे
अहले दानिस ने बहुत सोच समझ कर उलझाई है

By changing a political party in power today and putting another in power tomorrow and again electing and putting former in power or even replacing with the third, would make no difference in this state of affairs. It may be possible to put off fire by fire, light up fire by water or clean dirt by dirt but nothing could be remedied in the present **unethical**, criminalised political environment and **corruption infested** governance where **immorality, caste,** nepotism, money and sex work as **'isms'**, unless the form of governance and the Constitution are changed. The rotten and fallen system now only needs radical changes for restoration of good governance called Suraj, excellence and just human development environment based on equality and that would be real 'metamorphosis'.

The Question - Remedy and the Future

There is a well known proverb in Hindi "*Andhe peesen kutte khanyen*" (i.e. if blind are the grinders dogs will eat away) Today it all has changed. Today grinders and eaters are the same (*Peesne vale bhi kutte - khane vale bhi*) Therefore the 'Question' is what now, what next and what remedy for all these chronic ailments of body politic. What is the way out, what is the future – 'Suraj' i.e. good governance or living life as a worm of filth in filth, or living like human beings or as animals?

We have in India experimented with and have experiences of all alternatives, amongst all the experience of coalition governments proved the worst, the complete failure. It is absurdity as well as misleading to say that coalitions have come to stay in India or this is the age of coalitions or coalitions are time compulsions. Experience of last ten (10) years has proved and proved beyond doubt, that it is hundred eight (108) times better to have re-polls or re-election rather than to have coalitions.

Naturally, therefore, the question would be what is the solution; the way out? What is the remedy for all these evils, problems, and ailments; panacea rather, if any, for such ruptured and stinking system? All our experiments for establishing 'Suraj' failed one after the other which included changing the governments, changing the parties in power, single party rule, absolute majority, two-third majority, limited party coalitions, multi party alliances. All these experiments one after the other proved as bad, worse and ultimately worst as corrupt, horrific, and outrageous. Imposition of President's rule also similar to misuse of CBI proved more of a gimmick for capturing power than a remedy for good and stable government. There could never be any hope of good governance, fair administration, impartial legal system and fair justice under the present politico - legal - judicial system. Therefore, the only remedy, not simply possible remedy rather panacea for all ailments of the country and problems of the people - present and future is opting for Bharatiya Lok Jan Tantric Vyavastha or Paddhati for governance of the country and changing accordingly the Constitution that has otherwise also become obsolete, lacking amplitude, glossed with the total failures of Parliamentary form of government.

We have, in the past generally and in recent times completely forgotten our glorious past and intellectual inheritance as also rich treasures of cultural heritage. We generally aped and imitated West except when Mrs. Gandhi was Prime Minister. The amnesia made us forget our glorifying history, divine heritage, rich philosophical treasures, scientific wisdom of our ancestors and intellectual discoveries made. We aped Britain all along, Europe, generally now and US blindly. But callously enough, we aped and are aping everything rotten, everything junk, everything insensitive, obscene, vile, defile, porn, nude, homo, booze, aperitif, erotic incest sex, rudeness, lust, avarice, pelf, self, ostentatious, audacious displays, indecorous values and animalistic habits to name a few; otherwise what not?

Surprisingly, none of us, for that matter nobody including governments, aped the marvellousness of Europeans and their governments, including their decent qualities of humanity, sensitivity, values, ethos, compassion, quick decisions, speedy justice, impartiality of administration, honesty of police and investigation machinery, summary trials, cumulative punishment, commitments in transactions, fairness, decency, civility, good governance, service to the people, ethical morality in inter – personal relationships, obedience to law, road sense and obedience to traffic rules, housekeeping, cleanliness, hygiene, sense of duty, public accountability, and all that was needed for worth establishing *Suraj* - good governance. We all want to become *'Angrej'*, look like European without having any of their qualities. Still all our efforts are in looking sexy, smart, gorgeous and mod which is maddening.

Here also again, a natural innocent question, an anxiously inquisitive enquiry comes up and that is - if man has the habit of aping or capacity to ape why has he not aped angels and great men why demons, scoundrels, why not Rama, why Ravana? Therefore, the core, the substantive question and the most important question now is - why are we not aping the Euro - American system of governance i.e. the Presidential form that has speedy legal - judicial system including the system of punishment and administration, payment of or coverage of unemployment under insurance, cumulative punishment, summary trials and prima facie proof and vicarious liability of governance etc.?

We have aped no doubt, but everything bad of US and Europe - sex to porn, homo to nudity, junk to cheap lifestyles, boozing to bareness, individualism to capitalism but nothing worthy of good governance and lasting democratic value. We could not dare ape their system of rule of law, commitment to the service of the people and the nation, sense of duty, commitment to national prestige, dignity, patriotism, transparency etc.

If we could ape and have everything American - money to sex, employment to technology, if we could ape everything Western including their culture, and feel proud of having everything American or western - why not the form of government which will at least now ensure Suraaj, a clean, just and transparent society. Why we are not even aping the form of government that 70 per cent countries of the world have, amongst them all most all super powers, developed and most of the developing countries, big and small? Countries besides USA, France, Russia, China, Czech and Slovak republics, Indonesia, Pakistan, Philippines, Sri Lanka, S. Korea, Iran, Iraq, S. Africa, Zimbabwe, Kenya, Poland, All erstwhile eastern - south eastern European Communist Block countries viz. Romania, Bulgaria and others have Presidential form. All the countries which disintegrated from erstwhile USSR to name a few and Kazakhstan, Tajikistan, Kyrgyzstan, Turkmenistan etc and Bosnia, Herzegovina, Afghanistan, most of the African - Arabian countries Egypt, Lebanon and Syria to name a few and erstwhile eastern bloc (communist countries) have Presidential form.

Reasons for not opting Presidential form are very clear. As the present systems suits all corrupts and criminals, and befits all plunderers, squanderers, devourers, rapacious debauches, licentious looters, free for all not only without accountability but even without responsibility.

One reason why are we not debating Presidential form at least for future by creating national consensus is that nobody knew or knows how to bring the proposed change despite utter failure of present Constitution and parliamentary form of government, failure to come to the rescue of the people and the nation, failure to deliver.

The Constitution failed as it was made in haste as stop gap arrangement, copied without owning Bharat as an entity but India as territory, not Bharat as an emotional integrity but only India as land. Not as heritage, but simply an area for appropriating power, assuming offices and holding positions, not for selflessly serving the people or in service of the country, not a Nation of unity in diversity but of diversity in unity.

Till now crores have gone waste on committees and commissions just for recommending judicial, administrative, police, educational and other reforms but without any outcome. Even judicial directions for such reforms particularly administrative and police fell into deaf ears. The reasons are very clear - Judiciary herself has lost that regard over the period. The unfortunate situation is when judicial decisions are recalcitrated by not only the Govt but by recalcitrant fraternity of officials called IAS – to the detriment and agony of individual citizens. Bench and the Bar though talked of Constitutional supremacy yet always considered them above the sovereign people. They have always on some pretext opposed judicial reforms, time bound justice, simplification of procedures (Cr PC – CPC including other Rules of Courts) even opening up for foreign lawyers / Attorneys. The governments so to say Parliament succumbed to the pressures. Judiciary considers herself above all laws may that be declaration of assets or right to information or Judicial enquiry commissions to quote a few. Netas have mostly proved heartless already and government employees corrupt generally.

Therefore, there would be no use talking, writing, debating, weeping, and even crying any more. The time has come for acting, doing positive particularly by youth who have the future at stake with progeny in danger.

No other reform short of Presidential form that we call 'BLJT Vyavastha or Paddhati' could reform Indian polity and remove the ailments so deep inside. Once the people understand, and if really understand their power even once, all other organs of state and wings of government would understand it forever.

Our so called reformative legal - Judicial system has so far treated criminals not crimes, corrupts not corruption, offenders not offences the same way as medical science and medical practitioners treat patients not the ailments. None has the intention to do so, no intension to root out the root cause, as every one is afraid of losing his own root.

The inordinately delayed dispensing of cases under the pretext of hearing but factually accommodating Vakils has resulted in injustice more to the detriment of individual citizen and poor people. This has resulted in protecting criminals, mafia, musclemen, corrupt, big – guns and moneyed thus amounting to as much injustice as resulting from 'no' or absence of hearing or pretext thereof, in communist China or Arabian deserts.

The experience we had during the last sixty-five years is not only highly rich in depth, but widely extensive enough to make a fool-proof system for establishing Lok Raj or 'Suraaj' for the people and country. The structure so built now will have strong in-built auto mechanisms for checks and balances taking care of governance and the system every time – all the time - always. The built-in legal - constitutional processes will of their own take care of the people treating the sickness not merely the patient so that neither the individual citizen, nor the system, nor governance - nobody falls sick again. Entire governance will then become 'Seva', Law and justice 'Service' - all for the people.

People's participation in elections and electing their representatives at present is not the proof of their happiness with the system or liking for the governance. They are voting because they have to vote having neither an alternative nor being aware of any. Therefore have to vote and choose either a criminal or a corrupt - choose between the worse or bigger but scoundrel all the same, all the more. The per centage of votes polled in India reflects the above analysis. Alas! While voting they go on abusing the *Netas* and the system and after six months even the person they elected. An irony incomparable.

Clearly if a system of governance could not protect the poor that formed the real rich majority, how could it save the few poor, called the rich?

Golden Transformation and Suraj

With the failure of all experiments the only, perhaps the last golden opportunity now awaiting the people of India is the 'golden transformation' that only the people of Bharat could bring. People of Bharat have nothing to lose, only gain as they have already lost everything in the hands of India. Only the

Bhartiya Lok Jan Tantric called Presidential form of Government as proposed in the Draft Constitution presented in this book is the panacea not only for the people of Bharat but also of India for all their pains, sufferings, sorrows, anguish, dejection, discontentment, gloom, distress, agonies, woes, and the evils of corruption, injustice, exploitation, crimes, killings, rape, looting, plundering including hunger – starvation – squalor – poverty. Many of these have so far helped prosper India downgrading – suppressing Bharat (the sarcastic 'Aam Aadami' of TOI). The 'Form of Government and the Constitution' as proposed are the ones most suited to a country of the size of India with such magnitude of population and spectacular diversity needing a real participative democracy in which each citizen shall directly contribute in democratisation of institutions, in true sense. An electing head of the state and head of the government combined for the country besides for own state. This will set in motion the real and perennial process of 'Emotional Integration' of the people and unity of the country strengthening socio-political cohesiveness of the society, therefore, a blow to - factionalism (that is fractionalizing the psyche of the people) including casteism and regionalism.

The Presidential form with proposed Constitutional changes will set in motion the process of establishing real Suraaj – the good governance in action not merely in words, in practice not in speeches, seen in deeds not simply in principles. This will be Peoples Raj a genuine Lok Tantra, a Jan Tantra not Praja Tantra (subjects ruled by or under a King) a legacy of bygone days and British.

The proposed Presidential or BLJT system of government will bury political instability - the curse of Indian Polity – forever; otherwise also the biggest cause of its regressiveness and the cause of all causes: Corruption - political and administrative, crimes, immorality, injustice, frustration and alienation. This golden transformation will also for all times to come eliminate the vices of floor crossing (Aayaa - Gayaa Raams), threatening, browbeating or any Neta asking for political ransom – sharing in booty – sharing in power - threatening to quit or pulling down the governments. No MP,

MLA, or group of MLAs or MPs would ever be able to pressurise government in any manner. Therefore, no more fear of fall of governments with which will go all political uncertainties. Political bargaining of all or any kinds by or for vested interests will end. Race for ministerial births or pressure tactics for preferential portfolios will have no place. People and people's welfare will be the only aim and purpose of all governance - National Interests being above all. The system would ultimately lead to polarisation of political parties minimizing the number at national level, in real sense ensure sustainable economic growth and development with stability. Even at state levels polarisation would bring mushrooming of the parties to a halt.

Presidential/BLJT Form of Government

The Presidential or BLJT form of government and the new Constitution would be complementary to each other strengthening the system and the governance. The Draft Constitution proposed here attempts to remove all the inadequacies, deficiencies, defects, faults, paucities and imperfections of present Constitution. It would ensure speedy, quick, timely and time bound justice, summary trials, exemplary punishments, and politico - economic equality with a responsive executive, legislature and judiciary where no one would ever talk of corruption, ask for bribery, show inefficiency, or commit dereliction of duty. Gross, habitual or deliberate negligence never, not even dare negligence.

With the installation of Presidential or BLJT System would establish quality leadership and therefore qualitative governance and government of intellectuals, wise, eminent professionals, patriots and visionaries in the country including the states. Truly the governments for the people, of the people, not simply by the people and thus, would come true peoples dream of "Suraaj". This Suraj would be the replica of unity of mind integrated with unity of soul as one people, one country without class differences; a great nation with great equality and great unity of purpose. There would be no fear of fall of government or hung parliament and rarely a need for midterm polls. Above all, there shall be no scope for factional fights – intra or inter se including leg pulling or politicking for seniority or succession and no uncertainty in devolution of power. The government and the system together would constitute impenetrable, impermeable, concrete, cogent, potent, coherent, stable, steady, sound, effective, proficient, prudent, efficacious system of governance for the people and the nation.

Just as the increasing population is the root cause of so many rather most of the socio- economic problems, ailments and sicknesses so is political corruption, the root cause of all other kinds of corruptions, evils and crimes in India. All administrative, police, judicial and political reforms having failed and no possibility of any improvement now. The only alternative is to replace present Parliamentary form of governance and Constitution by new system as proposed rather than repent later at a stage when that would be too late.

In China or for that matter in communist states injustice resulted because of no or scant trials. In India it has resulted in excessive trials and excessive adjournments in the name of due opportunity or fair and proper hearing. This in turn resulting in inordinate - undue and excessive delays, frustration all around amounting to unfair - unreasonable hearings to tire out the poor, the common man, the middle classes leading into gross injustice ultimately. Such excessive hearings in India could only be called 'gross legal luxury' on poverty, ignorance and legal illiteracy or want of such consciousness.

USSR disintegrated within 75 years we are heading towards that morally, ethically, administratively, humanly, socially, judicially and politically just within 65 years. The western Bhogavad oriented culture of crimes, corruption, loot, exploitation, killing, kidnapping, ransom, rape, atrocities on women and poor, Mafia-donism, terrorism – Naxalism - Maoism, regionalism with its disruptive secessionism – separatism have within a span of 30 – 40 years shattered the conceptual entity we live in as a 'Nation'. Socio-legal-administrative chaos, anarchy, indiscipline have pervaded the entire psyche of society the same as the interference of judiciary has done to the governmental functioning.

The future of a country, where children are kidnapped for ransom, raped and killed routinely by or at the behest of the

Netas who otherwise call these children 'future of the country - future hopes even future leaders', could very well be imagined. Therefore, before the system and governance permits any more kidnap or kill the future, let people collectively and consciously kidnap that system and governance. Disrespect for law has, as a fact of matter, reached its nadir which is another name for state of lawlessness - an insult to governance, Constitution, and Constitutional freedom of the people.

Clinton Human Rights

The 'Clintonic Human Rights' have over and above, played a pimple on the ulcer making India a paradise for criminals, Mafia - Dons, offenders and a heaven even for terrorists. This is perhaps the only country where terrorists taking shelter under Clintonic Human Rights chant loudly "Jai ho judiciary ki" and are defended by communal - casteist politicians alike.

The biggest terrorist of the world of his times, Clinton, made India surrender in fact compelled and forcibly imposed Human Rights obligations on the country to save and serve his vote bank. He was the same Clinton who visited India at the fag end of his Presidency that too perhaps on the insistence of his wife. He was the one Democratic Party President in the history of Democratic Party of America who had so bad relations with India – the biggest Democracy of the world. A deep antagonist to India of his times, his policies were responsible for maximum terrorist assaults on the country by Pakistan. During his Presidency India suffered maximum. His wife now Secretary of State is equally anti India, who talked of diplomacy not relationships and repented leaving Pakistan alone after the dissolution of USSR. Clinton was responsible for maximum killings in the sub-continent and around the world during 8 years of his Presidency. A man who violated human rights the maximum in the name of Human Rights, responsible for Pakistani Dadagiri and Kargil adventure. Responsible for protecting, encouraging and compelling Govt. of India in the name of human rights to desist from dealing with the Khalistani terrorists. Since then HR avocation has become a business, a trade, a 'Dhandha' in India against which people also required to fight unitedly. These HR protagonists and their business centered – profit oriented yellow journalistic fraternity has also invaded defence forces particularly Armed forces of India including Para-military forces - the dispensers of protection and providers of security - including to these Rightists. By exposing and exploding forces and keeping them in the dock they have made defence of the country precarious and security vulnerable. Though, the country will always look to them for security and protection still services are not as a consequence getting personnel for manning. Such accusations and consequent vulnerability further abetted corruption in forces and services and demoralized them.

As a matter of fact, the eight years of Clintonic Terrorism culminated in the blasting of 'Two Heads of American Ravan, the consequences unfortunately were borne by President Bush. It was perhaps an irony that the great President Bush suffered himself, but saved America, saved the world, and saved India in particular, from the fatal consequences of terrorism. This may take some time for Americans and the people of the world to realize.

Nevertheless, the fact remains that people of India suffered injustice because of Clintonic Human Rights debauchery and with that suffered the criminal jurisprudence and therefore justice.

Dubious—Dubitative Decisions of Judiciary

Besides Clintonic human rights, so many decisions of judiciary destroyed the Politico – Constitutional - Administrative – Legal fabric of the country.

First, was encroaching upon the Constitutional - Legislative function and jurisdiction of Parliament particularly in respect of Constitutional amendments, in short Judiciary going into the Constitutionality of Constitution, therefore, devastating interpretation of Art 368 read with Art 13.

Second, was interpretation of Art 311 of the Constitution after its amendment in 1977 that did away with the right of government employees / civil servants to alleged 'double opportunity' variously called 'Show Cause' or 'Right to Represent' on the penalty proposed.

Third, was interpretation of Sec. 197 of Criminal Procedure code (Cr.PC) requiring the sanction of Governor or President before prosecuting the government employees or public servants even in cases of offences and crimes committed arising not out of bonafide due discharge of official duty or responsibility in good faith.

Fourth, was inclusion of Chief Ministers, Ministers and persons holding such Constitutional or public positions in respect of whom neither the Governor nor President is appointing authority even inclusion of political appointments of public nature within the above category not covered by Art 311.

Fifth, is deriving uncalled for intentions of the Legislature while interpreting laws passed by the august body without either referring it to her or limiting it to the aims and objects mentioned in the bill or final Act passed. At times such intention of the Legislature was derived by too much stretching and travelling beyond the aims and objects or history behind at the most or interpreting intention remotely that in many cases defeated the purpose of the enactment. Same thing happened in the interpretation of Art 311 after its amendment in1977.

The interpretation of 'Right to reasonable opportunity of being heard under Art 311' was extended even to the stage of departmental appeals though not born out of the language of the Article. Therefore, the very purpose and intent of amending Art 311 got frustrated and the remedy proved worse than the disease. Such interpretations proved boon to culprits and corrupts and have been responsible along with excessive bails, stays, injunctions for continuance of corruption, irresponsibility, inefficiency and gross negligence in government services including Public Sector together with criminalised scandalous rampant corruption in politico - administrative governance of the country. Sixth, was Bhopal Gas Agreement – a calamity in fact, on teeming community of people.

The individualised, discretionary rather than legal, Constitutional or based even on preponderance of probability approach of interpretations has led to cobweb of case law and a situation of parallel Constitution in the country. The hearings of cases particularly Constitutional – legal interpretations have in effect become legal luxury and the country over the period is practically working under a parallel Constitution. Value of human life, talks about abolition of capital punishment, perpetuation of 'reservations', amendment of Preamble and Fundamental Rights, ordering or withdrawing CBI enquiries or providing or withdrawing personal security to big or moneyed few, or hearing cases of big ones at the residences are some other examples. The fate of the people of that country vis a vis justice could very well be imagined where language of Law and Judiciary is not its own but a foreign language not even the 'Lingua Franca' of the country. That is the reason that a couple of years back one Honble Judge of Bombay HC remarked on the unfortunate situation that despite 60 years of freedom we could not have laws in our National Language i.e. Hindi while another Honble Judge of Gujarat HC a year back or so said 'Hindi in Gujarat was as good as a foreign language'.

The situation today has reached an appalling stage where culprits, criminals, offenders prefer to remain or stay inside jails. Lacs of public money spent on their facilities, luxuries and 'Shan – O Shaukat' i.e. public money spent on the enemies of public. They are treated as 'Damads' of Govt rather than enemies of the people, anti social inhumans, a danger to civil society and national liability hence the criminality and offensiveness remained unaffected and least unimpacted in this country. These dreaded criminals not only looked after well rather very well and enjoy jails as picnic spots. There is nothing that could be called exemplary either punishment or treatment or trial. The Human Rights reformist policy reformed nobody rather these criminals – culprits when free, start reforming the public with the 'Danda' and 'Dadagiri'. It is only the fear of police or their certain degree punishments rather than fear of law that works and has worked more effectively. It is rather respect for police torture and 'Danda' than judicial or legal process that keep crimes and offences under control if any, whatsoever. This is similar type of situation developing as was brought about by Judiciary during 1975–88 when workers asked for suspension pending enquiry when they wanted to start their own business or alternative work or otherwise indulged in deliberate indiscipline particularly with seniors to be suspended pending enquiry so that they get subsistence allowance hoping reinstatement with back wages thus similar to present criminals and corrupt ruling both the worlds.

Present Parliamentary form of governance, besides suffocating itself has clogged the system and choked the people. This system would succeed and has succeeded in countries like Britain, Holland or Japan and a few others only because in these countries even on a mere allegation of corruption, immorality, debauchery, dissipation to unethical pursuits the person or persons in power either resign or sacked or otherwise thrown out under public pressure making it impossible for them to seek power again or dare seek re-election. Alternatively, parliamentary system could succeed only where bureaucracy and administration both are of highly dignified meritorious caliber appointed on fair competition and merits, not on castes and reservations; or where bureaucracy works as a steel frame and not as in India where it is not even a 'Paper Frame'. British Parliament though vested with despotic powers, supreme amongst all the Supremes yet the most democratic, most dignified and most responsive. Unlike America, Britain has cultural ethos, value systems, ethical and moral orientations and public decency besides emotional attachment and commitment to cultural heritage and socio – national traditions. British as a people are committed to parliamentary form and Parliamentary system to Britons because of political legal discipline, personal decency, social civility, sense of public duty, responsibility, and above all accountability to service to the people and the country. Civil services there still are Steel Frame not caste corrupted or caste prejudiced. For these reasons, Parliamentary form of government has succeeded, is succeeding and will continue to succeed in Britain, Japan and some such other countries as Holland, Sweden etc. These are the reasons, corruption at times seen so openly at top levels in these countries particularly Japan and at times Britain, has never percolated down as in India.

The tragic working of whole Legal, Justice and Judicial System gets exposed under the present form of governance the moment Delhi Police (for that matter Govt) is directed to compensate Late Raj Bala a sum of Rs. 3.50 lac only for causing her death and somebody else is awarded ten lacs from a private individual for comparatively petty offence, if at all.

Judicial Activism and Parallel Anomalies

Many anomalies cropped up because of undue judicial activism leading to a confused lego–judicial cob–web akin to parallel Constitution awkwardly coexisting with legal luxury. Such pitiable state of affairs arose again because of corruption that pervades whole political scenario of the country particularly prevailing amongst Netas compelling them to chant 'Jai Ho' rather than debating, challenging and correcting the situation of deviations, unconstitutional interferences and usurping the jurisdiction of other Wings and state Organs by Judiciary. The legislative wing unfortunately, succumbed the most for obvious reasons giving Judiciary occasion to interference. This is detrimental to the principle of separation of power, a pathetic pathos of the functioning of present system.

Indira ji never allowed pulling down of the Constitution and the Constitutional institutions, impliedly the Sovereignty of the People of India, in the name of either constitution or All Pervasive Judicial Power even under the pretext of justice and would have taken the issue to public. But the present generation of Netas sunk head to foot under the mud has no such guts. Presumption of all pervasive power by any state organ is unconstitutional. No organ under the present constitution is all pervasive, and if at all, it is Legislature, that represents general will of the people. However, if any such power exists, it is not for exhibiting ego or superiority but for the good of and justice to the people in general. Wielding such power or superiority under the dint of threatening punishment other than for justice to the masses is not born out of the present

Constitution still that pretext of doing justice to the people is seen nowhere even after Judicial Activism. People have gone as worse politically as they have in getting justice – the fair justice. A referendum would remove all the misconceptions.

The first anomaly seriously concerns the power and jurisdiction of Judiciary to go into the constitutionality of constitution that arose with the additions – deletions of Fundamental Rights by Parliament through constitutional amendments and Judiciary deciding on their constitutionality. That was in fact sitting on judgment on the competence of Parliament to amend the constitution despite the powers vested in her as Constituent Assembly under Art 368. Thus going in to the constitutionality of the constitution is in itself unconstitutional. Under our constitutional system based on Parliamentary form; legislature expressly – impliedly represents people's sovereign general will, therefore in the absence of provision for referendum has the sole constitutional jurisdiction, power and competence to amend any article of the Constitution. Therefore, the jurisdiction of judiciary to go into the legality or constitutionality of any constitutional amendment is expressly and by necessary implication barred. Still bigger and unusual anomalies arose when such constitutional amendment bills for amending fundamental rights were treated and compared with the bills brought for enacting general laws falling under Art 13. Since constitution bars any law inconsistent with fundamental rights, therefore such amendments were also held to be unconstitutional without making a difference between bills for enacting general laws and the bill placed as constitutional procedure for amending the constitution may that be FR or other provisions. Presenting bills for all purposes is constitutional mandate and legislative procedure but constitutional amendments differ from all others because these are not bills for making a law but form part of a procedure for amending constitution provided under the constitution itself. If the interpretation, presuming constitution amendment procedure Bill also a Bill as for general law, is held to be correct the same would create much bigger awkwardness where laws would become the source of constitution rather than the constitution the source of all laws, thus rendering Constitution to a secondary position losing its position as the supreme law of the land. This situation has arisen and will arise where constitutional amendments are or held valid as in around 115 cases uptil now. In all such cases the same constitutional amendment bill allegedly amounting to law under Art 13 has been incorporated in and became part of the constitution and thus its source.

Second anomaly arose when Fundamental Rights though held sacrosanct, inviolable and forming part of the basic structure of the Constitution beyond legislative competence to amend yet Art 16 was amended in 1995 and 2000 incorporating clauses (4A) and (4B) respectively on the subject of reservations that played havoc.

Third, the most unconstitutional act, really beyond the power, jurisdiction, and competence of Parliament amounting to destruction of Constitution in real sense was amendment of Preamble in 1976–77. Preamble and Pt IV, the two only – none else – constitute really the basic structure of the Constitution and are sacrosanct therefore beyond the power of Legislature to amend. But then Preamble was amended in 1976–77, incorporating Secular - Socialist which continues even today. Where was judicial activism then? What of such activism that could not save the Constitution? What now, when the same preamble and Directives have been openly shattered and practically shelved consequent to porn liberalisation and incest globalisation of economy at the behest of West particularly America in utter violation and flagrant disregard to the basic structure? How any Govt could agree or succumb to foreign pressure or at their behest agree to destroy its own Constitution?

The other anomaly in complete contravention of Constitution was a decade ago, when Shri Romesh ji Bhandari was Governor of UP and Shri Jagadambika Pal an extra constitutional authority was allowed to sit on the one side of dais with Speaker besides the then CM on the other. Vidhan Sabha, the sovereign body in her functioning, was then directed, in utter violation of Constitution to act in a particular way and follow a particular method in choosing CM for the State.

The yet another was the directions in respect of appointment of CVC and the procedure to be followed, practically assuming legislative function by laying down the scheme.

The equally serious, completely unconstitutional, inconsistent with Art 12 of the Constitution was laying down quota scheme and formula in respect of reservations. These are only some examples the list would go on lengthening.

The Chief Justice of India has, also on 15th Aug 2012 while addressing Independence Day gathering as reported by media, given an indication that could be extended to any extent the same way as judiciary extends the intention of the legislature. Therefore, until system change through a new Constitution, judicial accountability and judicial reforms shall remain untouched and fairy tale in this country under this Constitution and judicial functioning above suspicion - as Caesar's wife.

Last but not the least, is shelving of Part- IV of the Constitution by the government i.e. Directive Principles of State Policy, which otherwise constitute the vision of the people, constituting basic structure of the Constitution. This has allegedly been done under the garb of hedonistic liberalisation, epicurean economics and perverted westernism. How big is the contradiction and glaring the contravention of the Constitution that went unheeded, unprosecuted and unpunished? All wings of government, all functionaries are simply show pieces, shedding crocodile tears to the public but in fact self centered and pretentious if said daringly - anti people.

The present politico – economic - judicial caucus system has divided the citizenry into elites and depleted classes exactly Marxian haves and have notes, former ensuring to delete the latter completely not realising how will it survive then.

The confusions and absurdities in India arose because of British rule and consequent aping of Western Jurisprudence particularly British by Indians defining Constitution in their ignorance as the 'Supreme Law of the Land' while it falls nowhere within that ambit whether called the Supreme, High or 'Super Supreme' Law. Constitution in real sense is the codified 'General Will' of the 'Sovereign people' how they would govern themselves. It therefore is the touch stone akin to 'Shastra' i.e. inviolable Governing scripture enacted and adopted by people of a country under their Sovereign Common or General Will for leading a blissfully blessed human life on this earth itself rather than after death as preach Guru – Babas, Swami - Swaminis.

Compulsive Anguish of the People

People of Bharat, frustrated with the Netas and the governance lost faith in the system along with and in that state of withdrawal and fixation even without caring for the consequences, ignorantly out of deep discontentment and anguish, allowed Judiciary to strike at their own roots. People knowingly allowed Judiciary to bang their feet, destroy the Constitutional Principle of Separation of Power, and go even into the Constitutionality of Constitution, the power otherwise vested in them. People were prepared even for judicial anarchy and legal chaos and suffered the consequences rather than be squeezed by the corrupt Netas and suppressed by despotic governmental system continuously every time. The consequences of such abdication by the people have however, been disastrous. Now Netas, Governments, executive and administration all playing safe by relinquishing their public duty and leaving things on Judiciary not only to decide but practically govern making it like a fish market, a mess, open mismanagement and misrule, resulting in chaos and anarchy never seen before and hardly heard of in history.

It is, said that before World War I, Germany had a Constitution of people's dreams, approximating in form if not in spirit to an ideal Constitution of 'Suraaj' i.e. good governance but in India unfortunately poor have no courage, masses dare not, middle classes have no time, rich are unconcerned, youth is '*mast*' (captivated) and 'Bhog' rules the rest. This all has made everything 'Rust'.

Mania for Rights without Duty and Indiscipline

India was under British Empire and won freedom from

foreign rule hence there was bound to be disobedience of law, orders and rules including violence and indiscipline. All this despite Gandhi's non-violence, truth and disobedience in a civil manner also known as the civil disobedience which was in the nature of a movement for good cause. That mindset unfortunately continued in its poorest form in one of the poorest free countries abetted by Communism and protected by Judiciary. Absence of duty under the Constitution of free India made people only Right conscious. Governmental corruption and putridness of Netas since the infancy of free India further added fuel to the fire. Nobody had either guts or dare talk about duty. All this collectively and coupled with vote politics resulted in slow poisoning of society and defilement of environment resulting in all-round decadence where disobedience, insubordination, gross and deliberate negligence became order of the day and all play no work common. Demands, strikes, bandhs, slowdowns, work stoppages and blockades frequent. The collective and cumulative effect of all this pushed the country to the condition we are in today, a condition beyond anarchy and chaos, a condition of revolt, terrorism, rebellion, subversion and insurgency appearing impossible to mend and if possible at all, only be changing the form of governance and the Constitution.

Ignorance and the Irony

This was perhaps the satire of the circumstances that neither the intellectuals, genius, learned, nor social reformers, judicio - legal luminaries, Human Right Activists and other experts ever had time - what of common man and Netas - to pause and ponder over the causes that ailed the society and continued ailing leading ultimately to this impervious state of affairs. None of them ever went in to the root cause i.e. the cause of all causes, the problem of all problems. We all failed to diagnose the disease therefore failed in the treatment. If diagnosis was at such variance, remedy automatically proved worse than the disease. The root of all problems of the country laid in the inaction of Judiciary, an unaccountable judiciary and passive legal system including the injustice that flowed in and out of law and Constitutional manipulations by pro or Anti government judges or pro – anti establishment or pro and anti worker judges resulting in present chaos - anarchy and lawlessness. This may in other words be called the death of Nyaya, the death of rule of law, the killing of principle of separation of power, hence the reign of 'Anyaya', misrule and bad governance. The system made governance rotten, failing to own the people making the system and the governance obsolete to own the nation. The power owned power, powerful own their selves. Power of politics owned politics of power that owned money and in turn power and money both, therefore the system. Nobody owned the people and the country who owned all of them just to play their games. Not people but the individuals own and owned the authority, system, and governance hence in the process no one owned the country and the people.

Therefore, the need for change now, change for the good the ultimate betterment – 'Changing the Form of Government and the Constitution'; opting for the Presidential or Bhartiya form - the only panacea for all ailments and problems, present and future, ensuring at the same time the future of posterity for all times to come - 'the new avatar - saviour of people, democracy, and the country.

If people do not now decide and go for the change the plundering state, stripping governance, criminalised politics, corrupt Netas, befallen socialists, unaccountable Marxists, marginalised Communists, barbaric Naxalites, robbing Maoists, blind legal–judicial system, unconcerned justice, 'Bhookh' and exploitative poverty would sooner than later make the country '*Mobocratically Plutocratic Lootocracy*' where everything would be decided on roads, snatched and eagled upon taking toll of the whole socio-national polity.

Expressing the General Will

Democracy in this country is not the Government for – of - by the people, which Suraj will mean. That will be democracy in action i.e. Government for the people – of the people – by the people unlike the present which is by – of – for. It is now only the question of expressing that general will also called the Sovereign will of the people by the people for the proposed change and how to express that. The future of youngsters, the educated youth constituting 35% of total population at present and likely to be more than 50% by the end of 2025 is linked to that change, reform, and system substitution or governance replacement. They will have to decide what system and form of government they would like to have or work with for their betterment including prosperity of the country, general happiness, and glorious future of society with clean governance based on justice and equality. Where law would be king of kings in action not in sermons, in practice not in words and where people would work neither for anybody nor under anybody but as in America under a system for the country and for everybody. Where nobody is a 'Sahib' but everybody equal citizen of a Nation.

British were bad because they ruled us and exploited the natural resources of the country but in turn at least gave India Institutions, ethos and values which system and the governance in free India slowly degenerated. One fine morning by 1991 - 92 India found itself at a loss with which began the ugly horrifying face of politics in the country that by the beginning of twenty first century reached a menacing state and since then started a deadly journey leading to a state that the country lost herself, her people and the governance, exploiting everything - men, women, children, resources, nation, society even hunger, poverty and starvation of the people. The grand creation of God or nature - the Humans reduced to resource – lifeless and dead.

We blame British for dividing us to rule in perpetuity but what after their exit. British divided us to destroy the very fabric, the texture of which has now been destroyed by elected rulers in free India. To save this texture and fabric forever, people will have to decide for proposed change here and now without losing time any more. There could be many ways for.

Sovereign Decision of the People

The sovereign people of the country have to decide between Caste - Community - Class divide corrupt, exploitative, mismanaged government - misruled governance vis a vis integrated, equal society based on justice and rule of law i.e. good governance called Suraaj. Good of a few or good of all is the question before the people of the country. They have to choose out of hunger - poverty – starvation – squalor – exploitation - unemployment and misrule, on the one hand and employment guarantee - prosperity – decent living – human existence - equality - welfare state and good governance on the other. Understanding very well that 'Reservations' would change the fate of nobody, only good governance will. Reservations otherwise also could neither be permanent nor such solution to people's problems, national evils and societal ailments, in any case, not at all a perennially perpetuating situation even under the Constitution because it in itself is an evil.

This is high time for people to feel the pain of scams, scandals, frauds at least of those have come on the surface. May that be Provident Fund scam by Judges of High Court, scam by the relatives of a CJI or misuse of office by judges of Supreme Court, fodder - sugar - wheat scams or mining – coal gate - land frauds, Commonwealth games corruption, 2G scandals or Haryana, Delhi, Tamil Nadu or UP, MP, Rajasthan, Maharashtra, Punjab, Jharkhand and Uttarakhand rackets. If people still do not, then God even can not help them. This is the time to feel the height and extent of corruption prevailing in the country at every corner, every step, everywhere as if it is the government of - for and by corruption. Examples of a police constable of fifteen years service in Bihar having Rs. fifty-one lacs and an accountant of equal number of years of service one crore as unaccounted money are an eye opener. Earlier we thought of just UP, UK, Jharkhand, Bihar, Haryana, Punjab, Delhi, TN, Maharashtra but now it reveals that MP is one of the morally – ethically failed states that has left all others behind. If people still do not open their eyes when would they? Debasement of saffron clad Swamis, Babas, Gurus and Mahants apart, Netas have fallen to such state of shame where shame itself is ashamed. Defrauding own parties and party cadres by selling even the election tickets are only the trailers.

Whatever we see or hear is only the tip of the iceberg. The real life situation is outraging - '*Jo Pakara Nahin Gaya*

Woh Shah' (Until caught is lord). The question is who would catch whom, if the whole system is Chor - thief? Even CBI requires a super CBI, Civil court needs District Court that needs High and then Supreme. A DM needs Commissioner who needs Secretary who in turn Minister and then Chief Minister and who also a governor. Most of the enquiries and commissions are political gimmicks for threatening or exploiting and remaining in power or enacting political drama to silence the mouth of opponents or public which again is a game playing at the cost of starving masses – hungry millions crores poor. Hardly ever are big fishes caught except those who either have many enemies or refused to please those who were to be pleased. Even in such cases hardly a few are proceeded against or prosecuted. Almost all are released on bail and rarely one out of million is punished, making no impact on the system. If defence forces could sink in high profile corruption, the time has naturally come for operation of the system the same way as Armed forces launch against enemies. The system has become monstrous and governance demonic.

The only solution now with the people is either to opt for Presidential form or Bhartiya Lok Jan Tantric form of government i.e. directly electing the Prime Minister or President and Dy. Prime Minister or Vice President for the country and Governor or Chief Minister and Dy. Governor or Dy. CM for the states with a new Constitution for governance. The working of present constitution during the last sixty-five years has proved its complete failure leading to around 115 Amendments basically changing its originality, therefore all the more need for the change.

Just as no court can decide the unconstitutionality of the Constitution, no one can the Constitutionality of the Constitution. Only the people of India can decide the nature, modus, pattern and the system of their governance – the form of their Constitution for ensuring their future, and their destiny.

Modus and the Alternatives for Transformation

It is the opportune time, proper time and the right time, before judicial anarchy, legal chaos, police despotism, cruelty of Netas, capitalistic exploitation and governmental animalism kidnaps the future of the country. Thus, compelling the people to decide everything on roads. The people should collectively kidnap bad governance and misrule forever and for all times and transform India into 'Bharat Varsh' of their dreams.

There are many ways of and for expressing that general will:

1. The best democratic and peaceful way is to hold referendum. In that process if 50 per cent of the total number of voters in the country (not merely votes polled) plus one (fifty-per cent + 1) cast their votes in favour of Presidential or BLJT System including naturally the modification of the Constitution the present system of Parliamentary Form would be replaced by BLJT Paddhati and the new Constitution.
2. The other way collectively for the people is not to participate in any election, not to caste vote, which will be an expression of their general will for change.
3. Third is to participate in elections but cast invalid votes by stamping more than one candidate or box.

Next is making this proposal for change an election issue for ascertaining general will but this hardly any party is expected to do.

Proposed Form of Government: A Fool Proof System

Bharatiya Lok - Jan Tantric Paddhati

The proposed form of government will be very much Democratic with elections or adult franchise rather very wide, extensive – intensive both. The fundamentals of present Constitution would remain. Probably more than 50 per cent provisions of the present Constitution will remain. It shall be a real democracy just, clean and transparent – truly a people's democracy. Parliament and Vidhan Sabha shall function *mutatis mutandis* and the members shall continue to be MPs and MLAs as at present. Various Commissions such as Public Service Commissions, Election Commissions, Auditor and Comptroller General, Attorney and Solicitor Generals, and Information Commission would not only continue but made stronger with certain improvements. Many more Commissions such as Water Commission, UGC, Lok or Jana Ayukt and Ombudsman would be created or made stronger by giving them Constitutional status. All India and State Services shall be made more responsive, accountable and people service oriented. There shall also be an Appellate Court of India but no 'Vidhan Parishads or Councils in states. There shall be no Vigilance Commission only 'Lok Ayuktas' for States and 'ombudsman' for Central Government employees or by whatever name called – Lok or Jan Ayukt - but will be made very - very strong.

Legal – Judicial system and Administrative structure including Executive functioning will have radically drastic changes and will function always in the service of the people and never as their masters. There shall hardly be any case of corruption. Load on the Judiciary i.e. cases in courts will reduce drastically within three years – just 25 per cent of the number today.

The country will have either a directly elected 'President as the head of state and government' or the Prime Minister with their deputies elected by the people of India and Governor or Chief Minister and their Deputies directly elected by the voters of the state concerned.

The proposed system would be fool proof against all corruption, crimes, all ailments of the country and problems of the people and may be called 'Bharatiya Lok – Jan Tantric Vyavastha / Paddhati' that would modify and replace about 40 % provisions of the present Constitution and remaining would continue.

Procedure for Bringing in the Change

Depending upon the outcome of expression of general will either thru referendum or elections or otherwise, Parliament so elected shall be converted into constituent assembly and will appoint a Constitution drafting committee of not exceeding 15 members including 5 expert members even from outside and not exceeding 3 from Rajya Sabha to draft the Constitution within four months.

The draft Constitution would be discussed and debated in Joint Sessions of Parliament. All the speakers and Dy. Speakers of Vidhan Sabhas shall be present in such discussions and shall for the purpose deemed to be the members of parliament. State legislatures may, if they so desire send their suggestions to the speaker of Lok Sabha. The Jt. Session of Parliament by simple majority could modify the draft and incorporate the amendments. The soul of the Constitution or the drafts including amendments will be on the lines as presented in this book and there shall be no substantial deviation from the intended purpose. Entire process would be completed within six months. Final draft Constitution would be read clause wise in joint session of Parliament relayed nationally and if desired internationally and codification shall be completed within three month. Finally it shall be put to the vote of the people of India within one month wherein all the voters would cast their votes. If 50% of the total voters plus 1 (fifty per cent plus one) cast their vote in favour the new Constitution it would be taken as enacted, accepted, adopted and approved by all the people of India in exercise of their collective sovereign general will and would come in to force as provided and accordingly the form of Govt shall also stand changed.

Election Commission will announce the results and within a week of such announcement issue notification and send the copy of finally adopted Constitution to each of the following authorities within seven days of such notification and get signed within 15 days : by the speaker of Lok Sabha, chairman, Rajya Sabha, Chief Justice of India, chairperson of the drafting committee, chairman law commission and rectified by not less than fifty per cent of the Vidhan Sabhas, governors and chief ministers. Thereafter the same shall be signed together by the PM and President. Alternatively Election Commission could organise a function for the purpose inviting all the above authorities for signing in ceremony of the Constitution finally enacted, adopted and accepted by the people of India thro referendum held for the purpose.

Immediately thereafter, in accordance with the new Constitutional provisions election commission will hold elections within three months of such signing until then existing working arrangements will continue.

3

Establishment of Bharatiya Lok Jan Tantric Shasan

New Constitution will have approximately 60 per cent provisions of the present constitution, Fifteen per cent (15 per cent) could be incorporated on the lines of American and French constitutions, Thirty per cent (30 per cent) provisions making all the difference would be as proposed in this book. The draft proposed in this Book as already explained is based on the problems faced by the people as also the experience of last over 60 years including the working of present constitution, functioning of government and system of governance at the same time ensuring the present and future of India and her people including the progeny.

This book is only an attempt perhaps the first ever attempt exhorting the people of the country for brain storming. It contains the Draft Constitution for initiating a dialogue, a national debate and may take a couple of years to materialise in our psycho-socio-political background.

One thing the people of India particularly the youth need to understand very clearly, that piece meal nothing is going to happen, nothing is going to succeed and nothing is going to be achieved. Therefore this book presents a system change with the main provisions to be incorporated in the Constitution to make it people's Constitution without which even the system change would not work rather prove it a futile exercise bringing us to same state wherefrom we had started.

For the present it is the substance not the legal shape that matters. Therefore presently it is in the language intelligible to as simple a man as we call common man in the lanes. The draft is being presented in simplified form understood even by a man in the corn fields, village and streets of cities.

It is a proposal to Youngsters, the future and the future hope of the country, the people in general and the masses to debate - argue and come to a consensus. This is for brain-storming of the public, the Aam Aadami, the poor, the middle classes and the intellectuals of the country. Presently it has nothing to do with the legal language, legal shape and terminology of drafting. This is a proposal to the people for establishing their democracy - people's democracy, a real Suraaj, a genuine Lok Tantra, a Jan Tantra in true sense in which rather than people going to justice, justice will come to their doorsteps. Rather than people running for and after services the same will come to their homes. Surprisingly, and for many astonishingly perhaps, 'Praja Tantra' in this country would come to an end forever. Crime and corruption will have no face to face their own face ensuring a system where rather than people running after the administration or government and public servants, they would run after the people.

New Preamble

We the people of 'Bharat Varsha' constitute Bharat into an Integrated Sovereign Lok Jan Tantra Rashtra (National Democratic People's Republic), secular i.e. Panth and Mujahab Nirpeksha (non theocratic theological) state, administratively decentralised into 'Pradesh or Anchals';

and

That Bharat shall be a Sarva Dharma Sambhav welfare state - for, of and by the People;

And therefore; 'We the People of Bharat solemnly resolve to secure to all citizens';

Justice — Social, Political and Economic; Liberty and Equality of status and opportunity; fraternity assuring dignity of individual,

And

Making Law the King of Kings in accordance with this Constitution - hereby in democratic manner enact, adopt, and give to ourselves this CONSTITUTION under our Sovereign general will.

Bharat and Central Government

Government of BHARAT will be, substituted for Government of India for all purposes including international transactions, treaties, or covenants whatsoever. All agreements, covenants, or transactions of international character or agreements, contracts entered into within the country with government of India or Union of India or central government shall be, deemed to, have been entered into with Government of Bharat.

Central Government of Bharat will be substituted for Union of India, and can sue and be sued in that name viz Central Govt of Bharat. In all litigations against Central government, the Central government of Bharat shall be, made first party, Secretary of the Deptt concerned as second party and the authority or authorities against whom relief has actually, been sought, may be made other parties.

The States or Pradeshiya Shasan

The 'Pradeshiya' Governments will be, known by name of their respective 'Shasans' e.g. Tamil Nadu Pradesh Shasan, Maharashtra Pradesh Shasan, Madhya Pradesh Shasan, Bihar Pradesh Shasan, Uttar Pradesh Shasan, and Kerala Pradesh Shasan.

State governments will sue and be sued in the name of that Pradeshiya Shasan as the first party and other matters the provisions shall *mutatis mutandis* apply as in the case of Govt. of India.

(Official Translation of this Constitution in different languages will have equal force but in case of conflict, Hindi or English translations will prevail).

State of West Bengal shall be, known as Bengal Pradesh,

Shasan and 'West' shall stand deleted.

Central Government: Prime Minister / Dy. PM - Direct Elections

1. There shall be a Prime Minister or President as Head of the Nation and Head of the Central Govt. of Bharat and a Dy. PM or VP to assist him and second in hierarchy elected directly by the electorates of India through adult franchise i.e. voters above 18 years of age.

2. Both of them shall be elected for six years and may seek re-election not exceeding three terms provided in case of a Deputy PM or Dy. President who has officiated as President on the death of or resignation or otherwise relinquishing office by the incumbents three terms will include the officiating period as well. Therefore, three terms will not necessarily mean 18 years. There shall be no Prime Minister if people opt for Presidential form instead of Bhartiya Lok Jan Tantric form. Similarly there shall be no President if people opt for Bhartiya Lok Jan Tantric form under which PM / Dy. PM and CM / Dy. CM shall be elected by the voters of India and the respective 'Pradesha' i.e. state as the case may be, people (Both of them shall reside in Rashtrapati Bhavan)

3. Prime Minister or President, by whatever name called, or VP or Dy. Prime Minister, could only, be removed by impeachment, by 2/3 majority of the membership of both the houses of Parliament, rectified by more than the half of the Pradesh Vidhan Sabhas by simple majority of total membership of such Vidhan Sabhas for serious misconduct, affecting security, safety of the nation, or of the people of Bharat, or property of the country, or propriety of the office, or for a crime or offence of serious nature inviting imprisonment, or for act of immorality, or Parliament by 2/3 majority of total membership of each house refer the matter for referendum of the people for approving such removal. If approved by the majority of voters voting in such referendum the incumbents shall relinquish the office immediately or be removed notwithstanding anything therewith in the Constitution by simple majority of members of Parliament present and voting within thirty days even if a special session is to be called for that purpose.

4. Sessions of Legislatures shall be called by the President or governor as the case may be, ordinarily in consultations with Speaker or Chairman as the case may be, and in case of an unforeseen eventuality or contingency by the President or the governor even without such consultations.

5. Deputy President or Dy. PM at the centre and Dy. Governor / Dy. CM in Pradesh or State, has if held the position of such deputy, for six or more years shall on being elected President or Governor hold office as such President and Governor for not more than two terms irrespective of the duration thereof.

6. After ceasing to be such President, Vice President, Governor or Dy. Governor the incumbent shall not hold any position in any government except that of a member of Sansad i.e. Parliament or Vidhan Sabha i.e. State legislature, or an advisory position or member or chairman of an ad hoc or special Commission under any government on honorarium or position in UNO, provided vice president may seek election for President and governor for President or VP and deputy governor for President /VP / governor as provided in the constitution.

Pradeshiya Shasan: Chief Minister / Dy. CM – Direct Elections

7. There shall be a Chief Minister or Governor and a Dy. Ch. Minister/ DG in each Pradesh elected by the voters of that Pradesh or Anchal and provisions in respect of the PM and Dy. PM shall *mutatis mutandis* apply.

8. Chief Minister / Governor or Dy. CM / DG in the states may be, removed by impeachment on the similar grounds as President / PM or VP / Dy. PM passed by 2/3 majority of total membership of Vidhan Sabha and rectified by Rajya Sabha by simple majority of total membership. If not rectified by Rajya Sabha (second house of Parliament) or prior to sending to approval of RS, if the Vidhan Sabha so considers it may refer the issue to the referendum of the people of the state and the provisions as provided for President shall *mutatis mutandis* apply.

9. The provisions regarding holding of offices and after ceasing to be such governor or Deputy, the provisions as applicable to President VP shall *mutatis mutandis* apply. Provided the deputy governor may seek the election for governor, vice president or president and governor for VP or President and Vice president for president in accordance with the provisions of the Constitution.

10. Notwithstanding, if any incumbent holding a constitutional position is removed by impeachment he may not be appointed on any position temporary, ad hoc, or in any Commission or advisory or any other under any government on fee or honorarium or by whatever name called except that of elected member of Parliament or state legislature.

11. Provided further that deputy governor may also, be appointed a cabinet minister in the state or at the centre and governor as cabinet minister in the central government.

12. There shall be neither confidence nor no confidence vote against the Govt or ministry but only against a minister. No confidence motion in case of Central Govt could be brought by a resolution in either house by 25 per cent membership of that house, and passed by simple majority of total membership of both the houses of Parliament jointly or separately. Similar provisions will apply to Pradesh and Vidhan Sabha in case of a Minister.

13. All election results including that of President, Vice President, Governor and Dy. Governor will be, declared on the basis, of valid votes polled and the candidate having polled maximum number of majority valid votes will be, declared elected.

14. Age for seeking election to President and Vice President would be 35 yrs and for governor and Dy. governor 30 yrs., for MLA and MP 25 years.

15. The work of Central Govt. of India shall be, carried in the name of President / PM and that of Pradesh /state government in the name of Governor / CM as the case may be as at present in the name of President or Governor.

16. Any candidate losing Presidential or Vice Presidential election or of Governor or Dy. Governor may seek re-election only once. Provided, if he wins at any time, his earlier term if any served on the position shall be included for computing 18 years tenure. Any person who has been President, Vice President, governor, or deputy Governor for any term shall not hold any office of profit under any public, private, or joint sector except universities and university colleges or study centers.

General Provisions for Governments and Uni–Cameral Vidhan Mandal (Legislature in the States)

17. There shall be Bi Cameral Sansad i.e. Lok Sabha and Rajya Sabha for Bharat and unicameral legislature i.e. Vidhan Sabha only for Pradesh elected for six years by voters above 18 years of India and / or state as the case may be.

18. There will be automatic devolution of power on the Deputies in the absence, relinquishment of office or death of the heads whether called PM or CM or President or Governor.

19. In the event of the death or resignation / relinquishment of office by Prime Minister or President or Chief Minister or Governor before the expiry of the term of six years, the Dy. PM or Dy. CM will be sworn in and hold the office of PM or CM for unexpired period or until Parliamentary / Vidhan Sabha elections whichever is earlier.

20. In case of death of VP/ Dy. PM / Dy. CM / DG as the case may be, the speaker of Lok Sabha or state Assembly subject to other provisions of the Constitution will be sworn in and hold office as such deputy in the same manner as provided in foregoing provisions for PM / CM and the concerned house will elect its speakers subject to other provisions of the Constitution.

21. Provided further that if the elected deputy acting as PM or CM also dies or resigns or relinquishes his office as such PM or CM, elections will be held for both the positions within two months in the manner provided and till then speaker acting as deputy PM or Deputy CM shall officiate as PM or CM besides his own position as such deputy. Provided further, if

he seeks election for any of the two positions and loses he will remain only the member of the house until expiry of the term otherwise will be revered back to his position as such speaker.

22. Lok Sabha shall have membership of one member for not less than ten lac population.

23. Rajya Sabha members shall have five years term, and the members will elect the chairperson / Dy. chairperson of RS for a period of five years. There shall be no ex-officio Chairman of RS. Lok Sabha will elect its Speaker and Dy. Speaker. Provided the members of RS shall rotate in the manner as at present.

24. RS will have not more than 250 members at present and the membership shall not exceed three hundred under any circumstances. Rajya Sabha shall have members elected by all such local bodies falling within corporations' viz-municipal corporations, metropolitan corporations, city corporations and Zila Panchayats of Pradeshas divided into constituencies but not less than one and more than three from any state. Only the elected members of above local bodies shall cast their votes in such elections.

25. Rajya Sabha shall have members not exceeding hundred elected by the recognised graduates and diploma holders with minimum three years course of all disciplines in the country professional, academic and technical - other than medical and practising lawyers - divided on the basis of population of each state and further divided into constituencies in such states, provided the number shall not be less than one and more than five from any state. RS will also have members not exceeding 15 elected by duly registered and approved practicing lawyers throughout India and not exceeding 25 by practicing medical practitioners duly registered and approved by Medical Council of India or such other recognised body for the purpose. Parliament with the approval of not less than half of the Vidhan Sabhas may provide for other mode or standards of electing members for RS other than from Vidhan Sabha.

26. The Pradesh Vidhan Sabha shall consist of the elected representatives of people of the Pradesh elected on the basis

of adult franchise and Lok Sabha will consist only of elected representatives of people of Bharat elected on the same basis.

27. President shall nominate at least five Christian members in Rajya Sabha as far as possible spread over all the four corners east, west, north, and south of India. Sansad may increase the number considering appreciable increase in their population. President in consultation with Parliament in a joint session nominate not more than 25 members from amongst the people of high order of social service, literary pursuit, scientific research, artistic caliber or intellectual, technical, professional expertise of high excellence.

28. The Prime Minister / President will have the ministry of not exceeding seven per cent (7 per cent) of total membership of Parliament and not exceeding half of them as cabinet ministers and not more than five from RS.

29. In Pradesh / states, total number of ministers shall not exceed 10% of the total membership of Vidhan Sabha.

30. Prime Minister / Chief Minister or President / governor as the case may be shall have the power to appoint any person of eminence, expertise, and professional knowledge or experience etc as minister whether or not a Member of Parliament / Vidhan Sabha but the number of such ministers will not exceed 50% of the total number of such ministers at any time.

31. President / PM shall be the Supreme Commander of all the defence forces of the country, assisted by a Defence Committee consisting of VP, Home Minister, Defence, finance and foreign ministers, three chiefs of staff and all Command heads of all the three forces, or such Para Military forces as he may consider fit which, shall meet at least once in six months.

32. There shall be a Defence Council to aid and advice the President/ PM in defence and national security matters consisting of three chiefs of staff, VP, Home, Defence, foreign Ministers, speaker of LS and Chairman of RS and co-opt such officers of other Para Military force as he may consider appropriate that shall meet once in three months or as PM may consider expedient.

33. The powers of Parliament or Vidhan Sabha as regards money bills and legislation will continue except that PM / CM or President/ Governor shall have the power to ask Parliament or Vidhan Sabha to pass special grants in case of extraordinary emergencies, natural calamities, revival of economy, national security, or defence or a crisis of general, national, or state level as the case may be.

34. Provided in case of natural calamity and state of war the President and the Governor may spend such amount in consultation with cabinet as urgently required to meet the emergency and take approval of Lok Sabha – Parliament or state Legislature, subsequently.

35. Lok Sabha and Vidhan Sabha shall have power over all money bills and passing of Budget as at present. Budget passed by Lok Sabha or Vidhan Sabha may be rectified by Rajya Sabha. It is for Lok Sabha and Vidhan Sabha to agree or not agree to such rectifications.

36. If, any grant or financial sanction is rejected by Lok Sabha the President / PM may call Jt. Session of Parliament for the purpose and get the money bill passed or sanctions obtained by simple majority of the Jt. Session of both the Houses of Parliament. Similarly, if Vidhan Sabha fails to pass a special money bill or financial grant, other than the Budget, as requested by Governor/ CM, he may send the same to the sanction of Rajya Sabha stating the reasons and background, and if approved by RS it shall be, presumed to have been, constitutionally approved.

Declaration of Assets

37. All and every candidate seeking election to any elective public position whether elections conducted by Election commission directly or under the authority of any government shall besides declaring his / their moveable, immoveable and other assets, in cash or kind shall also declare tentatively such wealth , assets, and property of his / their near and blood relations including of maternal side, and of married daughters side, on the side of aunt, on the side of fathers sister giving detail of their businesses, professions, details of incomes or

service along with copies of income tax return for the immediately preceding three years. Any person not complying with this provision shall be, debarred from contesting election and his ballot paper shall be rejected on this contravention and shall not be called in question in any court nor interfered with by any court.

38. If any person after being elected to any such position does not submit every alternate year the details of such assets, property, wealth, moveable or immoveable, in cash or kind as mentioned in foregoing article, the government or the concerned department of the government shall have the power and authority to enquire into any such assets, wealth, and other property and find the source thereof and seize such assets, wealth, property subject to such conditions and for such period as the court of competent jurisdiction may decide.

39. The government or such authority shall, if prima facie case is made initiate legal proceedings against such person and if he is held guilty and the case is decided within the tenure of his holding such elective position the same shall stand vacated and he shall also forfeit the right to contest any election for any position or elective office for next two complete terms of any such office or position for which he wants to contest.

40. In all such cases, if satisfactory explanation is not given for accumulation or earning of such assets or wealth or property the court will order seizure of entire un - accounted money, assets, wealth or property and also impose a fine of ¼ of tentative or exact value of such unaccounted assets together with sentence, which may extend to fifteen years but in no case less than five years.

41. All and every candidate seeking such election shall furnish all details of his prosecutions in criminal cases whether pending or decided together with nature of those cases and details of punishments if any. If any information so furnished is found wrong and incorrect the election shall stand quashed and cancelled and such person if reimbursed any expenses on behalf of Government shall refund that amount to government and shall be debarred from seeking any election to any elective

position for two terms of that position in addition to a fine of Rs 500000 towards the expenses for holding election to that position. Government may proceed to recover all above amounts as arrears of land revenue and no court shall interfere in such recovery.

42. If no party gets absolute majority in elections and running of government becomes impossible or against public interest or against security and defence of the country the President or the governor may after two years of constitution of new parliament or state assembly dissolve the Parliament or Vidhan Sabha and order fresh elections to be held within three months. Until then Rajya Sabha shall function as Lok Sabha and Vidhan Sabha if need be and the respective governors shall address the RS to that extent for the purpose.

43. Along with the elections of Vidhan Sabah of a state will be, held, the elections of governor/ Dy. Governor of that particular state and with Lok Sabha of President and Vice President as the case may be whether or not they have completed the constitutional tenure.

44. There shall be guidelines laid down by President and approved by Parliament by simple majority providing for general security to ministers and such other officials or persons holding strategic public offices. The category of security and number of personnel under each category shall also be, laid down under the guidelines that will have the force of law.

Provided, only on ceremonial or extra-ordinary occasions, or special national celebrations or such other occasions special security shall be, provided for which shall also be, laid down the guidelines. Provided no individual in his private capacity shall be provided state security paid or unpaid. Provided further, no court shall have power to order, decide, or take cognizance of any matter relating to provision of security to any person except by HC in case of violation of guidelines but not otherwise.

Power of PM or President / CM or Governor

45. Emergency power of the President including financial, external aggression and internal rebellion shall remain subject to the provisions of the Constitution.

46. President and governor shall have some wider administrative and financial powers as in America and France and function with appropriate checks and balances.

47. The President may declare external emergency on the advice of a committee consisting of Vice president, ministers for home, defence, foreign affairs, three services chiefs and Speaker and Chairman of Lok Sabha and Rajya Sabha. President may co-opt any member of defence committee in such decision-making.

48. Except in a situation of natural calamity and national or state level crisis or emergencies financial, external aggression, or state of war or internal rebellion, uprising, revolt or mutiny there shall be no power of issuing Ordinance to President or Governor as the case may be. An ordinance if not approved / passed by Parliament or Vidhan Sabha by simple majority within six months shall end on the expiry of six months or such disapproval whichever is earlier.

49. During emergency arising out of external aggression or internal rebellion or uprising or state of civil war the Parliament by law or if Parliament is not in session the President by Ordinance will have the right to suspend all/any of the fundamental rights not exceeding for three months at a time and in no case beyond six months. This shall not be, challenged in any court and no court will have jurisdiction to take cognizance of such challenge.

50. In case of financial emergency in the country the Parliament and in the state Vidhan Sabha may by law provide for any measure or measures for tightening up of the economy and controlling the crisis as the Parliament or Vidhan Sabha may deem fit not exceeding a year at a time and not beyond two years. This shall not be, challenged in any court and no court will have jurisdiction to take cognizance of such challenge.

51. No minister shall use 'I' while addressing the houses of legislature such as 'I propose' or 'I reduce or I increase' and so on but 'the government proposes' or government considers or government will increase or decrease' and so on.

52. PM shall, with the approval of Parliament, notwithstanding any power of framing any court rules or procedural rules to any court, amend, modify or delete such rules if these put any excessive burden including financial on the citizens and are cumbersome for common man.

Power of Clemency, Pardon and Remission

53. The power of clemency or mercy would vest in the President of India in accordance with the Constitution subject to the condition that death penalty awarded to a terrorist, hardcore criminal, enemy, person guilty of high treason or sedition, shall never be interfered with by the President. In other cases death penalty could be remitted to life imprisonment and life imprisonment to 25 years if the accused is below 60 years of age and 15 years if above 60 years of age. No other, punishment shall be, interfered with by the President. Governor will have no power of clemency, remission, or pardon.

54. Death Penalty awarded by the Distt or Sessions Judge shall be, confirmed by a Bench of three Judges of HC within two months and in appeal by a Bench of three Judges of AC within a month. Aggrieved party may appeal to President for remission immediately after the decision of AC. President will decide the appeal within one month unless for the reasons to be recorded he takes longer time not exceeding two months of such presentation, otherwise the punishment may be executed immediately on the expiry of said period of one month or two months as the case may be.

55. AC may continue to decide the case within the next one month irrespective of its pendency before the President. If the President, decides the matter before the decision of the AC, and reduces the death penalty to life imprisonment the AC will hear it no further. If the confirmation of AC comes after the decision of the President, the decision of the President to the extent of reduction of death penalty to life imprisonment will prevail.

56. Notwithstanding, if not merely the punishment but merits of the case are under challenge the same shall be decided as regular appeals by the HC/AC under this Constitution

and President shall thereafter decide petition for clemency in accordance with the provisions of this Constitution.

57. Provisions regarding citizenship, fundamental rights, and directive principles will *mutatis mutandis* remain except as provided.

58. Sharing of financial resources and constitution of Finance Commission by President / PM will continue as at present.

Three Lists

59. Union list shall be, renamed as 'Kendriya Vishaya Suchi' and State list as 'Pradeshiya Vishaya Suchi'. Concurrent list as 'Samavarti Suchi'.

Official Language

60. Sanskritised Hindi shall be the national official language of India, of all the services and offices including courts and the central government but English shall continue as secondary language in the Courts and All India Services. States may have Hindi or their respective regional language or both as official language emphasizing use of Hindi as link language.

Age of Superannuation

61. Age of superannuation / retirement shall be uniform throughout the country in all services whether government, public, joint, or private sector services.

62. President / Prime Minister may, after taking into account the increasing trend of population, unemployment conditions, or other economic consideration subject to the approval of simple majority of Members of Parliament present and voting reduce such age of retirement / superannuation not below 55 years.

63. Prime Minister and the Chief Minister shall have the constitutional power and authority to modify, amend, add or delete any existing service condition of government and public servants and employees at any time subject to the approval of the cabinet and after consultations with the speaker and chairman of Lok Sabha and Rajya Sabha and in case of Chief

Minister after consultations with the speaker of the Vidhan Sabha of the State.

64. Governments may use any foreign language in international correspondence with countries concerned subject to the approval of President or Governor as the case may be.

Provided further, if any Pradesh government uses its regional tongue as official language in the State, in correspondence with other states and the centre the correspondence shall be accompanied by authentic Hindi or English translation as may be desired by the state concerned but with centre it shall be in any of the two languages.

Parliament: Powers and Amendment of Constitution

65. Subject to other provisions, Parliament shall have exclusive power and jurisdiction of adding any provision to this Constitution but shall have no power of deleting any of the existing provisions. Parliament may add by way of explanation or proviso to remove any ambiguity or add to give a provision wider dimension but no addition or amendment shall in any, way change the intent and meaning of any such provision or change the substance or meaning of the Constitution or that provision in any way. Provided, Parliament may, altogether replace an existing provision and substitute by another only if such change has been approved by the people after a referendum in the manner provided. Notwithstanding anything in the Constitution, Parliament may even incorporate any draconian provision in the constitution temporarily or permanently or for a specific purpose but for specific period, if it has been approved by two third majority of voters voting in a referendum.

66. The Deputy Speaker of Lok Sabha, Vidhan Sabha in the states and Chairman of Rajya Sabha shall invariably be of largest opposition party whether or not allied or combined.

67. No Constitutional amendment, whether by way of modification or addition, or in any manner, will ever be challenged in any court of law if made in accordance with the provisions of this Constitution and by not less than 2/3rd majority of the total membership of each House of Parliament

subject to following proviso;

Provided, any restructuring, explanation, extension, or addition relating to appointment and removal of judges, constitution of EC, appointment and removal of Chief or other Election Commissioners, appointment and removal of CAG, Constitution of Information Commission, removal and appointment of Chief or other Information Commissioners, citizenship, Fundamental Rights, Fundamental Duties, Constitution of Supreme Court, AC, HC and appointment and removal of judges, changing Central, State or Concurrent lists, restructuring of any House of Parliament or Vidhan Sabha, constitution of University and Higher Education Commission, constitution of Public Service Commissions, constitution of Law Commission, Constitution of Lok Ayukt, and Ombudsman and appointment and removal of chairmen and members of all the above Commissions will require rectification by more than half of the state legislatures.

Restructuring includes increasing – decreasing membership of any of the Houses of Legislatures, Commissions, Courts, or other Constitutional bodies under this Constitution.

Parliament without prejudice may, through, EC refer any issue to the referendum of the electorate and if approved by the majority of voters voting the same shall have the force as if originally incorporated in the Constitution and that may include even any of the existing provisions

68. Parliament will have no jurisdiction or power to amend or modify or add to the Constitution or legislate to discriminate against any citizen of India on the basis of caste, creed, religion, community, gender or race or birth or create inequality of any kind. Any such legislation by any Legislature will be unconstitutional and void.

Provided subject to the ratification by more than fifty per cent of Vidhan Sabhas Parliament shall have power, authority and jurisdiction to amend, modify or substitute present National Anthem once but not National Flag and Rashtra Geet.

69. Sansad and Vidhan Sabha will have full power within

their jurisdiction as provided under this Constitution to make laws rules, regulations, and schemes there under to give effect to the provisions of this Constitution but not inconsistent with the provisions of the Constitution.

70. A Vidhan Sabha shall have the jurisdiction and power to pass a resolution for reference of an issue to referendum of people of Bharat including removal of a Judge of AC / SC / HC on moral and ethical grounds provided the same is duly ratified by more than fifty per cent of the members of more than fifty per cent Vidhan Sabhas of the country and in that event President / PM will have to act on such resolution and refer the same to referendum within a month.

71. Parliament will have the power, jurisdiction, and option to refer by simple majority any matter of high public or general importance, morality, ethics, and policy, whether economic, social, ethical, religious, or political to be decided by referendum of the people of India in the manner provided in this Constitution, provided for modifying, substituting or deleting any existing provision of the Constitution by referendum minimum 2/3rd majority of total membership of each house shall be required.

72. Parliament in the manner provided may also by simple majority refer any matter of high public, legal, or general importance arising out of any decisions of AC / SC to the referendum of the people for acceptance. The decision of the majority of voters will be binding and incorporated in the Constitution.

73. All the results of such referendums shall be notified by the EC and signed by the President before incorporation in the Constitution.

74. A Joint Parliamentary Committee or a committee of either House of Parliament or committee of Vidhan Sabha investigating into any governmental corruption or corruption by President, Vice president, governor or deputy governor or any minister shall only look into a prima facie case and submit report within three months. If a prima facie case is made out and put to vote of house or houses and accepted by simple

majority of members present and voting of each house of Parliament or Vidhan Sabha as the case may be, the same shall be sufficient for bringing a no confidence motion against the minister or impeachment against President, Vice president, and governor, or deputy governor, as the case may be.

75. Speaker, Deputy Speaker of Lok Sabha, Chairman and Deputy Chairman of Rajya or Speaker and Dy. Speaker of Vidhan Sabha could also be proceeded against in the manner provided under Art 68. In all other cases, they could be removed by bringing in a no confidence motion sponsored by at least 10% members of the house concerned and passed by 2/3 majority of membership of that House.

76. Any citizen of the country may, file a civil or criminal case against any official, authority, body whether incorporated and registered or not, or any person including a private person involved or believed to be involved in corruption or dishonesty, embezzlement, misappropriation, fraud and misuse of public or governmental or state money, property, assets or deprivation of general public or state or government of any money, property, wealth or assets in cash or kind, provided he makes a prima facie case at the time of filing the plaint/application/ complaint or case and the court is prima facie satisfied with, after hearing the case within a month.

77. The report of Jt. Parliamentary Committee or Committee of any house or houses of legislature or a Commission, or court of enquiry, CBI, or State bureau or any other investigating authority shall be sufficient for making out a prima facie case without any further hearing by the court. An indictment or allegation by CAG or AG or by any approved auditing authority, agency, or body shall also constitute a prima facie case requiring no further hearing by the court for ascertaining whether prima facie case has been, made out.

78. The court shall take a civil case as criminal case, and a criminal case as civil if it constitutes both and proceed simultaneously in accordance with the provisions of the constitution or law.

79. If any state, or central government brings a bill for making a law in any matter or proposes to introduce any policy change whatsoever, not covered by the election manifesto of the party in power or three largest parties in case of coalition, the Parliament or the Vidhan Sabha as the case may be, shall be under obligation to refer such issue for referendum of the voters of the country or the state concerned, for rectification before it is put into effect, or sent to the assent of President or governor as the case may be.

80. The decision of majority of voters so voting in all cases of referendum shall be binding but the voters who have not voted shall be, deemed to have impliedly consented and voted with the majority. Such consent of voters shall be final and will not be, questioned in any court of law unless the same is in contravention of the Constitution.

81. A record of all such referendums shall be maintained by EC, RS and LS Secretariats, ministry of home and Legal affairs with brief account of referendum and results. Where however the referendum is for making a change in the Constitution the brief account shall also be given in the Preamble to the Constitution amendment bill for incorporation.

82. All such references will be, made in a question form sentence to elicit 'yeas or ayes' and 'nays' of the voters and two permanent symbols shall be assigned for the answers in all cases of referendums. Voters will only put a seal or a sign or impression on the symbol of their preference in the particular box of ballot paper. Separate ballot papers will be, used if referendum on more than one issue or point is to be, held.

83. Notwithstanding, the Prime Minister may, in accordance with other provisions of the Constitution refer an issue to Parliament for referring it to the referendum of the voters of the country if it concerns the removal of Dy. PM or judge of HC / SC / AC including his own removal and subject to the approval of the Vidhan Sabha of the State concerned refer the issue of removal of the CM or Dy. CM to the referendum of the voters of the State.

84. Notwithstanding, in all such cases where Parliament is authorised to initiate impeachment against any of the elected or appointed authority including President or PM and Judges or refer an issue to referendum of the public fails to do so and if more than fifty per cent of the Vidhan Sabhas pass a resolution to that effect Parliament or President will have to take action on the same as if the resolution has been initiated by them.

85. Notwithstanding passing of impeachment in the manner prescribed, the President or PM or the Deputy and Governor or CM and the deputy shall only be removed if such impeachment resolution is confirmed in a referendum within a month by the voters of the country or the state as the case may be.

86. Similarly if state Vidhan Sabha fails to refer a matter to referendum of the voters of the state or pass an impeachment under this Constitution the Parliament may pass a resolution by simple majority of total membership asking the Vidhan Sabha to refer the issue to the referendum of the voters of the state including removal of CM or Governor and if the Sabha fails to do so within a month may refer the issue to the voters of the state in the manner as if referred by the Vidhan Sabha.

87. Any matters not covered by the Constitution or law of the Legislature shall in such emergency be decided by the President or Governor as the case may be in consultation with the respective legislature after notifying in the official gazette which shall have the force of law and shall later be ratified by a law.

88. All referendums under this Constitution shall be held and monitored by election commission in the same manner as any other election and send official communication to the President within three days who shall send the same to Speaker and Chairman of LS and RS for communicating to respective houses of Parliament within a week, for incorporating or not incorporating in the Constitution.

89. Doctors – physicians by whatever name called, teachers by whatever name called (primary up to University), Defence

personnel below the rank of captain of armed forces and Judges of courts under the Constitution shall be paid income tax free salary.

90. All offences of corruption, indiscipline and any act of ommission or commission, unworthy of becoming such doctor, teacher, defence personnel and judge shall be decided by all competent authorities, courts, commissions, committees within three months irrespective of nature of commission or ommission of offence, civil or criminal as the case may be.

91. The charges of corruption, incompetency and any allegation of unbecoming of a judge of High Court, AC and SC shall be investigated by a committee consisting of Speaker of Lok Sabha, Chairman of Rajya Sabha, Attorney General of India and Chairman of Law Commission of India presided over by Vice president / Dy. Prime Minister of India. The committee shall submit its report to President within two months who shall place the same before Parliament within a week along with his recommendations for further appropriate action.

92. State shall, besides payment of pension and other legal benefits, reimburse legal fee, legal hostel charges if any, and an appropriate amount towards books for two children up to Post graduation or equivalent in any discipline of an employee employed in armed or defence forces or Para military forces or civil police, or any other force or any citizen of the country who dies in combat operation or fighting enemy or defending the country or the people or the property or ensuring security of people, nation or property against any attack including terrorist attack, provided such children pass the exams continuously and successfully.

93. Where such person being a common citizen has no family, or is minor or is the only earning member of the family one of his family members shall be, given commensurate employment under the State.

94. Above provisions shall also apply if such person is permanently handicapped or incapacitated provided further his entire hospitalization charges shall be borne by the State.

95. Parliament or any other authority shall have no power and jurisdiction to nullify a judgment of the SC or AC, but in

exercise of inherent sovereign power of the people vested in her may amend the Constitution subject to the other provisions, or make a law or amend the existing law removing the prospective operation of the judgment.

96. No law of parliament will have retrospective effect if it deprives the citizen of any benefit or advantage or money except immovable property or asset or wealth subject to payment of compensation as per law. Any such law will also take into consideration the prevailing market rate and the reasonableness of economic conditions prevailing at the time.

97. Only Parliament shall have the power and jurisdiction to regulate and limit professional fee and charges in respect of any or all professional occupations and determine their categories.

98. Parliament and Vidhan Sabha shall be their masters in conducting their business and proceedings as at present without any judicial interference or direction and all members shall be immune and free of any contempt of court or any other action for whatever they say or do within the house.

Reimbursement of Election Expenses

99. Parliament subject to ratification by more than half of the Vidhan Sabhas may provide for reimbursement of elections expenses of winning candidates for President / PM, Governor / CM, their deputies, members of Lok Sabha and Vidhan Sabha not exceeding 50% of fair expenses calculated rationally from time to time and 25% to RS members.

100. Parliament may by, law provide for tax-free donations to political parties recognised by election commission nationally or at Pradesh level, which may not exceed 33% of the yearly expenses or of the Accounting Year of such party.

101. Parliament on the recommendations of election commission shall by, law provide for the limit of election expenses for all elected positions and conditions for quashing of election of any such person exceeding such expenses. Election commission while determining the limit of such expenses shall take expert opinion, general economic levels, and an overall public view of the matter.

102. CAG shall appoint such number of recognised qualified chartered accountants or firms of accountants as may be reasonably required to audit the accounts of any recognised political party and may ask any such party to produce her accounts for inspection. The fee shall be, reasonably determined by Election commission in consultation with CAG, subject to the approval of President and 50% of the fee shall be, reimbursed to the auditor by election commission and rest by the party concerned.

Judicial Administration and All India Judicial Service

103. There shall be a Supreme Court of India, an Appellate Court of India and High Courts in the States with the powers of Prerogative writs subject to the provisions of this Constitution.

104. There shall be an Akhil Bharatiya Nyayik Seva (All India Judicial Service) for selecting the Chief Judicial, Ch. Metropolitan Magistrates and Additional DJs or equivalent posts/cadres for which examinations / tests will be conducted by UPSC in consultation and coordination with the CJs of Supreme and Appellate Court of India. The Commission shall be free to take advice from any Chief Justice of a High Court but in holding tests / examinations including setting of papers and conducting interviews the committee consisting of two CJs as above and the Chairman UPSC shall decide all the issues and matters. In case of any difference of opinion the decision of Dy. PM shall be final. The Dy. PM in all such cases shall act in consultation with the PM. These posts shall be transferable from one to the other state subject to the approval of CJs of the concerned HCs.

105. No Court in India, shall have the power to issue instructions to government or frame any scheme or procedure for conducting government business in any way or in a particular manner or direct the Legislature to act in a particular manner or conduct business in a particular way except for acting in accordance with the Constitution or as provided under the provisions of the Constitution, or any Law and shall limit itself only to the interpretation of Constitution or the law or constitutionality of any law and direct implementation of its

judgment or order including compliance of stay, injunction or prerogative Writs.

106. The judges and the Chief Justices of AC and SC will have equal status and will be, addressed as the CJ and judges of the Appellate Court of India, or the Chief Justice and judges of the Supreme Court of India.

107. The Supreme Court will have only nine (9) judges and the appellate court 31, but parliament may by law increase or decrease the number of judges of AC subject to the need of country, justice, population, and frequency of litigation and pendency of cases. The Supreme court shall co-opt the judges of the Appellate court but at no time the bench shall consist of more than 15 judges for deciding a constitutional matter of extraordinary public importance and that of Appellate Court more than 9 (nine).

108. All cases, in SC/AC/HC will be, decided by not less than three – judges including admission of writs and appeals.

109. No court shall have the power and jurisdiction to stay and issue any writ to stay or prohibit or quash any proceeding pending before any subordinate court, Ombudsman or Lok Ayukt if it relates to corruption defined under this Constitution.

110. No legal notice for filing suit against any government shall be necessary if a citizen had sent three registered letters to concerned department of the government or concern authority for meeting or deciding the claim, dispute, or matter whatsoever, giving at least one months' time under each notice for the purpose.

Appointment, Promotion and Removal of Judges

97. The judges of all the three courts shall be appointed by the President / PM on the recommendations of an expert committee based on the guidelines given in the constitution.

98. The Expert Committee appointed by the president shall consist of not less than seven eminent persons including Chief justices of Appellate and Supreme Court of India provided the CJ of the high court where vacancy is to be filled shall be co-opted in respect of that High court only. Other members as far

as possible will include Attorney General of India, Chairman Law Commission, Chairman and Speaker RS and LS, and Public Person of repute in any field who shall preside over the Committee as an independent member.

99. The committee will consider seniority wise names of not more than one and a half times the vacancies and recommend a panel of names to President not exceeding one and a quarter times more than the vacancies. President in consultation with the cabinet and for the reasons to be recorded shall have the power to change or deviate from the seriatim list recommended by the Panel and make appointments accordingly. But in all such deviations only President will take approval by simple majority of the membership of both the houses of Parliament present and voting. If approval is not given, appointments shall be, made in the order either recommended by the penal, or from amongst the remaining names of the penal as Parliament may decide by simple majority of members present and voting.

Provided, that no judge to the Supreme and Appellate courts will be, appointed at an age less than 50 yrs and to HC at less than 40 yrs.

100. The expert committee while recommending the names for filling the vacancies of Chief Justice in a HC shall empanel the names of two senior most judges of the HC out of four senior most. Similarly for the CJ of AC two names out of five senior most judges of AC and for CJ of SC two names out of three senior most judges of that court. The President may appoint any person so recommended subject to the approval of Parliament by simple majority of members present and voting if any deviation is made from the panel. If not approved by Parliament the President will appoint the other judge of the panel as recommended by the committee the CJ of the court concerned. However, while, counting seniority the period of service of a judge before transfer, transfers, or deputation if any, will also, be taken into account.

101. A Judge or CJ of any HC may be transferred to any other HC and a judge may be appointed Lok Ayukt or Ombudsman as provided and such transfer or appointment

shall not be questioned in any court of law. The judges, CJs of SC, and AC will be transferable inter-se.

102. Appointment of judges to HC, AC, or SC will not, be questioned in any court of law unless appointed in violation of the procedure laid down in the Constitution.

(A) All vacancies of Judges in the Supreme Court and Appellate Court besides transfers will be filled from amongst the Chief Justice of the HCs. The PM / President may, in very special cases; subject to the approval of Parliament by simple majority of members present and voting, appoint a legal luminary or a person of legal eminence and repute including sitting judge of HC directly to the AC or SC.

(B) Vacancies in the HC will be filled in from amongst the DJs except 25% that will be filled from the Bar of that particular HC including any legal luminary or person of legal eminence. All such persons other than the DJs must have practiced in the HC and Supreme Court or equivalent court for not less than 15 years. In case of DJs the incumbent must have been DJ for not less than 5 years and must have 3 years service remaining.

Explanation:- No promotion or appointment as a judge to HC, AC or SC shall be made on any grounds or consideration other than wisdom, intellectual acumen, knowledge, expertise and caliber braided with honesty, reputation, professional knowledge and ethics or such merits of the person concerned.

(C) The Judges of SC and AC shall hold office till the completion of 65 yrs of age retiring on last day of the month in which such judge completes 65 years and the judges of HC on completion of 63 years of age in the same manner.

103. Subject to other provisions of the Constitution a judge or Judges of all the above three courts could be removed by impeachment passed by more than 50% membership of each house of Parliament by bringing a resolution in any of the houses by not less than 25% membership of that house clearly making out the grounds for such impeachment. In case of a High Court judge if the Vidhan Sabha passes a resolution by more than 50% majority and sends that to Rajya Sabha the

latter would be bound to take up impeachment in the manner as if initiated by its own motion and the procedure as laid down above will be, followed.

104. A Judge or Judges could also be removed by the President or Prime Minister as the case may be, if he or they are found guilty of violating any Constitutional provision recommended by a committee of not less than six eminent jurists of the rank not less than Chief Justice of HC of India presided over by a reputed public personality including not more than two Judges of ICJ or Supreme Court of a foreign country if PM or President so desires for maintaining impartiality.

105. Transfers of judges to and from SC- AC will be decided by the CJs of both the courts unanimously in case of difference of opinion the President shall decide the matter after considering the report of both and take his own decision which shall not be questioned in any court in India.

Provided further that in case of transfer of judges from or to HCs the CJs of all those HCs will be consulted and their concurrence obtained. CJ of any HC may recommend transfer of a judge for reasons to be recorded and communicated to CJ of AC and SC and the President. The majority decision of four CJs i.e. two of HCs concerned and of AC and SC will be binding and in case of equal division, the President will decide the matter in the manner provided above.

Supreme Court of India

106. Supreme Court shall hear and decide all Constitutional matters that would involve interpretation of any provision of the Constitution whether referred to it by AC or HC or directly by the President including any contraventions by any organ of government or authority or body. In former three cases, the matter would be decided within two months, in latter within three months. In all other, cases within six months.

107. Subject to the provisions of the Constitution, SC will decide the constitutionality of all laws or legislations including byelaws, rules, regulations, or schemes made by Sansad or

Vidhan Sabha but shall have no power to look even into the constitutionality of the Constitution or any provision thereof.

108. Supreme Court will decide all the disputes between Union of India and States or States and States.

109. An Appeal to SC against the judgment of HC in all election petitions will lie if HC has committed an illegality in fact and law on the face of record.

110. Violations of legal and constitutional rights of citizens will be decided by either the HC or SC but PILs will lie only in SC and only in cases of violations of rights of citizens in general or of masses and not otherwise.

111. PIL will, lie only if the matters are of such urgency as to invite interference of the SC that concerns safety, life, health or hygiene of people, or matters of very vital importance to masses, or the nation, or security or defence of the country, or the life and property of the people, or welfare of general public, and not otherwise provided such violation (s) were brought to the notice of concerned authorities, officials, Deptt, and Govt at least once every month, and thrice within a period of three months.

112. All disputes of International character, including international crimes, criminals, fugitives, political asylum, and extradition.

113. All boundary disputes between India and a foreign country, or countries, interpretations of international treaties including agreements, contracts, and covenants, between India and any other country.

114. Subject to other provisions of the Constitution, Supreme Court will be the court of record and shall be, bound by the precedents of a larger Bench unless over ruled by a Bench larger than the earlier one that decided the matter. The decisions of SC shall be binding on all courts in India and every individual, citizen, person or groups or bodies and all Govts.

115. All cases by the Supreme Court, except of international character shall, be decided within six months and for reasons to be recorded not exceeding a year.

116. Constitutionality or legality of any law made by Parliament or Vidhan Sabha, or rules regulations, bye-laws, schemes made by any legal authority or body and of notifications or orders issued by any authority including governments shall be decided by SC within four months from the date petition is admitted.

117. Appeals in respect of all offences committed within the territory of India including terrorism by foreign nationals or citizens of India settled in foreign countries or by an NRI will be, decided by SC within one year or for reasons to be recorded within one and a half years.

118. All crimes, and offences of international character involving international criminals and fugitives, shall be decided by SC as far as possible within two years.

119. All appeals, in respect of terrorism committed by foreign nationals within the territory of India shall be decided by SC within a year and only in exceptional cases within one and a half year.

120. Interpretation of constitutional provisions and constitutionality of any law will be heard and decided by not less than a bench of five judges.

121. All constitutional issues referred by President for opinion shall be decided within three months.

122. Working of the court will be, so arranged that minimum six Judges always remain present in the court.

123. AC and SC shall be duty bound to protect the constitution and if at time any of them finds destroying of Constitution by any organ the court by a unanimous resolution of all the judges request the PM / president to refer such issue either to a Jt. bench of 25 Judges of both the courts or referendum of the people. Provided if the PM does not do so within a month of such request the court may in the manner above direct the Election Commission to refer such issue to the referendum of the people.

Appellate Court of India

124. The Appellate court will hear and decide all appeals

Civil and / or Criminal including taxation, excise, labour, customs, service, companies, business, revenue, insurance, or any other matter of civil or criminal nature, except as explicitly barred under this Constitution, or fall within the exclusive jurisdiction of Supreme Court, against the final decisions, judgments, and final orders, of HCs, or judicial, and quasi judicial authorities, and bodies, throughout the territory of India.

125. All civil, criminal, or other appeals will be decided within one year except as provided under this Constitution.

126. The judgments, decisions and orders of the AC will be final and binding on all courts, tribunals, quasi judicial authorities, all Govts, other authorities, individuals, persons, groups, and bodies, public or Pvt, companies and corporations throughout the territory of India. AC will be the court of record and bound by its own precedents in the same manner as SC.

127. If there are conflicting judgments of equal Benches of SC or AC or any Bench of either court holds a contrary view than earlier bench of equal number of judges, the matter shall be referred to a larger Bench for decision.

128. All appeals concerning accidents or accident claims, rent or landlord-tenant disputes and insurance claims will be decided by summary hearings on ascertaining primafacie case and within four months and for reasons to be recorded within six months. All other property disputes shall be, decided within a year.

129. All appeals concerning rape, rape with murder, abduction, abduction with murder and abduction for ransom or offences and crimes connected therewith shall be, decided within a year.

130. All appeals concerning kidnapping, rape, murder of minors below 16 years of age, or for ransom will be decided by summary hearing and prima facie proof within six months.

131. All appeals arising out of offences constituting terrorism or crimes falling under terrorist activities within the territory of India and committed by Indian nationals, will be decided within one and a half year.

132. All other cases of murder, murder with dacoity, or any offences and crimes involving life imprisonment or death penalty or other offences or crimes involving imprisonment exceeding 15 years or fine with punishment exceeding Rs. five lac shall be decided within two years.

133. All corruption cases against public servants, which include Govt employees, Public sector employees, cooperative sector employees or any other person, body or company involved, conspired, or connived in such corruption shall be decided by summary hearing on making a prima facie case within a year.

134. All other cases not covered herein will be, decided within one and a half year.

135. All appeals and cases in AC will be heard and decided by not less than three judges.

136. President, shall have the power to refer any judgment of public importance, or of wide repercussions, and of general import delivered by a bench of SC or AC to a larger bench of the same court consisting of twice the number of judges including the judges who delivered earlier judgment but in no case larger than 15 in case of SC and nine in case of AC.

137. President may, in exceptional cases, with the approval of cabinet or on the request of a governor duly approved by the state cabinet refer any matter of current urgency or import, being of general importance to the state falling within the respective jurisdiction of SC or AC for opinion of that court and such opinion will be given not less than a bench of five judges within three months.

138. In all matters majority decisions of judges of a bench of HC, AC, SC will prevail.

High Courts

Functioning and powers of HCs will generally remain as they are at present subject to following provisions;

139. An election petition will lie in HC, but only on the ground of arbitrariness, discrimination, apparent legal or factual malafides, or favouritism of administration or Govt. or any official /employee of any Govt, illegality, unconstitutionality,

fraud, or malpractices, whatsoever committed by Govt, administration, or the officials or the candidate, or his agent, or under their directions, or any act against the directions of the Election Commission, or Code of Conduct agreed to by majority of political parties and accepted by EC.

140. Legality and constitutionality of any notification issued by State, Central Government, or any order, rules, byelaws, or subordinate legislations of any kind made by any Govt, authority, corporations, or legal entity or local body, shall be decided by HC; and in appeal by SC. The decision of SC shall be final and binding on all courts, citizens, person, groups, bodies, legal entities, and Governments.

141. No bail will be, granted where death sentence, life imprisonment, or imprisonment for more than five years has, been awarded by the lower court.

142. HC will decide all such cases, within one and a half year where ultimate punishment is either death penalty or life imprisonment or imprisonment for not less than five yrs or fine along with any other punishment amounting to five lacs or more.

143. No bail will be granted if the charges relate to committing murder, homicide, dacoity, rape, rape with murder, kidnapping, kidnapping with murder, kidnapping for ransom or corruption, forgery, embezzlement, fraud and misappropriation of public or government money, property, wealth or assets whatsoever or of public in general or citizens in common.

144. Not less than a bench of three judges will decide a case in the HC including admission of appeals or writs.

145. All other cases of civil and criminal nature will be, decided by HC within one year except accident cases not resulting in death.

146. All cases of compensation or damages arising out of accidents, insurance claims of all types, rent and proprietor-tenant disputes and all disputes of trivial nature shall be, decided within six months by summary hearing on making of

a prima facie case. Accident cases, resulting in death will be, decided as a case of murder.

147. No appeal or writ will be, admitted by HC where imprisonment awarded by lower court is upto three years, and fine not exceeding Rs five lacs or both.

148. No stay will be, granted without hearing the other party or his counsel. The order, judgment, award, appealed against shall only be, kept in abeyance by the orders of the court until stay is granted. It will be the duty of the court and of the petitioner / appellant to ensure service on the opposite party / defendant / respondent within 15 days and only if service is, proved and opp. party or its counsel fails to appear, stay will be, granted if the court thinks fit to do so.

149. No stay against prosecution, proceeding or FIR will be granted by any court including High court in any case where charges are of terrorism, murder, rape, rape with murder, kidnapping, kidnapping with murder, kidnapping for ransom, dacoity, leaking defence secrets, endangering or likely to endanger life of the people, or general public, or security and defence of the country or corruption of any kind.

150. High court, after one month of filing of the writ petition or appeal or any other petition or at any stage thereafter will get a notice, or summon, or warrant published in any reputed daily of the state or of the country, at the cost of such party found avoiding service or otherwise absconding or not traceable, by giving 10 days time to appear and thereafter, may proceed ex-parte. No such publication shall be obligatory for AC or SC.

Explanation: Granting stay and bail will not be the absolute discretion, jurisdiction or power of any court but an exception subject to the limitations provided under the provisions of the constitution and for ensuring justice to litigants and safeguarding misuse and abuse of judicial process.

151. The HC will decide all cases relating to corruption against govt. employees, public servants or persons holding public or governmental posts or positions including that of public sector and cooperative sector, within one year and against

persons holding quasi public, and quasi governmental posts and positions within six months but in all cases by summary hearing and evaluating a prima facie case only.

152. All cases of dismissal and any other punishment awarded to government, Public Sector employees including of joint or cooperative sector will be decided within one year by the court or courts before whom such cases are pending.

Explanation: Jt. Sector means any venture where any government or governments have minimum 51% shares.

Explanation: Parliament or Vidhan Sabha will have the power to constitute special courts or tribunals for deciding particular nature of cases within their constitutional jurisdiction not, inconsistent with the provisions of this Constitution and subordinate to HC, AC, SC.

Procedure before Judicial, Quasi Judicial Bodies and Authorities

153. Subject to other provisions of the Constitution, all courts, Tribunals, Judicial or quasi judicial bodies and authorities throughout the territory of India, not being the High Courts and above, having original jurisdiction in any matter whether civil court, sessions court, revenue courts, labour courts, taxation authorities or tribunals, excise, customs, insurance courts or Central or State Government tribunals or courts or by whatever name called shall decide the cases and disputes, matters or suits, complaints or criminal proceedings or by whatever name called within two years and all appellate or revision courts, authorities and bodies within one year from the date of institution or filing of the case, suit or prosecution, petition, plaint or appeal or revision as the case may be.

154. All jurisdictional issues shall be raised in the first instant at the first hearing before any court, authority or forum. Thereafter no suit, writ, appeal or litigation whatsoever shall be stayed, dismissed or annulled on the ground of jurisdiction if that court, authority or forum has the jurisdiction of trying such type or nature of cases.

155. All Jurisdictional issues shall be decided within 15 days. If any court, authority or forum finds having no

jurisdiction it shall transfer the matter, case or litigation, etc as above to competent court, authority or forum within ten days but shall not dismiss, annul or file the case, matter or litigation.

156. Not more than five witnesses shall be examined in a case constituting the main case whether criminal, civil, labour or any taxation and revenue, accident, motor vehicles, rent, insurance, land revenue or any other whatsoever and not more than three on any new, additional or ancillary point arising in any such case.

157. Once a date of hearing is reasonably believed to be communicated it shall be the duty of the party to appear before the court, tribunal, authority or as the case may be and ascertain the further date of hearing. No party will be given more than one adjournment before a particular forum during the course of hearing of the case except;

(A) Adjournment for seven days in case of death of the counsel,

(B) Ten days adjournment in case of death in the family or similar reasons.

(C) for any other reason subject to payment of cost amounting to Rs. 2500 for first adjournment not exceeding 10 days and second adjournment for 10 days on payment of cost of Rs. 5000. Thereafter the court or the authority will proceed exparte but no adjournment will be given.

158. If any party absconds or does not appear because of none service of summons, or warrants, or avoids service thereof, the courts or authorities would within a month of first date of hearing, irrespective of the gravity and nature of offence, or crime get a notice, summon or warrant published in a language daily or dailies of repute in the state or states where party or parties are believed to be residing or ascertained to be residing on the basis of addresses obtained or provided or are on record of the case giving ten days time for the party or parties to appear. If the parties do not appear the court will decide the case / matter exparte. In such a situation the time limit of court or authorities to decide the cases would stand

extended by one month. The cost of such publications would be, recovered from the party as arrears of land revenue and until such recovery will be borne by the government.

159. If any party or parties manage to go out of India in any manner and do not return within the period permitted or otherwise escape, a notice in the reputed national daily directing the party or parties, giving minimum fifteen days time, to appear on the date and time fixed, before the court which will suffice to meet the ends of justice and no further opportunity will be required to be given and the case will thereafter be proceeded with and heard exparte.

160. Above provisions will also apply if the offender or culprit absconds to foreign country clandestinely or otherwise is a fugitive.

161. If, any court, including quasi judicial forums after complying with the provisions of the Constitution find that the counsel of a party has not appeared on the date the court shall provide an '*Amicus curiae*' in all cases irrespective of the nature of the cases and decide in accordance with the provisions of this Constitution subject to the condition that in such a contingency the court shall give seven days extra time to the party and the Amicus to prepare the case, over the limit provided for such cases under the Constitution and decide the case. Provided the reasonable fee as laid down by judiciary in such cases shall be borne by the party.

162. Any litigant whether petitioner, respondent or plaintiff and defendant could conduct his / their own case before any court throughout the territory of India and if asks for *Amicus Curiae* for helping in procedural matters, the court shall provide such Amicus at reasonable fee payable by such litigant.

163. Any plaintiff, petitioner and complainant can file a suit, appeal, writ or case in any court by post or other method with due proof and the court shall be bound to hear the case giving opportunity of hearing to such litigant through the quickest mode if any provided by him in his application, petition, complaint or appeal giving five days time for such appearance or hear exparte and decide if litigant fails to appear. If however

the court fails to hear and decide the litigant will have the right to file appeal in the higher court on this ground alone.

164. In cases where courts/authorities or bodies or such other forums find the litigation, prosecution, proceedings, cases, plaints/ suits, complaints filed or brought before them as frivolous, vexatious or misuse or abuse of judicial process the courts or authorities would have the power to impose damages, fines or cost on the erring party/parties to the extent of Rs. 2,00,000 depending on the nature, extent, and value of suit, case or matter and intensity and extent of harrasment to the aggrieved party but in no case less than Rs. 50,000 and such further amount as to compensate the party/ parties harmed or aggrieved or harassed by such vexatious or frivolous litigation.

165. Above provisions however will not apply to any court of enquiry or commission appointed by Governments meant for investigation of a special matter or facts finding purposes or for making recommendations on a particular issue.

Explanation: the provisions regarding adjournments and cost will apply to all courts including HC, SC, AC.

166. Any party including any government asked by any court to produce any document or evidence within a particular time being not less than ten days for any government and five days for others, if fails to produce the document or evidence adverse inference could be drawn by the court against the party in whose favour such non production is likely to go, including the government where it is a party, except where the party proves that despite due diligence, efforts, and power within its limits, the other party in whose possession such document is kept or supposed to be kept has failed to make the same available. In such situation the court may order such party to produce the document within a week or / and after hearing all parties concerned proceed in the matter as justice may require including prosecution of a party and punishing for default.

167. Any liability falling or coming on the government on account of such non production shall be realised from the employee or employees or group of employees which the court deciding the case shall determine prima facie.

168. Appeals will lie in the High Court against all the decisions of subordinate courts, judicial, quasi-judicial and other authorities in the matter of corruption cases and in the Appellate Court against the decisions of Lok Ayukt and Ombudsman. HC or AC as the case may be shall decide the matter as provided in respect of the appeals under this constitution. The courts may at this stage, if justice so demands partially or fully stay the operation of decision / judgment, orders appealed against.

169. All court fees under rules of any court shall increase by 5% every six years unless Parliament or Vidhan Sabha provides otherwise. Similarly, all fines, penalties, or damages by way of penalty shall increase by 10% every five years until Legislature provides otherwise, sentence of imprisonment shall, in all, cases enhance by six months every five year but not beyond three years of its present limit.

Jurisdiction of Courts, other Provisions and Punishment

170. All Judges of the SC, AC, and HC shall, be addressed as 'Nyaymurti' or 'Nyaya Moortis' in the courts and in no other way. The system of addressing as 'Me Lord' etc is to be, discontinued. The judges of all other courts will be, addressed as 'Shriman' Shrimaan 'or Maan-niya or Mahodaya.

171. The procedure regarding adjournments, cost and hearing will also apply to SC, AC, HC subject to the exceptions provided to them under the Constitution.

172. Writ jurisdiction of the courts empowered to issue them shall be, subject to the provisions of this Constitution and shall be, exercised only, if it has not been expressly or impliedly barred.

173. No court shall have the power of granting interlocutory stay and / or anticipatory bail in any matter or offence under investigation by any investigating authority unless three months have elapsed since the initiation of such investgation (s). No bail shall, be granted to the accused if final investigation report has been submitted within three months.

174. Any High Court if it considers in public interest so to do, may take suo - motu cognizance of any offence of corruption against a Central Government or Central public sector employee and the High Court of a State of any offence of corruption against an employee of the state government or state public sector employee within its jurisdiction.

175. The High Court of a state may in general public interest also direct any subordinate court working under it to take suo motu cognizance of any offence of rape irrespective of gender, kidnapping and atrocity (atrocities) on women or children or corruption case of any kind and nature, committed within the jurisdiction of such HC and direct such subordinate court to transfer the case to the court of competent jurisdiction. Appellate court may exercise such power throughout the territory of India.

176. All civil cases involving any liability of any nature including claim for damages or compensation up to Rs. 25,00,000 will be decided by a civil judge and up to Rs. 2,00,00,000 by a Sr. Civil judge or equivalent judge as may be decided by Distt judge. All such cases shall be appealable to Distt judge. Distt judge may hear any dispute involving any liability.

177. If there is no dispute or controversy on facts and admitted liability exceeds Rs. 2,00,00,000 the same may also be decided by the High Court.

Explanation: Distt judge for all purposes includes Session judge and any Asstt. Distt judge, Addl. DJ, or by whatever name called.

178. High court in special cases may constitute special courts to decide any civil, criminal, taxation, property or land or estate disputes and cases within a specified period not exceeding one year.

179. An accused shall, either be punished or held not guilty. There shall be, given no benefit of doubt to an accused by any court, judicial or quasi-judicial authority. If, the court or the authority is doubtful, of an accused having committed an offence, but finds some evidence or proof of his having either committed the offence, or involvement, or abetment, though not conclusive;

the accused shall be punished proportionately but not less than 1/3 of the maximum punishment provided for the offence or fine in the same proportion or both.

180. Nobody, whosoever shall be, awarded capital punishment, or imprisoned for life on the ground of such doubt or suspicion.

181. Notwithstanding anything in the Constitution, the exclusive onus for proving his full innocence shall be on the accused in all cases of rape of children, minor, women or rape with murder or abduction of any person for whatsoever reason or abduction coupled with ransom or rape or murder or all combined, dacoity, murder and corruption shall be on the accused.

182. Notwithstanding anything to the contrary in this Constitution, an attempt to commit an offence if circumstances so indicate shall be deemed to be offence committed and prosecuted and punished accordingly.

183. If, any investigating authority, including any police official deliberately, malafidely, intentionally, with any ulterior purpose, or motive apprehends, or falsely fastens, or hooks any innocent person and the court in the course of hearing finds it to be true or of substance, such official or authority shall be charged for abetting, instigating such offence or acting as an accomplice and shall be prosecuted and punished accordingly.

184. No accused shall be, given parole for more than ten days under special circumstances if Distt and session judge deems it necessary. In case of ill health or sickness the judge after getting the accused examined preferably by a penal of three senior doctors if available, grant parole as may be considered just and proper but ordinarily not exceeding fifteen days at a time.

185. Notwithstanding, no court shall have the power to grant anticipatory bail where FIR has been filed for committing murder, rape, kidnapping, dacoity or corruption in connection with govermental, public or social property, wealth or money in cash or kind. In all other cases bail shall stand discharged

and cease to have effect as soon as charges are framed by the court of original jurisdiction.

186. No court shall infer or interpret the intention of legislature beyond the Preamble of the Act or where Preamble is ambiguous the history of the bill originally introduced in the Legislature or amended at the time of passing the law by her. This will also apply to the modification of a Section or sections as the case may be.

187. Any death of any person in police custody arising out of police excesses or harassment, or rape of any person in police custody, could be, taken cognizance by any court civil or criminal in that district and if taken cognizance by civil court the same shall be transferred to any criminal court within 15 days and shall be summarily decided by such court within three months even if ultimately capital punishment is to be awarded to culprits.

188. Any complaint, charge, litigation or prosecution or proceedings found vexatious, frivolous, fabricated, or trumpet up shall not be allowed to be withdrawn, or any proceedings or litigation or complaint found to be misuse of judicial process or abuse of legal system the party that initiated or on whose behalf such proceeding were initiated shall pay such damages, compensation, expenses or penalty as the court may fix after taking into account the time, resources, money and man-power wasted and cost incurred by government and the loss of other party or parties in the case.

189. In the course of hearing, if any court finds prima facie that any police personnel or government employee or public servant or any citizen has deliberately or falsely misused or abused the process of law or judicial system to harass, or to revenge or take personal vendetta against the accused the guilty if a police personnel shall be punished upto five years, any other government or public servant for three years and any other person or citizen for two years and all of them shall reimburse the cost and expenses of litigation to accused and shall be fined if a police personnel, government or public servant Rs. 25,000 and others Rs. 15,000.

190. All Private sector companies or corporations or partnerships or businesses whether incorporated or registered or not would fall within the Writ jurisdiction of the High Court if they have taken or have been advanced loans or advances or credit exceeding rupees one crore from the Govts. or public or governmental financial or other institutions including such Insurance companies or corporations in the Public Sector; or if any govt. or any of the above financial or other institutions have invested or have share capital in them exceeding rupees one crore including any rehabilitation package. This will also include all such private sector companies in which public in general have invested by way of shares an amount exceeding Rs. two crores.

191. The court may scrutinise the working and functioning of such companies or corporations before they become sick and direct the board of directors or management of such bodies, subject to the approval of such economic experts not less than three as the court may think proper, to work in a particular way in the interest of profitability or future of business or in the interest of workmen or general public.

192. The court may direct the Govt. nominee director to act in a particular way until the company or corporation, firm turns around, or anomalies removed and fix the liability or suggest action to be, taken including removal of any person responsible for such mess or mismanagement.

193. If however the business of the companies or corporations etc., is found to be running smoothly in good condition or the company or corporation etc., is or are in good shape and there is no likelihood of its falling sick in near future looking to the trends of profitability and business the court will not interfere in any way.

194. Every company, or corporation, or body corporate in private sector will have minimum two government directors if its share capital is less than 100 crores and three if the share capital is more but less than 1000 crores and one additional director for every 500 crores not exceeding seven irrespective of share capital. No company or body corporate shall have

more than 5 (five) directors where government directors are two (2) and in no case more than 11 directors in the board excluding government directors.

195. Every company or body corporate whether in public or private sector or joint or co-operative sector shall spend 5% of its gross profits on tangible, verifiable and visible public welfare schemes to discharge their public accountability. Any three judges of the HC having jurisdiction over the territory may inspect, verify and certify such spending by any such company or corporation during an accounting year subject to the approval of Chief Justice of the HC. If any company or corporation, is unable to spend a particular percentage of 5 per cent, of such gross profits in any particular account year, it shall seek permission of the High Court under whose jurisdiction it is located, and if the HC is satisfied it may grant such permission with such conditions but in no case the permission shall be given for more than three years and for more than 2% of such spending, subject to the condition that entire balance amount shall be spent within next five years. The amount so spent shall be permissible deduction for the purposes of IT or other tax laws.

196. Age shall be no bar for inflicting punishment except to the extent provided under this Constitution.

197. No government or public scheme shall be named or launched after or in the name of any individual unless he died for the cause nation or society or the people or while saving public or national property or died for recognised social or national or public purpose.

198. No court shall ever hear any case or petition and or decide any matter at any place other than in the court and seat of justice meant for the purpose. The court may sit on a close day or after working hours only if grave or serious injustice is likely to be caused to a poor citizen or a pauper or otherwise there is likelihood of civil or other commotion or arson or looting or imminent danger to life of people as a community or in general or social or property or safety and security of the country.

199. The right of a litigant for justice and power of the court to find the truth and dispense justice will extend to any limit subject to the provisions of the Constitution.

200. In awarding punishment or taking and putting in custody there shall be no discrimination on the ground of education, age, status, position or on any ground whatsoever and all offenders and criminals shall be, treated alike.

201. No criminal case pending before any court in respect of offences of rape, murder, dacoity, corruption, offence causing death, and abduction, shall ever be, compromised, compounded, or withdrawn by any party. However, in case of other offences or crimes if the case or cases are not withdrawn or compromised within six months of institution in the court the same shall not be withdrawn and shall only be, compromised with the permission of the court on the terms and conditions, as the court may consider legal, justified, and reasonable to meet the ends of justice.

202. Court fee for individual citizens throughout the territory of India in all courts shall be 10 per cent if the value of the claim whatsoever including property movable or immovable, compensation or damages does not exceed rupees one crore and 15% in all other cases provided such fee shall be realised only after the litigant has succeeded in the lower court or High Court and at each stage of appeal or writ, litigants will have to attach the certificate of lower court if he or they have or not deposited the prescribed court fee. If the litigation, claim or case is decided by the SC the litigant shall be required to pay 5% extra fee if succeeds in SC. Subject to the above the court fee in case of governments, companies, corporations, societies, partnerships, businesses and firms shall be 15 per cent up to twenty crores and 20 per cent above that amount.

203. All litigations including suits, writs, appeals and attached documents to be filed before a court throughout the territory of India shall be sworn or authenticated or verified by an authorised Notary cum Oath Commissioner while before quasi – judicial authorities and government authorities by Oath Commissioner if so required by such authority and in all other cases by Notary.

204. A complaint including that concerning corruption, suit, writ or litigation whatsoever must have ten per cent substance otherwise that shall be treated abuse and misuse of legal, judicial and constitutional process and procedure inviting heavy penalty including cost and fine determined by the court.

CBI and SBI

205. There shall be an institution of CBI at the centre and State Bureau of Investigation (SBI) in each state or more than one state, as Parliament may by law, provide and shall work under the Vice President or Dy. Governor as the case may be. Organisationally SBI will be part of CBI and inter transferable but SBI will investigate cases only within the state while CBI throughout the country. If any case needs investigation beyond the state SBI will assign the matter to CBI for further investigation.

206. No court below the rank of High court except Ombudsman under the institution of Ombudsman, shall ever order Central Govt. to hold or conduct a CBI enquiry in any matter pending before such court or authority mentioned above without the permission of President or Vice President, if the court or authority for the reasons to be recorded and communicated to the President or VP, finds such enquiry the only alternative for ascertaining the truth of the matter. Such request shall not ordinarily be, refused.

207. No court below the rank of HC except the institution of Lok Ayukt will order SBI enquiry except as provided under the Constitution.

208. Whenever or wherever, a request is, made to President or VP both will take a unanimous decision in that matter.

209. Any Distt or Sessions Judge including those empowered to act as such may however, order enquiry by State Bureau of Investigation if all other alternatives have proved ineffective and the Governor or Dy. Governor / Chief Minister or Dy. CM as the case may be, has / have been, informed about. An application or request made either to the Governor or Dy. Governor shall be decided by them unanimously.

210. If any committee of Parliament or Vidhan Sabha by majority decides to hold or considers it necessary to hold a CBI or SBI enquiry into any matter that shall prevail notwithstanding anything to the contrary in this constitution.

211. No court shall interfere with any law made by Parliament with 2/3 majority for a specific purpose of public importance or meeting a national or general crisis for a specific period not exceeding six months. National interests shall supersede all other interests.

212. No court shall interfere with any policy of government if it is covered by the election manifesto of the party in power or three major parties with maximum number of MPs in case of coalition government, unless it is patently on the face of it illegal and unjust or violative of any law or Constitutional provisions.

213. Where an accused is charged of an offence or offences of accident resulting in death or grievous hurt likely to cause death, or rape of any nature, or rape with death, kidnapping for ransom or kidnapping with death, dacoity whether or not accompanied by death, and corruption as defined in this Constitution, the onus will be on the accused to prove his innocence and / or rebut the charges.

214. Neither law nor judicial process will be open to luxury nor will anybody abuse or misuse the legal-Judicial processes. This will invite an imprisonment of three years and a fine extending to Rs. three lacs subject to minimum of Rs. 50,000 after a summary trial.

215. All fines, and penalties mentioned in this Constitution refer to present level of economy and will stand proportionately appreciated with the enhancement, growth, or progress of the economy and changing times subject to the condition that no change or modification shall be made unless five years have elapsed since the earlier change or modification.

CBI and SBI Enquiry

216. CBI enquiry once ordered or started by any Govt. or

court will not be discontinued or called off till CBI submits its final Report and ;

217. All such CBI enquiries shall be completed and final report submitted within three months as far as possible but not exceeding six months under exceptional cases and for reasons to be recorded except where it is in respect of an alien or foreigners.

218. CBI investigations will not be reopened once CBI has submitted final report unless fresh material and or evidence substantive in nature, which could not have been placed earlier despite due diligence, has been brought or placed before the court or the Govt that will substantially alter the conclusions or decision in the matter.

219. Gazetted Officers of CBI and SBI shall be, transferred inter se anywhere throughout India. Provided, CBI and SBI enquiries will not overlap and once SBI enquiry has been, held and completed CBI enquiry will be ordered and held only if there is proof of dishonesty, gross or deliberate negligence, corruption and manipulation against any of the SBI officials investigating in to the said matter.

Cumulative Sentence and Punishment

220. All sentences of imprisonment where there are more than one i.e. except fines, damages or penalties payable in cash, awarded by a court shall be undergone simultaneously in phased manner starting from lowest to the highest.

221. Notwithstanding, anything to the contrary all punishments other than penalties and fines in cash awarded along with life imprisonment or capital punishment shall also be undergone in the manner provided under Art 200.

222. Pecuniary punishments or sentences by whatever name called fine, penalty, damages, or compensation, shall be payable at one time or recovered in the manner provided as arrears of land revenue.

223. Additional Directive Principles

(a) Government will ensure maintenance of public health, hygiene, pollution free environment including essentials of life to the people.

(b) Protecting environment, ensuring living human life for people, government will make resources available for sustenance of human life and welfare of the masses,

(c) Government will ensure prohibiting manufacturing of any mechanism like RO that result in wastage of water, or Gutka and tobacco of all types in any form, liquor and such intoxicants including drugs except for medical use under a authorised license.

(d) Except river water, Government will ensure prohibiting exploitation of underground water for bottling or commercial purposes except for agriculture, irrigation and authorised water supply for mass consumption.

(e) Government will ensure rationalisation and systematic use of vehicles, transport system including the use of private vehicles, transport, and regularize the same in public good.

(f) Government will ensure garlanding and linking of all rivers throughout the country to assure flood control, availability of potable drinking water and management of crises.

(g) All additions to Directive Principles shall be in addition to existing ones and none of them shall be, deleted.

Other Constitutional Changes

224. Art.136 i.e. Special Leave to Appeal to SC shall be deleted and there shall be no provision like Special Leave to Appeal.

225. Notwithstanding anything inconsistent therewith in this Constitution, no court what and whichsoever shall have the authority and power to stay the proceedings of a case or hearing of a matter before any forum, court or authority despite staying arrest as provided in other provisions of this Constitution.

226. No court shall have the power and authority to grant Anticipatory Bail.

227. Art. 370 giving special status to J & K state shall be deleted and all states i.e. 'Pradesh' shall be integral parts and equal units of Bharat without discrimination.

228. Fundamental rights shall be renamed as the 'Rights of Citizens'.

229. Suicide shall also be deemed to be self murder and inciting anybody to commit murder shall be deemed as an attempt to murder.

230. There shall be no Mercy Killing and all persons desiring such killing shall, without becoming a burden on family, parents or relatives, be nourished in protective home which shall be financed by the incomes of religious trusts, temples and religious places and incomes of Jogi, Baba - Gurus, Swamis, Joginis, Mahantas, Sanyasinis and Acharyas or by whatever name called. Parliament by law shall provide for taxing of such income only for the purpose up to 33 per cent.

231. Only such of the Jogis, Joginis, Babas, Gurus, Gurains, Swamis, Swaminis, Mahants – Mahantanis, Jagatgurus or Mathadhis, monks and the like by whatever name called under different religions and/ or sects shall be exempt from tax of all types who have provenly invested / expended or contributed fifty per cent of their income on social services like provision for education, including construction of buildings, hospitals, providing medicines, road, water, electricity, libraries, housing, construction of Dharmshalas, employment generation schemes and such other substantive welfare and entertainment provisions to public or children free of cost, including cleaning of rivers and so on and 25 per cent on health – hygiene, stipends, bounties, gifts to girls – women - poor, free food – clothing to poor and the like.

232. No government functionary whether elected or appointed shall enjoy any privilege, benefit or facility at public or government cost and shall be allowed only such expenses or reimbursements whether private or public as may be laid down by law either by state Vidhan Sabha or Sansad. Any unauthorized use or spending of government or public money for personal use or spent on any guest or colleagues or employees shall be deemed to be misuse and abuse of public and government money and treated a serious crime and moral turpitude.

233. All crimes involving misuse, abuse, misappropriation, embezzlement, dishonesty with and defrauding of public or government money, shall besides punishment, invariably imply recovery of such money from the individual, his property, wealth, assets movable or immovable including of his sons, daughters, parents and such other near relatives suspected to be involved in and successors, assigns and heirs etc.

234. There shall be no exploitation, misuse, or abuse of children upto the age of sixteen years for any purpose individual, social, political, or public and under excessive weather conditions likely to endanger them mentally, physically or psychologically. This however will not include any purpose concerning their development, academic, and potential, intellectual, including public exposure of potential, sports, games, art, or skill within reasonable human limits.

235. Any institution, individual or group by whom or any person for whom such exploitation, misuse, or abuse is committed shall be imprisoned for three years, and fined up to Rupees fifty thousand. All such cases shall be decided on summary trial basis and completed within three months to make out only a prima facie case.

236. Any person engaged in any illegal, unjustified, or immoral – unethical act or deal, clandestinely, directly, indirectly or as an accomplice, to defraud or deprive any citizen or group of citizens of their legal, due or justified right, entitlement, or claim shall after summary trial and prima facie evidence be liable to not less than five years imprisonment and damages not less than the quantification of such fraud, deal or illegal act and a penalty or fine of Rs. 1,00,000, plus expenditure on litigation duly quantified by the court taking the prevailing cost and economic conditions of the time into consideration.

237. All trusts, except religious trusts, purely for spiritual and philanthropic purposes; and their income, through all or any business, trade or profession, property, gift, wealth, Dan / donations in cash or kind and carried on for profit or invested for earning profit will be covered by taxation laws but

will be allowed 10 per cent extra standard deductions of their net profit, over those provided under Finance Act as may be applicable.

238. All the laws, rules, bye laws, including Cr.PC (Criminal Procedure Code) and CPC (Civil Procedure Code) conduct, service, or appeal rules, schemes, regulations and notifications, etc to the extent of repugnancy with the provisions of the Constitution will be ultra-vires whether made before or after coming into effect of this Constitution. This however will not affect and apply to the actions already taken in good faith and bonafidely under any law or any of the above instruments or provisions having force of law.

239. All constitutional or other authorities appointed under this Constitution or any other law shall frame their procedural rules for regulating their functioning and procedure not, inconsistent with the provisions of the Constitution, or law made by Parliament or Vidhan Sabha and the rules made thereunder. The President or Governor as the case may be shall assent to all such rules.

240. All Acts, rules, regulations, notifications, will otherwise be, approved, notified, and enforced in the manner as at present.

241. No governmental, public, or official contracts of any kind by way of auction or tender or otherwise shall be given to any person without verifying his antecedents and previous record and only if found authentic, professional and ethical on record subject to depositing a security of 33 per cent of total cost whether within or outside the country or whether undertaken by a foreigner or a citizen, or NRI within the country. However, 15 per cent of the security will be refunded only after 50 per cent work has been completed and verified by an expert committee consisting of not less than three senior cadre officers not below the rank of Dy. Secretary of Central government presided over by an officer not below Additional Secretary.

242. Any person or body of persons found guilty of manufacturing or producing any spurious item for consumption or drinking or forging, faking or adulterating any food article,

eatables, including drinks, and drinking items used by humans or likely to be used by humans, or used for animals or likely to be used for animals, or medicines of any kind shall be liable to be imprisoned for minimum ten years with a fine upto Rs. 50,00,000 but in no case less than Rs. 5,00,000 excluding the distributor, and sales persons as the court may decide but there shall not be imprisonment for less than two years and fine of not less than Rs. 1,00,000 up to Rs. 10,00,000. However, if, death of a human being or human beings occurs all such person or persons shall be liable to death penalty or life imprisonment as the court may decide, with a reasonable compensation to the family of person or persons who died as a consequence, but in no case less than 10,00,000 by the manufacturer in each case of death and ten years imprisonment to distributor or salesmen with a fine of Rs. 2,00,000 each payable to government.

Provided if death occurs to an animal or animals all the penalties shall be, reduced to one third. Provided further, trial in respect of the offences under this article shall be, held on summary basis with prima facie proof of evidence.

243. Any person found guilty of misusing or abusing, faking, or adulterating, or contaminating any food article or eatable item including drinking water for public distribution or diverting it to any other purpose or selling to any unauthorized person or body of persons for purpose other than for which it is meant or over charging or under weighing, or otherwise misappropriating any public procurement or embezzling in or defrauding with such procurement shall after summary trial and prima facie evidence be liable up to life imprisonment but in no case less than ten years imprisonment with a penalty of Rs. 50,00,000 and fine of Rs. 5,00,000, and the abettors, conspirators and accomplices shall be liable to fifty per cent of the above punishment.

244. Any person or body of persons found guilty of creating artificial shortages, or charge higher rates or prices, illegally holds, stores, or artificially conceals or holds for selling in black market any food, cereals, grains or eatable items, or water including a middleman or commission agent who for the purposes of profiteering exploits the farmers, pays them less

than fixed price or under weighs any such item or adulterates to deprive the farmers or public in general of genuine and pure items or exploits any natural calamity or takes advantage of any crop failure shall be punished for life with damages of Rs. 50,00,000 and penalty of Rs. 10,00,000 and each abettor, conspirator or accompiice shall undergo fifty per cent of the above punishment.

245. Parliament or Vidhan Sabha may provide for direct selling of food grains or eatables items by farmers to fair price shops, retailers or other outlets or fixed wholesalers on the conditions and price as may be provided under such law provided if there is any conflict between sate and central law the central law will prevail.

246. Summary trial whereever referred to in this Constitution shall mean, if no limitation is provided, a period of six months and prima facie evidence means proof not to the hilt but even if two views are possible, the view an average man would take in such matters, not necessarily a reasonable view but preponderance of possibility. Benefit of doubt in all cases of summary trials and prima facie evidence cases will go in favour of public, poor masses, society, and then to law, or government and not in favour of offenders, criminals or culprits or their accomplices or conspirators.

247. All unaccounted money, corrupt, unclaimed or black money and moveable wealth within the territory of India shall vest in the Central government and all other such property including assets which are immovable shall vest in the state government concerned having jurisdiction over but in all cases outside the territory of India, in Central government. The dispute, regarding such vesting, if any, shall be decided by Supreme Court.

248. No treaty, agreements, or covenants, will ever be entered by any 'Pradesh Shashan' / State government, with any foreign government or national without the approval of Central government, and shall also be signed by not less than the Secretary of the department concerned, on behalf of the President and no agreements, covenants or treaty shall be entered by Central government with any country against the

provisions of the Constitution or any law of the country, morality or ethics or against public interest or for dishonest or illegal purposes.

249. Any person imprisoned for a term not less than one year for committing any offence/ crime or fined not less than Rs. 15,000 shall be debarred from contesting to any public office for which holding of electiions is either the duty of Election Commission of India or of any government or public authority.

250. Any persons against whom charges have been framed by any competent court in connection with committing of murder, booth capturing, terrorizing voters, obstructing elections, rape, dacoity, kidnapping, terrorism or corruption or any offence of similar nature or conspiracy in connection there-with or abetment of such offences including any offence connected with national defence, security and safety of the people and property shall be debarred from seeking any such election.

251. If the election of any person is quashed by HC and not challenged in Supreme Court or quashed by Supreme Court for corrupt practices he shall be, debarred from contesting elections for next ten years from the date of such judgment.

252. Any person who has been, held guilty of any offence or crime and twice sentenced to imprisonment or fined by a competent court or legal authority after trial shall be debarred from seeking any election irrespective of the period of imprisonment or amount of fine. Such punishment shall be the proof of his being a habitual offender.

253. No person, or body of persons shall be members of a body, committee, or commission, constituted by any government for enquiring into any matter, if such person or his relatives are or were involved or connected with the matter of enquiry or such person or persons have any connection or relationship with any other person or body of persons against whom enquiry is being held.

254. If any investigating or other authority empowered to check, enquire, inspect, or investigate, any violation, contravention, ommission, or commission, uses any power or

authority or means in excess of what is vested under the law, or rules or needed under the circumstances, and the aggrieved makes a complaint to higher authority, it shall be the duty of such authority to enquire into or send the same to appropriate authority if he is not such authority. If none of the above authorities hear the complaint within fifteen days and decide within next fifteen days in accordance with law or natural justice or the complainant is not satisfied with, he may approach any civil or criminal court for relief and civil court shall be treated a criminal court and the court shall prima facie decide the matter within three months and award appropriate relief to the aggrieved and punishment to culprit extending two to five years and fine extending to Rs. 1,00,000 but not less than Rs. 25,000 depending upon gravity of complaint.

255. Parliament shall have the power of prohibiting any strike throughout the territory of India and passing any law on the subject including fixing of personal and general liability of such persons or any person to compensate or pay penalty or damages to sufferers and provide for other punishments.

256. Similarly, Pradesha Vidhan Sabha shall have exclusive jurisdiction to prohibit any strike in the state and provide for punishment in case of violation including damages, or compensation.

257. Wherever government and citizens are under obligation to perform a duty under any law, scheme, or rules, etc., the department or ministry concerned shall specify those obligations to be performed step by step and communicate to the concerned citizen or citizens. If because of governmental failure, limitation if any citizens act upon the same that shall not be called in question and loss if any suffered by the government shall be recovered from employees or employee concerned found liable after a summary preliminary enquiry, which, if challenged shall be decided as a civil case in accordance with the provisions of the Constitution.

258. In case of all industrial disasters, besides the company, all directors by whatever name called including chairman, Managing director, partner, owner, occupier or head or chief executive of the establishment shall be severally and jointly

held liable for payment of compensation, damages, penalty, and punishment not less than 10 years, to life imprisonment, and if death occurs, depending upon the extent of responsibility, and liability, to capital punishment.

259. Provisions of above Article will mutatis mutandis apply to localised pollution, environmental decadence, natural or ecological damage, degeneration or defilement of flora and fauna.

Service Conditions, Leave - Salary - DA etc.

260. There shall be not more than 15 festival holidays in government services, 10 in public and private sector, and 20 in schools and educational institutions in a year.

(a) There shall be not more than 15 earned or privilege leaves, 12 casual leaves, 12 sick leaves in government services, private, and public sectors. Casual leave shall not accumulate beyond three days at any time, and shall not, be taken more than three at a time, only one CL will be given in advance. Earned leave shall accumulate and encashed only for three years and sick leaves shall accumulate for five years, provided sick leaves shall not be encashed. However, if sick leave of an employee for 36 days lapses after three years and he or his espouse falls sick requiring hospitalization for not less than three days at anytime duly certified by authorised physicians such employee shall be, reimbursed and allowed upto ten days paid leave as may be certified by the surgeon. All the three leaves shall be, earned by an employee only if he has actually worked for not less than 20 days in a month or 240 days in a year, excluding all holidays and weekly offs.

(b) Any employee legally and validly officiating on any other post for more than three months shall after the expiry of third month be paid from the fourth month a consolidated adhoc allowance equivalent to 40% of basic and DA of the post if any he is officiating.

(c) Except as provided above schools upto senior secondary or higher-secondary i.e. 10 + 2 shall work throughout the year except for the months of May and June and 15th December to 15th February during an academic session depending upon the weather conditions to be, decided by appropriate governments. Other Higher Education Institutes shall however, be, governed by their own rules in the matter.

(d) All Government employees shall be in grades and scales as may be prescribed and except in a situation of declared financial emergency, shall be neutralized to the extent of 50% escalation in cost of living or dearness because of inflation if any, every six months. Grades and scales shall be, revised every five year by a Pay Commission appointed by the PM / President. State governments may also appoint their own Pay Commissions not recommending higher salaries than central PC or follow the recommendations of CPC fully or partially.

(e) State governments depending upon their paying capacity may have their separate grades and pay scales not, higher than the Central government and reimburse DA in the manner by Central government.

(f) Government employees whosoever, shall not be entitled to any other benefit, amenity, or concession free of cost. They shall not enjoy any service or privilege over the people of India and share the same public services, amenities, and facilities as provided to all other citizens of the country;

(g) All government employees will pay for the facility and amenity as all other citizens of the country and shall not be, reimbursed any other cost towards any other facility, or amenity, or convenience. Their salary, grades, and scales will therefore be inclusive except reimbursement of DA every six months.

Misconducts and Disciplinary Proceedings

261. Present Art 311 will be amended and modified to the extent provided below; 'Notwithstanding anything, the provisions regarding Lok Ayukt and Ombudsman shall have precedence over all other enquiries and shall have effect in the matters of corruption pending before them in respect of a government employee and shall also be treated as departmental enquiry for misconduct of corruption'.

262. No govt. servant holding permanent post or cadre under State / Pradesh or Central government will be dismissed or otherwise punished unless he has been informed of the charges and given an opportunity of explanation thereto and further opportunity of hearing in an enquiry to defend himself by producing documentary or oral evidence and of defence if any.

263. Enquiry in respect of the misconducts for which punishment provided is less than dismissal, discharge or termination, shall be completed within six months and one year in all other cases, subject to;

264. Irrespective of punishment if charges relate to the security, safety and defence of the country, or leaking of defence secrets of the country, or endangering human life or property, or leaking of any strategic or military or defence information, making out of a prima facie case only would suffice to take appropriate disciplinary action against the delinquent. In such cases enquiry will be completed expeditiously within six months.

265. Irrespective of punishment, in the cases of charges of corruption, a summary enquiry will be conducted wherein delinquent will be given the opportunity of expeditious hearing to ascertain only a prima facie case. If after such hearing a prima facie case is made out that will suffice for taking disciplinary action. In all cases of charges of corruption enquiry will be completed within four months.

266. If any government employee, public servant, or a person holding constitutional position hides, conceals or suppresses any evidence, or information, oral or documentary in or within his knowledge, relevant in and for a case or suit, whether pending or decided and publishes it orally or through print, afterwards including retirement shall be guilty of an offence of abetting, conspiracy, and being an accomplice in the offence and prosecuted, punished or charged as if in service and if punished he shall also lose his pension for remaining life.

267. Notwithstanding, armed and defence forces personnel shall not be liable to any human rights violation if engaged in

enemy or terrorist, insurgency or rebellious or such combating operations in any part of the country or the world.

Corruption: Meaning and Enquiry

268. Corruption for all purposes 'means ill gotten, immorally amassed, unethically accumulated or unjustifiably collected money, wealth, asset or property movable or immoveable, in cash or kind, whether in India or out of India, beyond known means or supposed possible resources or ordinarily expected means in general background of the accused person or government servant, or connected with the affairs of the State or of any government or public in general, affecting the economy or the affairs of the State, government, or society under any Law, rules, regulations, schemes or other instruments throughout the territory of India' and includes:

"Taking and giving bribe including in the name and style of, or under the garb or nature of gift (except to the extent permitted by rules or bye laws or order of competent authority with the sanction of the President or governor) irrespective of size, value, amount, in kind or cash, for any favour or disfavour, for commission or ommission of an act, or any act of illegal gratification, fraud, dishonesty, misappropriation, embezzlement of Govt. or public money, property, wealth, moveable or immoveable in cash or kind, or putting public life in danger arising out of poor quality of material used or work done or any construction work of inferior quality likely to endanger life and property, purchasing material at high cost, or purchasing inferior quality material or purchasing such material at higher or lower cost for gratification or favouring any person or persons including group or body corporate, partnership or firm whether incorporated and registered or not, and includes any conspiracy or abetment thereof or actual commission of an act to deprive real and bonafide claimants of their legal claims and rights or diverting any government or public money or property or wealth or assets to a purpose other than for, which it was or is meant (except with the written permission of competent authority), or depriving a rightful claimant or claimants or beneficiary or beneficiaries of his or their rightful claim, entitlement or benefit or legal right and diverting or misusing or misappropriating any money or property movable or immovable to a purpose or person other than for which or for whom it was meant".

269. It will be the duty of the delinquent to ascertain the date of hearing if he absents on any day of hearing. Not more than one adjourment will be given to either party and for not more than three days unless it is a case of death in the family when it could be upto maximum of ten days. In case of serious accident of accused a material witness enquiry would be held at the earliest opportunity at a convenient place as may be decided by the Inquiry Officer.

270. No enquiry in any case will extend beyond six months except in case of serious accident or such bodily injury or serious illness which incapacitates the delinquent to such extent that conducting enquiry will not at all be possible to be held, if so certified by approved penal of doctors. In such cases, it will be held within reasonable period but at the earliest. In such cases, Enquiry Officer will have to give the details of steps taken and problems faced in not holding the enquiry in time.

271. There shall be no right of personal hearing at appellate stage in corruption matters or allegations. In all other cases, the appellate authority may on the basis of evidence on record and for the reasons to be recorded reconsider the punishment. Authority will inform the delinquent within 15 days the reasons and outcome of its decision on the appeal or representation of delinquent but that shall not be necessary or obligatory if there are any corruption charges.

272. Disciplinary cases will not be reopened under any circumstances unless fresh evidence has been found or ascertained or revealed within six months, which is of such a nature as to materially affect the merit and substance of the case and punishment, both could not have been reasonably with due diligence be produced at the earlier stages of enquiry proceedings. In such cases, fresh enquiry may, nevertheless be held in the manner as if the delinquent is being charged for the first time.

273. No government employee will be represented in the enquiry by a practising lawyer. Only an employee upto the rank of gazetted officer shall be allowed to represent the delinquent.

274. No gazetted officer charged of misconduct shall be allowed to be represented by any other employee whosoever in the domestic or departmental inquiry.

275. Similarly no Govt. or any other authority or corporation or agency working under any Govt or control of such Govt. or such authority shall be represented by any practising lawyer except by an employee of the deptt. to which delinquent belongs to.

276. In all such cases, where charges are of such nature that punishment will be either termination of service in any form, or withholding of grade, increment or promotion for life. Enquiry in all cases of employees irrespective of rank and position or grade will be held by an enquiry committee not exceeding three gazetted officers, and in all other cases by two employees of not less than two grades or cadres above the delinquent including gazetted officers of any rank or grade.

277. Govts. or disciplinary authority may discharge an employee or simply terminate his services if found guilty of an offence in the manner provided, if the offence is of such a nature or the employee is holding a position of confidence, trust or strategic nature, that trust or confidence cannot be reposed on him in the interest of defence, security or safety of the people, country or property or finances of the society or the country.

278. In all those cases, where video clip or video or a visual cassette or any such visual evidence of committing any crime, offence or excesses against citizen or citizens, not arising out of and in the course of performance of official duty or bonafide discharge of official responsibility, is / are available against any government or public servant, and after preliminary investigations by two gazetted officers in the presence of such accused person, the same stands corroborated, or found not cooked, forged or appears genuine, no further enquiry or

evidence shall be necessary and such servant shall be, punished as per law or service rules on that basis only.

279. No government employee will be terminated, dismissed, or otherwise discharged by an authority below the rank of appointing authority. All other punishments may be, meted out by an authority as may be authorised by appointing authority but not below the rank of delinquent.

280. No order of discharge or termination or dismissal will be legal unless the employee has been provided with a copy of the Report of enquiry along with such order.

281. No discharge, termination or dismissal will take effect unless employee has been paid or validly or legally offered three months salary, cash or by cheque simultaneously.

282. All other dues of such employee will be paid and cleared as far as possible within three months or else he may file a suit for recovery within six months of such termination or dismissal at the cost of concerned authorities liable or responsible for delay.

283. All or any person allotted government or public accommodation on account of holding a particular position, post, authority or status, whether constitutional or not including a public servant and a foreign national under contract shall vacate such accommodation within one month of ceasing to hold such position, post, authority or status. Whether on the expiry of the tenure or term or retirement or discharge or superannuation or otherwise termination of service, contract or tenure. No court shall interfere and go into the matter any further if prima facie such cessation is established and no court at any stage shall take more than two months in deciding such disputes and cases subject to the imposition of the penalty five times the normal rent or fee or charges of such accommodation.

284. All existing service rules applicable to government servants or employees or employees of statutory and other bodies, local or other authorities and public corporations shall stand modified to the extent provided herein above and any rule, regulation or order or notification including service and

conduct rules to the extent of repugnancy shall be null and void.

285. In all other cases employee may ask for enquiry report which shall be provided within fifteen days.

286. Suspension pending enquiry shall not be interfered with by any court whether or not such right exists in any rules or service conditions, if it is for any act of corruption or leakage of defence secrets or strategic information likely to endanger or put security or safety of nation, people or property in danger. No suspension or subsistence allowance shall be, payable in any of the cases covered by this clause and if charges are found not proved only then the payment of full salary shall be made.

287. Punishment will include besides termination in any form, withholding of increment - promotion - grade for life or any length of service and fine but not suspension in any way. Fine shall be imposed only in cases of simple negligence or neglect of work where public or government has not suffered any financial or other losses, absence without leave or from place of work, sleeping or gambling during duty hours, or the like shall if not habitual be covered by fine, which shall not be less than Rs. 2,500 for first misconduct and may go up to Rs. 10,000 thereafter depending upon the facts and circumstances of each case.

288. In case of dispute between Pradesh / State government and Centre, concerning disciplinary matters in respect of any employee of All India Services the decision of centre / president shall be final and binding on all concerns.

289. Any authority neglecting its duties or responsibilities or obligations shall, if any liability is incurred by the government because of such negligence, in addition to other punishment, be liable to compensate the govt. or such other authority to the extent of such liability.

290. Notwithstanding to the contrary in the Constitution, if any person, or any government servant, after preliminary investigations by CBI, or State Bureau of Investigation, or by a judge of any court, is found prima facie guilty of

embezzlement, fraud, misappropriation or dishonesty in connection with any grant, subsidy, exgratia, aid, or payment posthumously sanctioned and authorised to be made to the family or dependents of any personnel of defence or armed forces, or Para military forces, or personnel of civilian forces, or any citizen of the country; shall if a public, or government servant, be terminated or discharged, from the services and such action shall not be called in question in any court in India.

291. Such government servant will reimburse to the government the entire amount so misappropriated which, shall be realised from his property, movable or immovable assets or business if any including of his family, heir, successors, assigns and shall; also be liable to imprisonment which may extend to ten years but not less than three years in any case. All other persons not being government servants shall reimburse the government in the manner provided for government servants and recover as arrears of land revenue, but the punishment in his / her or their case shall not be less than five years but not exceeding 15 years.

292. No Govt servant of the Central or State holding the post of a gazetted officer and above shall be transferred for two years and all other employees for three years, from the date of his / her posting on a post / cadre or place unless the President or the governor under exceptional circumstances of public revolt or visible public rebellion or commotion against him or after prima facie investigation of charges of corruption against him / her for reasons to be recorded decides to transfer him / her earlier.

293. There shall be no wholesale transfers by any government and not more than 10 in a month. There shall be no transfers during January to May of the year;

(1) Any Govt. servant aggrieved by transfer in violation of these provisions may after joining approach the court of Distt. Judge of his posting for injunction and the Distt judge shall decide such cases, whether or not injunction is granted, within three months after hearing the matter prima facie and

interfere only if transfer is in violations of these constitutional provisions.

Explanation: Distt judge under the constitution also means Sessions judge and includes Addl. or Asstt. DJ or SJ of the Distt.

Fixing Liability Vicariously

294. Till a law is made, not inconsistent with the provisions of the Constitution, if any person or group of persons or citizens collectively suffer any loss or damage or destruction, whether of life or property, movable or immovable or in terms of money; due to deliberate, or habitual negligence, or gross neglect, of work or duty by any Govt employee, group of employees or Deptt. of Govt, he or they may sue, such employee or group of employees or deptt. for damages or compensation against such loss or damage or destruction in a civil or criminal court of original jurisdiction within three months of such loss or damage or destruction provided:

295. The Govt. concerned would be held liable only if the loss or damage or destruction was due to the wrong policies of the Govt. or absence of a policy on the subject, directly resulting in such loss or damage etc. and not otherwise.

296. Provided further, no govt. or employee will be, held liable or responsible in any such case in any manner if such loss has resulted because of a law passed by the legislature of a state or parliament or decree / order / judgment of any court, or orders of any other authority or body legally competent to do so.

297. In all other cases whether arising out of deliberate, habitual negligence or gross neglect of work, or wrong implementation or none execution of policy or any work, orders or systems the employee, employees or group of employees personally and / or employees of Deptt. concerned jointly as the case may be shall be liable or responsible for payment of such damages or loss or compensation to the concerned person or persons, group of persons or public as the case may be.

298. The court shall objectively determine the amount payble depending upon the loss or damage etc.

299. The court will fix the liability of each employee or employees of the deptt. individually and also lay down the criterea for distribution of the amount of compensation or damages amongst the claimant or claimants as the case may be.

300. Provided, when Deptt is held responsible and liable the court will fix the liability right from head or Secretary of the Deptt by whatever name called, down the line, including specific liability or responsibility or specific guilt if any of a particular employee or employees and extent of their liability if any, along with the liability of others and action to be taken against such persons.

301. All such plaints, claims or suits for damages or compensation or relief shall be signed by the plaintiff or complainant. If however, the claim is of general nature or concerns a group of people or number of persons the same shall, besides one of the affected or concerned individuals, also be countersigned, duly sealed / stamped by the gram pradhan or Block pramukh or panchayat pramukh or Zila panchayat pramukh or chairman of municipality, notified area or any corporation which fall within the definition of local body, or MLA or MP of the constituency where the cause of action arose or the plaintiff /complainants resides or reside.

302. Any suit or complaint found frivolous, unfounded or baseless would make the complainant and the authority countersigning the plaint or claim liable to criminal prosecution and payment of fine as may be decided by the court but in no case less than Rs. 25,000 and more than Rs. 5,00,000.

303. All legal notices issued by any court or notices issued by any Govt shall be, published only on page two of the Newspaper or papers throughout the territory of India.

304. No person below the age of 14 years and no woman or girl shall be imprisoned or put under custody by police or any other investigating agency or authority to compel presence or attendance of any offender or criminal or suspect nor will his property be attached for the purpose except when found guilty by a competent court.

305. A woman or a girl below 14 years of age and above 10 years if accused of committing any offence or crime shall be sent to central or district jail before 5 pm as and when called for investigation by police station or Thana and shall not be called for the purpose before 8 am. Any police personnel violating these provisions shall be liable to summary prosecution, imprisonment and damages payable to woman, women or girl or girls as any court of the area may determine.

306. Any act or conduct which is a crime or offence under any Act of Parliament or Vidhan Sabha will not be protected by any prerogative parliamentary, Judicial, administrative or executive and will need no permission and sanction either of President or governor or any other authority for prosecution. Any law providing for such sanction shall, to that extent be void and ultra vires.

307. A law made by Parliament will prevail in all incases of repugnancy with state law. If however state law is, made subsequent to the parliamentary law and having obtained the assent of the President, the same shall prevail in that state to that extent despite such repugnancy.

308. However, if Parliament subsequently enacts a law or amendment the existing law overrides any state law despite such assent provided the matter falls in concurrent list and made applicable for whole of India or that particular state the parliamentary law shall prevail.

309. Political parties may obtain political funds from business houses, firms, companies, or corporations in the private sector for contesting elections upto ten crores without tax liability to such business, and up to 50 crores subject to payment of tax on the amount above 10 crores. Alternatively, political parties may obtain without tax liability upto Rs. five lacs for the election of a candidate contesting the election of an MLA and fifteen lacs for a candidate contesting for MP provided; they submit the details of income and expenditure to tax authorities and election commission.

310. Said amount for political parties from the sources as mentioned in the above Articles may extend to seventy-five lacs for presidential candidate, fifty lacs for VP and thirty lacs

for Governor, and twenty lacs for Dy. Governor without any tax liability only submission of returns under tax laws will apply.

311. Any Act passed by Parliament or Vidhan Sabha will become law enforceable only after receiving assent of President or Governor as the case may be. State may reserve any Act on concurrent list to the assent of President to prevail in the state in accordance with the other provisions of the Constitution.

312. No citizen, or body of citizens, or any person, whether natural or artificial will be deprived of life, property, or wealth, movable, or immovable without following the process of law or where there is no law without giving an opportunity of hearing in an unbiased manner in accordance with the principles of natural justice.

313. No person shall ever be punished without giving him the opportunity of hearing, and no person shall ever be the judge in his own case including in case of his relatives or of those he has ever been an employee, or paid servant, or a counsel, or adviser, or consultant.

Explanation: Own case includes family, relatives and any matter in which any such person or persons have or had any interest direct or indirect.

(A) Where there is no law there shall be right of hearing in accordance with the principles of natural justice. Where however, under any law, rule, procedure or scheme, regulations including the service rules, right to hearing or opportunity of hearing as above has not been, provided that shall be deemed to have been amended to the extent of this provision read with other provisions of the Constitution.

Explanation: No right to hearing shall extend beyond the provisions of the Constitution. If the right has been provided under any law, rule, procedure or scheme the same shall be governed by those provisions provided those are not inconsistent with the provisions of the Constitution.

Explanation: opportunity of hearing means reasonable opportunity of hearing the aggrieved or wronged and includes opportunity of defence to such delinquent or accused, in an unbiased manner, by an independent person as provided in the Constitution or any law or instrument not, inconsistent with the Constitution, and will not mean due opportunity or due process of law.

314. No law made for acquiring any property, wealth, or assets, movable or immovable including payment of compensation shall be, called in question in any court of law if such acquisition is for national and societal purposes or in general public interest; subject to payment of such compensation as may be laid down by Sansad or Vidhan Sabha. In case of conflict between State and Central law regarding payment of compensation, the Central Law will prevail.

315. Public sector employees shall not be treated at par with or similar to Govt. employees on the ground of government holding the share capital. Public Sector units will run as independent business centers for profits in competition with others including the private sector but with high standards of integrity, honesty, efficiency, professional ethics and economy. No Public Sector Corporation, company, or organisation will be created under any statute but only by incorporation under Company Act or registration under Societies Act, unless it is a question of nationalization of a private sector unit under a law. However, despite such acquisitions all such units shall be, treated only Companies as if incorporated under Company Act.

316. Acquisition of any specific private property including nationalisation of any private sector company or organisation or corporation or business shall be, made by a decree of the President or the governor as the case may be subject to the approval of simple majority of members of Parliament or Vidhan Sabha present and voting.

317. Any bill once placed in any legislature and defeated could be, placed again only after one year or 365 days from the date it was rejected by the legislature.

318. Nothing in this article shall prevent government, or governments, to enter into joint ventures within or outside the country either on equal partnership or sharing of management or profit with the private sector or individuals or

body of individuals, subject to other provisions of the Constitution. However, central government may ask for any information from the state and impose such conditions, as it may consider necessary in the national or societal interest, which may include defence and security.

319. There shall be only three political alliances at the national level and the fourth will be of independents that shall be, treated as non-aligned. Election Commission will ensure the modus operandi of and frame rules under Representation of Peoples Act or recommend for amendment in the Act if necessary for giving effect to these provisions. The Commission may classify the political parties into principal and secondary parties and ask the latter to ally with any principal party for contesting elections, thereafter the party may not ally or form alliance with any political party. Three alliances could also be, formed on the lines Right – Left - Centre or by such names as NDA - UPA - leftist / centrist, as the Commission may approve.

320. No Member of Parliament or Vidhan Sabha will cross floor and join any other political party unless he resigns in which case Election Commission will hold elections within three months. Despite resignation, he will continue to remain member until the date of declaration of election results. Nothing in this Constitution will apply to cross voting by any member.

321. Any member of any Legislature, found prima facie guilty by a committee of five members of any house of legislature, two each of the treasury, and opposition, presided over by a sitting or retired judge of not less than a High Court, bribing or receiving bribe (s) in any form i.e. cash or kind for voting in any form or in any manner in or outside Legislature, will resign immediately on such pronouncement by the committee and debarred from seeking re-election for next two terms, or ten years whichever is later. If such member does not resign, the speaker or Chairman of the house shall make a declaration of cancellation of membership and vacating of seat by such member automatically. The judge so presiding over shall be, deemed as the member of that house for that purpose and period. The committee shall decide the matter

finally and pronounce the decision within three months by sending the same to the speaker or Chairman of the house as the case may be.

322. No individual, or body of individuals, or Company, or partnership, or corporation, registered or not, shall open an account in any foreign bank, without prior permission of the Central Government. All such accounts shall be illegal if opened without such permission, and open to forfeiture by the Central Government, at any time after a summary inquiry on making out of a prima facie case.

323. Parliament will have the exclusive jurisdiction and power to enact a law prescribing for or laying down any dress or uniform or civil code for clothes, wear, and garments, for maintaining decency, propriety, and civility of life in society, national festivities or any code for maintaining civil behaviour in general.

324. Parliament may enact any law or prescribe for standard or standards to be followed by media- print or visual, news-papers, channels, TVs and film industry so as to maintain decency, ethics, civility and morality in the society or saving it from degeneration, or in the interest of the security, safety and defence of the country, people and the property.

325. The word 'due' or any phrase with the word due occurring anywhere in any Law, Rules, regulations, Scheme, or service conditions, with reference to hearing or opportunity of hearing such as due opportunity of hearing, or due opportunity of defence, or due chance of representing, and the like shall be deemed to have been omitted; and read only as 'opportunity of".

326. Notwithstanding, Art 325 performance of duty, responsibility, and accountability, shall always and under all circumstances obligate such performance with due diligence, due care, due intelligence, due effort, and so on.

327. Media will have freedom only of presenting the news, facts, events, and reports as they are and not of interpreting them or making deductions or intention therefrom or from the speeches of anybody except in Panel discussion of not less than three experts.

328. Media will have no freedom of reporting or displaying any security, or defence operation undertaken or carried by defence or armed or Para military forces anywhere or against terrorists or enemy, or revealing and making public any defence secrets or defence strategy of the country unless it reasonably involves corruption.

329. The state or the government shall not advertise in any print, or visual media, any political, social, or economic or developmental scheme at its expenses with photographs of any person except the benefits of the scheme and procedure for getting such benefits, including authorities, place and time etc., or by way of information to general public without eulogizing, or idolizing any party, or individual, including inauguration, and laying of foundation stones of any government or government aided project or scheme.

330. If any person, or body of persons, or legal person whether incorporated or not, partnership, whether registered or not or governmental or public or co-operative sector authority, exports any goods or material to any destination in India or abroad and if on confiscation or checking, the same is / are found to be other than what has been declared, the exporter shall be guilty of non bailable offence and the goods shall be confiscated immediately and sold by auction. Similar provisions will apply if any goods are imported and in that case, the importer shall be, held guilty and liable. In both the cases where it is difficult to fix liability, the head of department or head of the section, or any director, or occupier, or person responsible for importing, and exporting of consignment, secretary of government department, or any of the partners or proprietors of corporations, companies, firms or business or societies shall be imprisoned for 15 years if found guilty; and fined to the extent of the value of consignment as the court may deem fit, which shall be realised as arrears of land revenue. However, in case of, any casualty arising out of such misdemeanor the amount realised by auctioning the consignment shall be, paid to victims in addition to the compensation if any. All such auctions shall be, completed reasonably within three months. Remaining liability if any

shall be, decided by the competent court as per law and Constitution. However, the auction shall not be, challenged in any court unless corruption or favouritism is prima facie, made out including violation of any law and Constitution.

331. Parliament may provide for limit on expenses of each functionary of the State including President, Judges, ministers and officials and so may State legislature in the State including of Governor or Ministers or other functionaries and its audit by AG or CAG as the case may be.

332. If any authority, employee, or government, either malafidely, or for political or extraneous reasons, or for any other consideration fails to discharge its duty or obligations under any law or rules or regulations or scheme and the limitation expires as a consequence; any citizen, body of citizens, society or any other legal entity may despite such expiry challenge the same before the competent higher authority, authorities, or courts for justice or decision and the authority or court will decide the same as a regular matter.

Provided, however, if any person or official is found by the authority, or court, deciding the matter, responsible for any of the lapse as above, including the person on whose behalf such lapse is committed, they/ he shall bear entire burden of litigation as may be assessed by each authority or court at each stage, together with a fine up to Rs. 5,00,000 payable by each such person or official as determined by court but in no case less than Rs. 1,00,000 each.

333. Any liability, falling on the government on account of the lapse, negligence, habitual negligence, or gross neglect of any employee or group of employees or any department, or office, the same shall be recovered from such employee or group of employees or employees of the office concerned, their assigns, successors, dependents or heirs of the property, wealth and assets belonging to any or all of them.

334. Similarly, any person held guilty of fraud, embezzlement, deception or dishonest misuse or misappropriation of government or public money that is money belonging to general or common public, the amount shall be,

recovered in the same manner as provided in the preceding provisions.

335. If any government has to pay any amount by way of compensation or on compassionate grounds to any person including any employee for the fault of any government employee, the same shall be, recovered from the employee or employees concerned in the manner provided in foregoing provisions.

336. If any attempt to commit suicide, or of suicide, by anybody results as a consequence of unwarranted, uncalled for, inhuman treatment, or sentimental exploitation, or excessively undesirable behaviour of any person including brutality, excessiveness, exploitation, or unwarranted coercion, by any official, police personnel or authority, such person, police personnel or authority as the case may be shall be guilty of culpable homicide individually or jointly as the case may be or situation may warrant.

337. Misuse, improper use, illegal or fake use of any benefit, privilege, concession or facility provided to any individual, person, group or class of people or community of citizens by any other person or persons, class or community shall be non-bailable offence and treated a criminal offence inviting fine up to Rs. 1,00,00,000 and imprisonment upto 25 years or both.

338. Notwithstanding, anything to the contrary, all courts shall decide all or any amount of damages or compensation, wherever not provided in this Constitution, if a case is made out in the course of hearing for loss and damages or such compensation.

339. If rape, or rape with murder, or murder of the accused or apprehended person is committed during police custody by any person or police, personnel, the Inspector Incharge of the Thana or officer incharge of police station within whose jurisdiction such act or acts have been committed shall be personally held guilty of abetment and tried as accomplice in the offence and the superintendent and Dy. Superintendent of police of the area shall also be proceeded with for deliberate and gross negligence under law and / or departmentally or both.

340. There shall be no discretionary power or quota with any authority in the matters of state involving public claims, benefits, rights or title of citizens, general masses, or in the matters of public nature and the same shall be decided in accordance with the scheme, rules or regulations made or law laid down by the legislature.

341. No private conversation shall be deemed to be, secret if it relates to or concerns the affairs of the state or government, whether economic, political, industrial, defence, security, or touches any public policy, of any government or concerns the interests of the public in general.

342. No suicide by, or death of a woman, within seven years of marriage shall be considered a dowry death unless supported by cogent prima facie evidence including circumstantial evidence, or dying declaration, or correspondence, or communications preceding such suicide or death, leading to the apprehension that such suicide or death was committed under instigation of, or prompted by, or caused or arose, out of dowry demand or such harassment. In both the cases main accused shall be liable to be punished by way of life imprisonment and not less than 15 years imprisonment for those who instigated or prompted such act including fine extending up to Rs. 10,00,000 in former case and to Rs. 5,00,000 in the latter, as the court may decide. Provided if death is caused or prompted by anybody on account of dowry harassment or demand the offence shall be treated as murder inviting capital punishment to main accused and life imprisonment to instigators with a fine extending to Rs. 1,00,00,000 in former case and Rs. 20,00,000 in latter. The fine shall be payable by each accused in all cases and reasonable humanitarian amount shall be paid by the court to the heirs, successors or dependents of deceased and rest shall be deposited in government treasury.

343. If any person commits suicide as a result of emotional excesses or harassment or instigation of other person on any ground, such other person or persons shall be liable to be sentenced extending up to life imprisonment and fine extending from Rs. 5,00,000 to Rs. 15,00,000 on each accused payable to heirs or successors or dependents of deceased as the court

may reasonably decide and balance shall be deposited with government treasury.

344. Notwithstanding, anything in the Constitution, all damages, fines, penalties imposed on any person, persons, group of persons, government employees, government, body, authority, company, corporation, or firm, etc., the court shall still decide the reasonableness of payment thereto, to sufferers and balance shall be deposited with the government treasury.

345. Any emotional harassment, mental torture, or exploitation of any person by any other person or persons if leads to any nervous breakdown or mental, physical disorder or undesirable consequences such as madness, the same shall invite imprisonment extending to life imprisonment and fine extending to Rs. 25,00,000 as may be decided by the court, including on the abettor, and instigator, depending upon the nature and extent of injury and expenses required for treatment. If however, suicide or death results as a consequence thereof, the same shall be, treated as murder, and punished accordingly as provided under other provisions of the Constitution.

346. No court shall reduce the punishment of any offender or criminal on the request of any party, litigant or aggrieved and punish the offender in accordance with law.

347. Farming, growing, manufacturing, production, or sale of drugs, alcohol, other intoxicants, tobacco, cigarettes or Biri and junk food, shall be, prohibited provided manufacture and sale of alcohol, spirit and drugs shall be permitted for medicinal purposes subject to the assessment of requirement from time to time. Parliament or Vidhan Sabha as the case may be provide for punishment for violators depending on the seriousness and extent of offence but in no case less than three year imprisonment and fine of not less than Rs. 1,00,000.

348. Provided further, Parliament or Vidhan Sabha may prohibit drinking of alcohol, spirituous substances and smoking of drugs or tobacco or eating of such spurious substances in public or public places, as the legislature may deem fit. Anybody found drinking alcohol or using drugs or smoking or eating as above in public places or publicly, shall be imprisoned upto five

years and fined not less than Rs. 25,000. Habitual violation may invite imprisonment upto 15 years and penalty or fine up to Rs. 1,00,000 as the court may decide.

349. Common use and manufacturing of polythene shall as far as possible be, banned by law and be punished at a higher scale than provided in Art 325.

350. No memorial or statue or such symbols of honour will be constructed on government expenses and on government land for any person whosoever, except for martyrs or those who died for the cause of the people, country or saving life or property of citizen, in general or property of the nation, or for and in the defence of the country. However, no such construction will be undertaken during the lifetime of any such person. Parliament will by law lay down the guidelines for installation of such memorials including categorisation of such construction and limit of expenses and their audit by CAG or AG.

351. Courts will have no power of making law indirectly under the façade of interpretation of law or Constitution. They will only interpret the law and interpret it as far as possible from all aspects arising in a pending case and not simply to the facts and circumstances of that case to take care of future possibilities and ambiguities so as to minimise litigation. Therefore, 'Obiter Dicta' will have equal force as a ruling.

352. The Rule of Law will prevail in the country. All citizens irrespective of their birth, position, place, status, beliefs or faith, gender, or caste, community will be, treated equal before law and in the services of State or public appointments, imprisonment, common public facilities, and punishments.

353. Law will be the king of kings and Judiciary while deciding matters and issues will ensure the same within the limits of her jurisdiction under this Constitution.

354. Notwithstanding, no government employee, public servant or citizen shall be prosecuted if prima facie proved to have killed a terrorist, looter, dacoit, kidnapper of human being or a person likely to indulge in arson or endanger the defence of the country or security of the nation or people or endanger the societal property.

355. A police or defence or Para-military personnel could shoot a terrorist, dacoit, kidnapper or any person likely to endanger national defence or security of the nation or of the people or of national or societal property.

356. All courts, whatsoever and whosoever will maintain dignity of Constitution and law and respect and adherence to the principles of 'Separation of Power'.

357. All government servants and employees under the control and authority of the governments shall work with utmost efficiency, economy, ethics, morality, devotion, and service to the country and the people as their masters.

358. No publicity of an individual or party purporting to be official shall be carried out in media, whether visual or print on government or state expenses, except when it is for pronouncing or informing the public of any government order, public notice, scheme, notification, benefits, but ensuring minimum cost and minimum space. No communication regarding inauguration or laying down of foundation stone of any project / scheme shall be, published as an advertisement in any medium at government cost.

359. The legislature shall by law provide for prohibition of night partying beyond eleven pm, noise pollution of any kind beyond ten pm. However, Legislature may provide for restaurants providing food or snacks to remain open till 12 mid night and open at 7 am. Nothing in this article shall apply to Khomchas, huts and tea stalls or food provisions run by poor people or for poor people.

360. Money laundering of any kind shall be an offence punishable by imprisonment extending upto 10 years and fine upto Rs. 2,50,000 or both as the court may decide.

361. There shall be not more than one thousand guests in any 'at home' whether official or private, where food or cooked food items made of rice, wheat, and pulses are served, and no wastage, which appears shocking, unreasonable, or unnecessary, shall be, allowed. All waste of cooked food or apprehended or likely raw items or material shall be brought to the notice of local body of the area as may be notified; for

consumption of the animals or safe distribution to human consumption if need be and found hygienic.

362. The person or body of persons organising such at homes shall ensure that the waste, rubbish, and dirt is not scattered, around and is kept and collected at a particular place safely to be lifted by local body. All persons or body of persons organising such at homes or parties shall, as soon as the function is over or at the earliest opening of the office inform the local body for lifting the waste and food items and the raw material as the case may be. Any person or body contravening the provisions shall be liable individually to pay fine of minimum Rs. 1,00,000 and undergo imprisonment of minimum one year extending upto five years. The evidence of three government employees or three local persons will constitute conclusive proof for levying fine by the government or local body to be realised as arrears of land revenue. Provided if the local body despite such information or communication fails to perform its duty the persons or department responsible for lifting the material as above shall be liable to be imprisoned for three years and fine extending upto Rs. 1,00,000 severely.

363. No couple bonding by marriage relationship shall be gifted or given by way of dowry in cash or kind or otherwise more than Rs. 25,00,000. Any amount or valuation over Rs. 10,00,000 shall be taxable @ of 15 per cent. IT department shall have the authority to take any step to find the truth of and seize the excess if reasonably proved to have been gifted as above and deposit in government treasury. Any such person or persons found guilty thereof shall be liable individually to pay a fine of Rs. 2,00,000. Parliament or Vidhan Sabha may make law within their respective jurisdiction on the subject.

364. Legislature may provide for medical stores, hospitals, water, electricity supply, petrol - diesel or any other essential services as may be notified to remain open at any time of the day of 24 hours, or in the manner as may be prescribed including by rotation or otherwise.

365. To prevent crimes on women and maintain the dignity of fair sex the working hours of women shall not extend beyond 10pm and commence earlier than 6.00 am. Provided an

employer may employ more than five women employees in a shift from 10 pm to 6 am during any time of the year with one hour rest after four hours working.

366. In the matter of corruption of any kind, concerning public money, assets, wealth or other property movable or immovable, a whistle blower shall be given full protection, and if 25 to 50 per cent of whistle blown is found correct the whistle blower shall be given two increments immediately. If more than 50 per cent upto 75 per cent is found correct, he shall, besides two increments be given preference in promotion over all others and if more than 75 per cent, of the whistle blown is found correct, such person shall be given special promotion in rank or grade-scale immediately above his present one, with an increment of promoted grade or rank or scale.

367. Nobody shall ever obstruct, block, close, or hinder public road, pathways, or lanes in marriage or other celebrations by putting Shamiana or tent or any enclosure. The offence shall be punishable as may be provided by the legislature but not less than three years imprisonment and fine amounting to Rs. 1,00,000 for each offender or culprit.

368. The legislature shall put a limit on all money-laundering, displays of riches, wastages of money, food, water, and public resources including gala partying and provide for heavy fines, penalties and other punishments in case of contraventions.

Additions to Fundamental Duties

369. Every citizen of India will maintain discipline, social decorum, dignity of human beings, fellow citizens particularly of fair sex, children, and poor ensuring their safety, non exploitation in any form.

Educational institutions will be kept out of politics and in high esteem by students and teachers.

370. Any kind of ragging whether within or out of the premises of educational institution by whatever name called, resulting in death would be treated a murder and tried accordingly.

371. Any ragging resulting in grievous hurt or loss of limb as a consequence of, or any activity analogous to ragging or inhuman treatment under the pretext of introduction, will be treated a crime as defined under the law of the land relating to crime or any other special law and invite not less than a fine of Rs. 1,00,000 or equivalent to the expenditure incurred on the treatment subject to payment of above amount in advance.

372. The court in case of death as a consequence of such ragging, at the first hearing of the case, if a prima facie case is made out on the basis of dying declaration of the victim or otherwise, direct the accused to pay such compensation to the family of victim i.e wife, children or dependent parents as appears reasonable to the court taking facts and circumstances of each case and for the reasons to be recorded, but in no case less than Rs. 5,00,000 and not exceeding Rs. 2,50,0000 after final hearing.

373. In addition, the authorities of Educational Institutions will be at liberty to take any action including that of rustication and imposition of fine to be paid to the Institution depending on the nature and extent of offence but not being less than Rs. 25,000 and more than Rs. 1,00,000, fifty per cent of which shall be paid towards immediate medical expenses of the victim if warranted by the injury caused.

374. All citizens will show due respect and regard to all patriots and martyrs who have sacrificed their lives for the country, society, and the people.

375. All citizens will give due dignity to defence and Armed forces all the times and to Para Military forces if latter is engaged in combating or defence operations.

376. All citizens will show due respect to Judges by whatever name called, teachers and teaching professionals by whatever name called and doctors or physicians by whatever name called.

377. Parliament shall make special law for all teachers and teaching professionals, judges and physicians – doctors in respect of their conduct, service conditions, and for maintaining dignity of these professions including penalties not inconsistent

with the Constitution but such law will have precedence notwithstanding any other law in operation if any.

378. All citizens will keep, international, national or state awards in high esteem and will never let down or down grade national awards or show disrespect to any of above awards or such functions provided national award functions will have precedence over all others in case of conflict.

379. All citizens will work for and ensure socio- religious harmony, compassion and peace in the society.

380. All citizens will faithfully help, co-operate and devote and train themselves in managing and handling of natural disasters or contingencies.

381. Government shall make all efforts to create work culture all around in the politico - economic social field whether government or other services or production and ensure citizens commitment to purpose for which government will also provide decent environment.

382. All citizens will ensure compliance of traffic and safety rules and road discipline and further ensure that all vehicles ply and move in their respetive lanes by making a row without breaking the 'Q' to avoid traffic jams. Any person violating the rules will be liable to pay fines as below at the present state of economy:

Fine for cyclist, two wheelers, four wheelers, medium vehicles, heavy vehicles and loaded buses and trucks being not less than Rs. 500, Rs. 1,000, Rs. 2,500, Rs. 4,500, Rs. 7,500 and Rs. 10,000 for each violation and in cases of pedestrians Rs. 200 each. If any accident results into death of a driver because of such violation, he will not be entitled to any insurance or other coverage or compensation.

357. All administrative heads of Distts and Distt police heads by whatever name called shall ensure within reasonable time completion of natural disaster plans and contingency plan for their Distt. which would include floods, earthquakes, famines, droughts, fatal gas leakages, fires, traffic jams, Rly or other massive road accidents, or air crashes etc.

358. The administrative head of the Distts and police Chiefs, will ensure that all such graduates and post graduates being paid unemployment insurance are trained in groups and batches for the purpose/ purposes as above and given at least 15 days training and 15 days refresher training after a suitable gap for which each individual shall be paid such pocket expenses as may be fixed by the appropriate government.

359. Such graduates may be trained for each block, tehsil or taluka or Panchayat area or Distt as may be decided by the appropriate govt. Any person in receipt of unemployment allowance or unemployment insurance coverage if refuses to attain and undergo such training shall lose his above allowance or coverage for one year in the first instance.

360. All citizens will respect and give due dignity to National Flag, National Anthem, National Song, National awards or decorations. All citizens shall maintain dignity and goodwill of the country. Disrespect to National Flag and National Anthem will invite minimum three years imprisonment and fine amounting to 5,000. In respect of all other offences as the court may decide taking the Constitutional intentions into account.

361. No channel, cinema or audio visual media will present, show or communicate any inhuman, cruel, vulgar, nude, nude exposures of any gender, indecent, porn or erotic, shooting, murderous, rape, dacoity and boozing, alcoholic, smoking scenes or shows unless based on actual life situation or presenting proof in evidence.

362. No channel, TV, cinema or any other audio visual media will address or communicate in any caste based or abusive or aggressive or filthy language or verbal or written unless presenting a real incident or actual happening or as an evidence to prove the same.

363. All citizens will maintain national amity, brotherhood, emotional unity and national integration, “Samarasata” and tranquility in the society. No citizens will indulge in any communal, regional, linguistic, racial or caste provocations or fomentations. All of the above acts will constitute crime severally and jointly punishable.

364. All citizens will protect environment, save, and preserve water, Endeavour to control pollution, and maintain cleanliness and hygiene.

365. Citizen will make optimum use of all resources particularly of economic resources without misuse and abuse and excessive use.

366. Govt vehicles, peon – daftari – staff, or official property, assets including ACs, shall neither be used misused, nor abused for private purposes, or work.

367. No pre poll surveys shall be conducted by any channel, newspaper, print or audiovisual media. No analysis pre or post poll or election analysis shall be conducted or political analysis including distribution of tickets shall be made on caste, creed, community, sect, or religion basis of any person or group or party.

368. Print or audio visual media shall not in any manner make any news analysis on the basis of caste, community, sect or creed basis, nor any public debate shall be so conducted in any channel. A panel of not less than three experts shall make comments on any news and event separately.

369. Media print or audio visual, whatsoever will only report the news and present the events before the public as they are. Media will not present any defence strategic news concerning defence operations or combat operations or news likely to help and assist any offender or criminal or vitiate the social, national harmony or the general morality of the people particularly of youth, armed, and defence forces in any way. Parliament may make such provisions including Constitution of a committee for overseeing the compliance by Media. Except to the extent provided, media will be free.

370. As far as possible, all language papers will use 'Hindi' constitutional terms and if possible and need be the language version within the bracket. Examples President (Rashhtradhyaksh, Shashanadhyaksh) Parliament (Sansad) Defence Minister (Raksha Mantri) Home Ministry (Swarashhtra Mantralay, Grih Mantralaya) Supreme Court (Sarvochcha Nyayalay, Uchchattam Nyayalaya), Rajyapal or Pradeshadh-

yksha, (Governor), Videsh Mantralaya (Ministry of Foreign Affairs) and so on.

Punishments and Prior Sanctions for Prosecution

371. All punishments within the territory of India for each offence proved or crime, even though a common or joint trial is held, would be awarded by all courts or judicial or quasi judicial authorities, individually or severally and will be undergone separately for each, but cumulatively for all. Thus, punishments for each offence or crime shall be awarded or pronounced by the courts separately, but carried on and executed cumulatively and simultaneously in accordance with the provisions of the Constitution.

372. No permission of Governor or President will be required for prosecuting any govt. employee or public servant or any person holding a public or governmental or statutory or non-statutory post or position under or under the control of any Govt., or public or joint sector or co-operative sector, whether or not employed permanently or employed on adhoc basis or for the time being, for any crime, offence constituting a crime within the territory of India, under any law or for any act of corruption, except for an act which may be a crime but committed in the bonafide discharge of duties or official responsibilities and functions in good faith with due diligence but under obligation of such office.

373. If any offence amounting to crime has been committed by such person or persons in due discharge of duties and responsibilities of his or their office, bonafide and in good faith as an obligation of the office, the court will not award any punishement to such person or persons and any compensation or damages if any payable to sufferer(s) including public at large will be borne by the State i.e. State or Central Government as the case may be or the corporation or company or sector or institution, etc. as the case may be.

Overriding Effect of the Constitutional Changes and the Existing Laws

374. The Central or the State governments as the case may be, shall amend the existing laws, rules, regulations,

schemes, bye-laws, service conditions, Cr. PC, CPC or other instruments to make them consistent with the provisions of the Constitution by removing inconsistencies therewith. Both the governments shall also provide minimum and maximum punishment including imprisonment and fine in accordance with the provisions of the Constitution provided in no case not provided in the Constitution imprisonment shall be less than one year and penalty or fine less than Rs. 10,000 taking into consideration the intention of the Constitution.

375. All fines and penalties under the Constitution are at present cost and economic levels and shall be enhanced by 5% after every five years as the Legislatures may deem fit depending on the extent and gravity of crimes including economic conditions of the country and people.

376. All governments will amend the Rules and Procedures including the schemes accordingly to make them consistent with the Constitution.

377. Provisions of the Constitution will override all inconsistencies in any law, rules, regulations, schemes, bye-laws, service rules or any other instrument and will prevail whether or not such amendments or modifications have been, made. Therefore, any, and all repugnancies with the Constitution shall be ultra vires.

378. Power of enacting would include power of amendment, modification, deletion, revision, and abrogation from time to time in accordance with the constitution.

Police and Action on FIR

379. Any citizen of the country, may file an FIR of general public nature, in connection with or arising out of any accident, calamity, disaster, natural catastrophe, fire, murder, dacoity, group or communal clashes, riot or shooting, commotion, connected with national defence or security or safety of the people or property in any nearby Police station by any means. Such police station without raising any jurisdictional dispute or legality thereof would take cognizance or charge and control of the situation. Such police station may inform the Distt police chief or Dy. chief or both about it, who will find the

concerned Thana or police station having jurisdiction over the area of incident or occurrence. However, the Police station where FIR was lodged or first information was given may also ascertain the concerned Thana having jurisdiction over and such police station will then take over charge of whole matter.

380. If a citizen, or tourist including a foreign national in India personally or through valid or acceptable communication lodges a pre-emptive complaint about an apprehended offence or crime, with any police station, or the police station having jurisdiction over, with a copy to Distt Police Chief or Deputy Chief, it shall be the duty of police to take due action on such complaint and if no action is taken and the incident happens, the concerned police personnel shall be held criminally liable for such happening.

Commissions and Authorities

381. There shall be a 'Law and Judicial commission', an Election Commission, Public Service Commission, University and Higher Education Commission, Information Commission, Planning Commission, CAG, Attorney or Solicitor General for India appointed by President and shall function subject to the provisions of the Constitution or law made by Parliament or the decree issued by the President.

382. The Pradesh / States may have their Planning Commission with Dy. Governor as Chairman and finance minister as secretary and no exceeding three expert members. States may also have Secondary Education Commission, Advocate general, AG, and Public Service Commission, In accordance with the provisions of this Constitution, and appointed by Governor or as provided by any law made by Vidhan Sabha.

383. No retired person shall be appointed to any of the commissions except Law Commission, Planning Commission, and University and HE Commission.

Law and Judicial Commission of India

384. There shall be a three-member Law Commission of India with a Chairman and two other legal experts as members,

which shall also function as Judicial Commission of India.

385. The qualifications, age and procedure for appointment and removal of the chairman shall be the same as that of a Judge of the AC or SC and that of members as Chief Justice of High Court, subject to the condition that the tenure of all members including Chairman shall not be less than three years at any time.

386. Chairman and members shall be transferable to AC / SC or HC and shall have seniority as sitting judges.

387. As Judicial Commission, the Commission shall enquire into, investigate, and determine prima facie cases of all complaint of impropriety, charges, or allegations of corruption, bribery or moral turpitude or such grave misconduct unbecoming of a judge of any of the three courts viz SC/AC/ HC. All such complaints shall be referred to it either by the President or a legally constituted Bar council, or Ombudsman or Lok Ayukt. However, in all such enquiries and investigations one of the Lok Ayukts as well as one of the Ombudsmen as may be, approved by Parliament by simple majority shall also be the members of the Commission for that purpose only.

Provided, if the matter is constitutionally pending as an impeachment motion before Parliament the Commission shall not hear such matters covered by such complaint until finally decided by Parliament. Pendency will arise from the date motion is admitted by Speaker of LS or Chairman of RS for discussion or debate and will end the day voting results were finally announced.

Provided further, the Judicial Commission may co- opt any of these authorities not exceeding two and not making it a forum of even numbers viz Speaker of LS, Chairman of RS, Attorney Gen of India, Solicitor Gen of India, any Advocate General, Chairman of any Bar council, if the Council is not one of, or a complainant in such case. Majority decision in case of difference of opinion shall be, deemed to be, the decision of the Commission.

Provided further that the complainant Bar Council (s) shall be represented by its President or Secretary or both and other complainant associations, societies, public or legal body or bodies also by their respective Presidents or Secretaries or both and accused Judge or Judges if so desire by a co judge only. No party shall be represented before the Commission by an Advocate except to the extent provided.

388. The Commission shall, after hearing the Judge or Judges complained or charged against and the complainant, send its reports and findings to the President / PM as the case may be, and if a prima facie case has been made against such judge (s), the President shall, notwithstanding any provision to the contrary, terminate the services of the judge or judges. But before such termination may call upon him to resign. Neither of the actions of the President shall be, called in question in any court of law. If no case is made out the Commission shall inform the President and the parties accordingly with a copy of its findings.

Planning Commission of India

389. Planning Commission shall be, headed by Vice President or Dy. PM (depending up on the form of government) and Finance Minister shall be its ex - officio vice chairperson. It shall have other expert members not exceeding five who shall be for not less than three years on such terms and conditions as President / PM may decide subject to the approval of Parliament, provided they shall have the rank of not less than a secretary of government of India.

Public Service Commission and the New Services

390. The members of Public Service Commissions of the State will be appointed by the Governors and that of Centre by the President in consultation with respective cabinets and approval of the Parliament.

391. State Public Service Commission shall administratively and functionally report to Dy. Governor / Dy. Chief Minister and Central Public Service Commission to Vice President subject to overall control of Chief Minister or the President as the case may be.

392. The members of the Commission will be the persons

of national or internationnal repute or persons of extraordinary calibre or research work or distinguished reputation or literary laureates or the awardees in their respetive fields, subject to:

393. That the tenure of a member will not exceed three yrs. Subject to extension in extraordinary circumstances up to maximum two years and may be removed only by an impeachment brought by 1/4 members of each houses of Paliament or State legislature as the case may be, and passed by more than 50% membership of the both the house or house as the case may be.

394. There shall be an 'Akhil Bhartiya Lok Seva' and 'Akhil Bhartiya Jan Seva' in place of present IAS and Allied services. Out of ABLS will be selected officers for administration, police and foreign service out of ABJS will be selected for all other services. All services under ABLS shall be *interse* transferable in equivalent ranks, positions and grades or cadres, after five years of service in their respective Seva and before such placement shall be given one months training.

395. There shall be a separate 'Bhartiya Lok and Jan Seva Training Sansthan' and under it shall function 'Regional Lok and Jan Seva' training Institutes to provide training varying from ten days to one month to all services and employees even on promotion right from peon to a clerk, Hd. Constable to Sub-Inspector and above the line until one reaches class I service cadre including refresher courses from time to time to equip the employees for transfer or promotion to higher post / position. All existing administrative academies for IAS and Allied Services shall be renamed 'Akhil Bhartiya Lok – Jan Seva Training Sansthan.'

396. Similarly, in each state there shall be a 'Pradeshiya Lok Seva', e.g., Maharashtra Pradeshiya Lok Seva, U. P. Pradeshiya Lok Seva in place of existing provincial civil or administrative services wherefrom will be selected personnel for provincial Administrative / Civil Services, Police Services upto the rank of Sub – Inspector and first class gazetted officers of all other services. Similarly there shall be 'Pradeshiya Jan Seva' in each state from where shall be selected personnel for all other services and cadres / positions.

397. As far as possible the training module provided under Art 395 shall also be followed in the States.

398. All such personnel whether of All India cadre or State cadre shall also undergo psycho-behavioural modification training including managing, etc., imparted by reputed behavioural scientists/experts or HR training experts of repute along with professional, routine and regular training.

University and Higher Education Commission

399. There shall be a University and Higher education Commission with a Chairman, Vice Chairman, Secretary, and maximum seven members to look after higher and university education, syllabus, course of studies, discipline, research, academic standards and recognition of colleges / universities including grants, subsidies and assistance for such educational institutions technical or academic, and universities. The Commission may also suggest courses and changes in curricula at 10 + 2 levels to State governments to synchronize with higher and university levels taking into needs of the changing times, inculcating culture, values, potential development and wisdom.

400. The Commission shall report to the President through the Minister concerned, and its recommendations shall be, placed before the Central Cabinet for approval and there after sent to states.

401. The Commission will relentlessly ensure that education becomes a profession and first priority of intelligentsia over all other professions.

402. The Commission may after due scrutiny co-opt educationists of repute for the purpose and constitute study groups for a period not exceeding three months to recommend improvements, transformational reforms, radical changes and high standards of combinations in all matters relating to such education.

403. Secretary shall be either class one officer of Central services on deputation or an academician not less than a Reader of the University.

404. The chairman and members of UGC will be nominated by the President in consultation with the cabinet for a minimum period of three yrs in the first instance, but not more than two years extension under special conditions and shall be the persons of national and / or international repute, awardees, distinguished academicians, or educationists of excellence having distinguished research work or have been distinguishingly associated with research and education or literary work or professional expertise.

405. The members including the Chairman and Dy. Chairman of UGC, excluding secretary, may be, removed from office only on an impeachment passed by the Parliament by simple majority for serious misconduct or incompetency or failure or inability to discharge duties efficiently.

Election Commission of India

406. There shall be an Election Commission for India and State Election Commissions under it for conducting free and fair constitutional and statutory elections and exercise such other powers as vested under other provisions of the Constitution.

407. Election Commissioners of India shall be appointed by President / PM of India for a period of five yrs in consultation with the cabinet and approval of the Parliament. Chief Election Commissioner of India will be the administrative as well as the functional head of all Election Commissioners throughout the country.

408. (a) The members of Election Commission will be the persons of high administrative or legal experience, professional experts of caliber and of distinguished reputation, nationally or internationally.

409. All decisions by the Commission will be taken by consensus. In case of difference of opinion, the decision of Chief commissioner will be final subject to the approval of the President.

410. State Election Commissioners will be appointed by the President in Consultation with the Election Commission of India.

411. The Chairman and / or members of Commission or Commissions may only be removed by Parliament by impeachment passed by 2/3 majority of total membership of each house provided a resolution to that effect is brought by not less thant 1/3 members of either house.

412. In all cases of impeachment wherever Parliament or Vidhan Sabha has such power, the resolution brought by members shall clearly set out the grounds of impeachment and the reasons. In the absence of such clarity, Speaker or the Chairman shall have the right not to admit the resolution for discussion.

413. If at any time it appears to EC of India of its own or recommendation of State EC that any political party directly or indirectly aiming at any election as a vote catching device is enticing or alluring the voters it can stop, prohibit or ask for withdrawal of such actions, concessions, announcements.

414. If the Commission finds deliberate or continued violation of its orders or code of conduct by any political party, the Commission may proceed either to cancel its registration or status or candidature of its candidates in any election.

Lok Ayukt for 'Pradesh or States

415. There shall be an institution of Lok Ayukt consisting of not less than two Ayukts and one Lok Ayukt as the Chairman in each State or jointly for more than one State depending upon the number of cases and population of such states as Parliament may decide. The Ayukts will hear all corruption cases involving the value estimated over Rs. one crore against employees of state government, including on deputation, public sector, co - operative and joint sectors under such government including the ministers of the state / Pradesh Shasan. Lok Ayukt may divide and distribute the work as deemed fit but final findings shall be signed by all. In case of difference of opinion, the matter shall be, referred to the CJ of HC of the State and his decision shall be binding and final.

416. The Institution, of L A, will enquire, investigate, hear, and decide any of the allegations, charges, and complaint concerning the matter of corruption as defined under this constitution provided a prima facie case is made out, and presented against such person or persons including any person holding public post or position, whether political, or otherwise but paid by government whether as salary or allowance or fee or in any other form.

417. There shall be no Vigilance Commission or Commissioner in States or Centre.

418. Subject to the provisions of this Constitution, Ayukts for reasons to be recorded may take '*suo – motu*' cognizance, of any corruption allegation, or charge against any government employee or such other person as defined above and proceed accordingly.

419. Ayukts shall also recommend action to be, taken against the accused depending upon the extent of charges proved.

420. Ayukts may examine any material and any witness for and against the charges not exceeding three on the same point so as to make a prima facie case after hearing and confronting the accused on all the available material oral or documentary and conclude the findings on summary trial basis.

421. Ayukts, may examine and cross-examine any witness to come to a just findings and direct SBI enquiry in accordance with the provisions of the Constitution, and SBI in such cases shall, submit its report within two months enabling the Ayukts to conclude hearing, and submit findings within six months to Governor / Chief Minister, (depending upon the form of Constitution), for action.

422. No lawyer shall be permitted to appear and Evidence Act shall have no application in any matter before Ayukts.

423. All cases of corruption involving less than the value of Rs one crore shall be heard by the courts in the hierarchy of courts in the state in the manner provided under this Constitution.

424. No writ will lie against the Ayukts except where he violates the provisions of the Constitution in which case the high court may direct the Ayukts within a month after hearing the matter prima facie to act and comply with such provisions. No further appeal will lie against such order / judgment of HC. The power and jurisdiction of courts to punish for their contempt will apply to Ayukts also. Ayukts shall be, deemed to be, court for enforcing attendance of witnesses and evidence including any document from any authority or government.

425. Ayukts shall fix and communicate the date for pronouncing its final orders and there shall not be part pronouncements of order.

426. An appeal will lie against the final order or decision of Ayukts, in Appellate Court of India within one month of the order or decision and the AC will decide the same within three months after summary hearing to satisfy itself if prima facie case has been made out. AC may entirely or partially stay the order of Ayukts or stay with such other conditions as it may deem fit. A citizen of India may file an appeal in AC of India if the quantum of punishment imposed by Ayukts is not reasonable or commensurate to the act or acts of corruption or is arbitrary, or unconstitutional or illegal.

427. If government fails to act on the findings of Ayukts, within two months any citizen or Ayukts may approach Appellate court if no appeal has been filed against or pending, to direct police officers to arrest such employee or person and further direct the concerned authorities to recover entire amount, wealth, or assets usurped by such employee and comply with all other findings or directions of Ayukts within a month.

428. AC after satisfying itself on such application or where appeal has been filed decide the matter within two months on summary basis and direct the authorities to comply with its own order or the order of Ayukts within a month.

429. Any government official, or authority imprisoned for contempt under these provisions shall also lose its job under the government, unless he proves to the satisfaction of the Ayukts that non-compliance was because of some other official or authority and not due to his fault. If the Ayukts find its

statement correct, then that other authority or official shall face such punishment as may be decided including losing job by way of termination, resignation, or pecuniary fines of not less than Rs one lac depending upon the gravity, damages or imprisonment or more than one punishment.

430. Recovery could be, made from the personal assets, wealth, cash, or kind of employee and shortfall from the assets, wealth, property, cash, or kind of his heirs, assigns, or successors.

431. Benefit of doubt, in all matters of enquiry and findings will go to the nation, the people of India, and the masses, not to the accused. Lok Ayukt will decide and recommend the proportion of recovery of the loss caused to the nation, people of India, and the citizens as a community.

432. No person or employee found guilty of corruption shall ever be employed by any government and the employee will in any case lose his employment with the government immediately.

Ombudsman (OBM) for Center

433. On the model of Lok Ayukt, there shall be an institution of not less than three 'Ombudsmen' one of them Chief Ombudsman, for Central Government employees, Central public sector employees including Joint Sector as Parliament may by law decide in accordance with this Constitution.

434. Ombudsmen will enquire into, investigate, hear, and decide the allegations, charges, complaints of corruption against the Central Government employees and central ministers including those on deputation.

435. All other provisions of Lok Ayukts shall *mutatis mutandis* apply to Ombudsmen except that OBM shall in accordance with the Constitution direct only CBI enquiry if the case warrants.

436. In all cases Ombudsmen, shall submit their unanimous findings and recommendations to President within six months, who after shall after discussing the same with his cabinet proceed to take action within a month of such submission. If

however, the ombudsmen fail to submit unanimous findings the same shall be, referred to Chief Justice of AC and his decision shall be, deemed to be, final.

437. President / PM, Vice President / Dy. PM, Governor / CM or Dy. Governor - Dy. CM, (as the form of government may suggest) and Judges of HC, AC, SC shall only be removed in the manner provided under this Constitution. All allegations against them including their conduct shall be enquired into only by a Parliamentary Committee of either house or jointly by both the houses and shall be beyond the jurisdiction of any Lok Ayukt, Jan Ayukt or Ombudsman or any such authority.

438. Provided further; any enquiry or investigation against Speaker and Chairman of Lok Sabha, and Rajya Sabha, Speaker of Assembly and Chairmen or commissioners of all the Central and State Commissions under this Constitution, including CAG, Attorney General of India, and Advocate General of State, whether serving or not, shall be conducted by not less than two Ayukts, or Ombudsmen as the case may be. President or governor shall take action against them in accordance with the Constitutional provisions only after addressing the Parliament or Vidhan Sabha as the case may be and obtaining approval of the houses / house.

439. Notwithstanding anything to the contrary, Criminal law will also take its own course in all cases of corruption.

440. If no action is taken by government within the time limit laid down at each stage, LA / OBM will themselves try the cases as if the competent courts constituted within the territory of India for trying criminal and civil cases and proceed with all legal actions against the culprits / accused including punishment and recovery of money, wealth, property, assets and disciplinary actions if any, under service and conduct rules.

441. However, despite impeachment, dismissal or resignation, recovery proceedings will apply and continue as provided in other cases under the provisions of Constitution.

Service Conditions of LA and OBM

442. Lok Ayukts and Ombudsmen shall be the sitting judges of HCs who have worked for three years as such judge and

shall be, appointed by the President with the approval of Parliament and all conditions as such judge shall apply to them. They shall be treated as sitting judges of high court for all purposes including transfers and promotions provided if any of them are found promotable to AC / SC or CJ of HC, within any tenure of three years as such LA / OBM he shall continue to serve on the position until expiry of tenure with all benefits of salary, position, and privileges of promoted position/post.

443. They shall be, appointed for three years in the first instance without affecting their seniority for promotion as such Judge and both the positions shall be inter-transferable.

Water Commission

444. There shall be a Water Commission appointed by the President in consultation with the cabinet and the CJs of AC and AC consisting of five members out of which two shall be legal luminaries and three highly technical experienced persons of National or international repute.

445. The Commission shall administratively work under Supreme Court of India, and suggest, advise and project management, preservation, linking, planning and integration of water resources of the country with long term perspective and equitable prosperity of all regions and the country as a whole so that tomorrow if any country or the nature or the science or Bhogvad creates any water crisis the country and people do not suffer.

Explanation: Management and linking of water resources includes linking, regulating and controlling of all rivers, canals, trading, and exploitation of water resources for business purposes and preservation of underground water, rainwater harvesting, water storage, and pollution. The Commission may take expert advice or invite national / international experts for the purpose.

446. The members shall be appointed for three years in the first instance and during this period could only be transferred or removed on the advice or recommendations of CJ of SC.

447. The recommendations of the Commission approved by CJ of SC shall be, placed before the President from time to time and President shall address Parliament on them accordingly.

448. All water disputes arising between the States, or States and Center shall be, heard and decided by the Supreme Court only and the court shall take the help of the Commission in investigating the issue and recommending the solution so that there is no conflict of any kind in the matter.

449. Government shall fix the service conditions and remuneration of the members of the Commission in consultation with the CJ of SC.

Information Commission

450. Right to Information: All citizens of the country shall have the right to information from any functionary of the Govt.; State or Central, executive, judiciary and legislature, any authority, corporation or body corporate including local bodies working under them or under such authorities and bodies whether in public, co-operative or Joint sector, provided:

(i) There shall be no right to information so far as it concerns defence, security, and safety of the nation and /or the people and / or national property, or any strategic information relating to war, combating operations, defence strategy or diplomacy, or

(ii) Its revelation may endanger or likely to endanger the country or the people or national - social property or create civil commotion or riot or civil strife, rebellion, or religious or communal or caste or class struggle, revolt or restlessness in defence forces or seriously jeopardize international relations or relations of the country with any other country, or

(iii) Combating strategy against - enemy, terrorism or terrorists, rebellious or disintegrative, seditious, secessionist forces or any activity connected therewith, or

(iv) Any matter which is under investigation till three months of such investigation, or

(v) Any matter likely to vitiate international diplomacy or diplomatic relations with any country or countries or community of nations.

(vi) The Chief Information Commissioner or Commissioner may satisfy himself before deciding the relevancy of all such matters and issues and may for that purpose call for the record or information from any government or authorities or bodies or organizations working under them or under their control and decide the controversy accordingly. His decisions or orders shall be final on the point of relevancy and none appealable and beyond challenge in any court.

(vii) Provided, any corruption matter or issue, negligence, apathy or non-performance of work or duty, arbitrariness, partiality, civil excesses on any people, constitutional and legal violations by government and its employees shall always, be treated as open matters.

451. There shall be a Chief Information Commissioner of India and Information Commissioners under him for one or more states as the Parliament by law provide.

452. Chief Information Commissioner will have the status of a Judge of the High Court and all conditions of a Judge will apply to him accordingly subject to:

(a) All Information Commissioners shall have the tenure of three years in the first instance and could not be removed during that period except in accordance with the provisions of this Constitution.

(b) Such appointment will not hamper or affect his seniority for promotion.

453. The President will appoint Chief Information Commissioner of India and the Information Commissioners for the States. Chief Information Commissioner will report to President administratively and functionally.

454. State Information Commissioner shall be not less than the rank of secretary of the State government having worked as such secretary for minimum three years. He will functionally and administratively report to CIC of India till he holds such position and will practically discharge the same

functions in the state as CIC at the centre.

(a) Such appointment will not in any way hamper or affect his or their seniority for promotion, if any if he / she or they are from services and serving.

(b) An Information Commissioner including CIC of India could be removed during the tenure only in the manner as is provided for a High Court Judge. Information Commissioner may however for reasons to be recorded, be transferred to any other state only once during the period of his tenure.

455. However, only such government, judicial, executive, or Legislative officials shall be appointed to above constitutional Commissions who still have minimum five years term to serve barring the exceptions as provided in this Constitution.

456. All persons holding specific constitutional positions provided in this Constitution with fixed tenure shall continue to hold such position until expiry of the tenure despite any promotion but with all benefits of salary, privileges and position of promoted post.

Commissions of Enquiry

457. The term of all Commissions of enquiry or enquiry committees constituted by any govt. for any purpose will not extend beyond one year to complete the enquiry including submission of report unless the culprits are aliens or the crime partakes the form of international crime, in which case the enquiry may be completed expeditiously within three years;

458. All such Commissions and committees will concentrate only on making of a prima facie case and not a case to the hilt;

459. Traffic rules shall not be relaxed to any person despite the status or position he holds. Tour or travel by any authority whosoever, will not create any inconvenience or nuisance to the public. All of them shall travel as general - public and the timings of such travelling shall not be made a 'show business'.

460. In appointing or filling of constitutional positions created under the Constitution, where no procedure is laid down the President or Governor as the case may be shall

consult the cabinet and take approval of the Parliament or Vidhan Sabha by simple majority of total membership of the houses or house. Provided the President or Governor before taking the approval of legislature shall place before the house entire service, moral, ethical, record of such person, his achievements, contributions, past performance, experience and record of cases pending or decided against him if any and outcome thereof.

461. No person punished for any criminal offence under any criminal law accompanied by imprisonment shall ever be, considered much less appointed to any public, constitutional, or governmental position or post.

Juvenile Delinquency and Punishment

462. As children are getting mature at very early age courtesy mod.-Ed., TV-Channels and western lifestyle therefore there shall be given no benefit of Juvenile delinquency to any person above ten yrs of age and /or who has passed 5th class. Such offenders shall be treated and punished as any other offender or criminal except that a juvenile shall not be awarded capital punishment or life imprisonment till the completion of fourteen years of age.

463. In case of any dispute or doubt regarding age, the higher secondary or equivalent recognised certificate or the age recorded in any authorised register, or as may be determined by a committee of three govt. doctors / physicians appointed by the court or authority shall be final and shall not be called in question unless a fraud, dishonesty, malafides or manipulation has been reasonably revealed or proved prima facie to the satisfaction of the court or authority.

464. All disputes and matters regarding determination of age in any matter throughout the territory of India shall be decided and determined in the manner provided in Art 459 above, whether by the courts or any other authority or body, legally obliged to determine or ascertain such age.

465. If in the determination of such age, fraud and dishonesty of any doctor / doctors is proved prima facie he / they shall be liable to such exemplary punishment which the

court or authority may think fit including cancellation of their registration to practice as such doctor or direct the appointing authority to withhold increment for not less than ten years or promotion for not less than fifteen years and impose a fine of not less than Rs. 1,00,000 each.

Payment of Unemployment Allowance

466. All State Govts in their States, and Central Govt whereever it applies to her as an appropriate Govt, shall ensure payment of Unemployment Allowance or Insurance coverage in cash per month for five years, equivalent to the minimum wages notified by the Central Govt under the Minimum Wages Act in respect of general or residuary employments to every unemployed graduate of any discipline not exceeding two children in a family of same parentage provided the post graduates would be paid Rs. 500 more than that payable to graduates subject to:

467. Three years legally recognised diploma holders shall be treated equal to graduates;

468. As soon as a recipient of un employment allowance or insurance coverage gets an employment the payment will be discontinued about which he shall inform the Govt or authorities as may be prescribed;

469. There shall be no mid day meal instead the State shall by the end of five years besides ensuring free education upto graduation shall, pay an amount towards the cost of books beginning 8th class onwards upto intermediate classes prescribing same curricula throughout the country in government and private institutions. State shall; within five years ensure payment of unemployment allowance for six years to each person who has passed intermediate on the terms and conditions applicable to graduates but the amount which shall be equal to fifty per cent of the amount paid to graduates. Provided further, this payment shall cease on becoming graduate.

470. Parliament may according to economic conditions of the country, growth of economy, well being of the people or welfare of poor masses extend this scheme to 10th class pass

persons who shall on the above terms be paid such allowance being 50% of that payable to intermediate pass persons for three years but payment shall cease once the person becomes entitled to higher allowance.

471. All payment shall be made to first two children of the family of one and same parents without any gender discrimination.

472. Provided, further that payment shall be made from the next of the month of submission of valid and legal proof of certificate or degree in support of having passed the examination.

473. It will be the duty of every such candidate to inform the concerned authority and the Govt concerned duly in writing as soon as he obtains an employment and the payment from such date will be discontinued;

474. Third child shall be entitled to this benefit only if one of the two recipients dies a natural death or as a consequence of act of god or nature.

475. Subject to the law or scheme made in this behalf an adopted child shall be entitled to the benefit only if there is no other including step son or daughter of either of the spouse already and availing the benefit.

476. Any candidate, claiming such payment fraudulently, dishonestly, or for any period against the provision of the Constitution or law made if any, shall be guilty of committing crime punishable with imprisonment for five yrs, and recovery of the amount so paid or claimend illegally together with a fine double of the amount claimed and penalty being equal to the expenses incurred on recovering the amount including litigation.

477. Any candidate, if he so desires may inform the government in writing, or the authority concerned declining such payment and he shall not be entitled to such payment from that date or thereafter.

478. Anybody including a govt. or public servant misappropriating or embezzling with the insurance amount or fund including the person conniving and conspiring, will be

held guilty of a crime punishable with imprisonment for ten yrs and a fine not less than double the amount misappropriated or embezzled together with a penalty equal to expenses incurred in prosecuting the case.

479. Vidhayak and Sansad Nidhis will be discontnued for ever and the fund shall be transferred to 'Unemployment Allowance Fund'.

480. Cricket shall stand banned for next 50 years. wrestling shall be national sport and Kabbaddi national game. Games such as lawn tennis, hockey, football, volley ball, basket ball, badminton, track events, gymnastics, shooting, weight lifting and others of Olympics or international level shall especially be encouraged.

481. Nobody will use any governmental or public, land, property, house or accommodation other than for the purpose authorized by the competent authority.

482. All employees working under any employer in any sector shall vacate the house or accommodation given to them as such employee, within three months of retirement, voluntary retirement, resignation and within a year of discharge, dismissal or termination failing which they would be forced to vacate by police action without any further court or legal proceedings.

483. Any illegal possession of government land for any purpose not authorised by competent authority including for social, religious, public purpose or purposes will invite imprisonment for minimum five years and fine not less than the income or profits notionally earned therefrom as the court may reasonably determine. In all other cases upto Rs. 1,00,00,000 as the court may reasonably determine after considering the facts, circumstances, gravity and chances of earning. In both the above cases, together with all expenses incurred in prosecuting the litigation.

None Applicability of Human Rights

484. Defence and Para-military or any other forces engaged or deployed in combating enemy forces, or enemy actions or

enemy groups or terrorists - internal or external or tackling of internal or external terrorists or secessionists, separatist or rebellious forces or groups will never be brought under any human rights violations under any circumstances.

485. Nobody who is accused of murder, dacoity, kidnapping, kidnapping with murder, rape, terrorism, looting, arson, indiscriminate shooting and corruption will be given any special treatment and shall be treated as all other criminals or offenders irrespective of his birth, education, age, status or position.

486. Human rights will apply only to democratic political omissions and commissions of petty, or minor nature and to minors below 14 years of age, women, infirm, physically handicapped, and old people over 60 yrs of age.

487. All young persons below the age of fourteen years and all women not tried for three years from the date of imprisonment will be, set free by the government or jail authorities after producing before any court of competent jurisdiction in the area, Tehsil, or Distt. Provided their trial shall continue as usual. The Judge, police, and jail authorities shall make a detailed entry of all such prisoners alphabetically or case wise, offence wise, village, city, or Mohalla wise as may be easy and convenient to retrieve. If any of them commits or found committing or repeats an offence (s) thereafter and is imprisoned, no such immunity or concession would be given to him anywhere in India and the offence would be tried in its normal way.

Prohibition of Strikes

488. There shall be no right to strike unless incorporated in the service rules or contract of service or service conditions. Any statute giving right to strike shall be void and no political party in power and running the Govt whether singly or in coalition whether in a state or at the centre will ever resort to strike and will be deemed to be guilty of offences subject to:

(i) Where it may not be possible to assign or contribute the guilt to any person or persons the Chief Minister or Prime Minister and the cabinet ministers along with the Président of the party or the State or the country and the secretary or general secretary or Secretaries will be held liable severally and jointly and punished irrespective of the duration and period of such strike, work stoppages, or halting of work.

(ii) The offence of strike, if not accompanied by any other offence or violence will carry the punishment of six months imprisonment to each such person found guilty, and a fine up to Rs. 1,00,000 on each such person.

(iii) Strike if accompanied by other offences or violence, will carry an imprisonment upto five years and fine upto Rs. 5,00,000 on each person found guilty.

(iv) Where it is not possible to fix responsibility on any person the court shall proceed in the manner provided under clause (i) above.

(v) The court shall also determine the value of damages caused to public or governmental property and proceed to recover in accordance with law.

General Liabilities of Govt. Employees or Public Servants

489. Recovery of money and punishment: (i) Wherever, a public servant, government employee, employee of statutory body, public - co-operative sector, or any statutory body, corporation, society or any other authority, or any individual or person, natural or fictitious, a citizen of India, or an alien is involved or found to be involved or has committed singly or jointly, or conspired in committing any offence so as to deprive or has deprived the exchequer or the Govt. or any authority, body, institution, corporation or company, whether incorporated, or not or any association of persons statutory or not, of any property, wealth movable or immovable, or money or assets, fraudulently, dishonestly, malafidely or illegally or unjustifiably; shall compensate such loss to such Govt., body, association, person or authority as the case may be, and the short fall or none payment shall be recovered and made good from the assets of his family including heirs, assignees, successors, and other relations or persons claiming entitlement to and on the property or assets or wealth of such person, or benefitted from such acts of the accused or derived advantage pecuniary or

otherwise from such act or acts of accused.

(ii) Notwithstanding, all or any of such persons will be guilty of the crime under the law or laws for the time being in force in any state or territory of India and will be punished accordingly. Any person charged for and found guilty of more than one offence shall be, punished for each offence separately, and will undergo punishment for each severally but cumulatively.

(iii) In the course of trial of offences or crimes, within the territory of India, whether offender is tried jointly or singly, if any offence other than for which trial is being held, is or are established or made out, or comes to the knowledge of the trial judge, or quasi judicial authority, or any court, the offender, offenders, will be tried or punished for that offence or offences also; provided he or they shall be provided opportunity of rebuttal and defence before such punishment.

Negative Voting

490. There shall be right to negative voting subject to the conditions that:

(i) Any voter who wishes not to elect any of the candidates contesting in a particular constituency or area whether for Vidhan Sabha, Lok Sabha or local body being not less than Zila Panchayat or a Corporation, may indicate his intention by stamping in the box meant for the purpose.

(ii) If the number of negative votes is 33% of total votes polled, re-election will be held in the constituency within a month as far as possible but not exceeding three months in any case, in which none of the candidates so rejected will be allowed to contest for next five years.

491. No person engaged in the profession of education or teaching in a recognised institution, whether in Pvt, public or Jt. sector or in any Govt. will seek elections to any legislature or to Zila Panchayat or a corporation unless he has resigned from his position prior to filing of nominations. This will debar neither him from being, appointed nor the President or governor to appoint him a minister or on any other unelected body.

492. Sansad or Vidhan Sabha may by law, passed by 2/3 majority of total membership provide for re calling of any elected member of Lok Sabha or Vidhan Sabha or above local bodies within their jurisdiction on such grounds and conditions as may be laid down.

Explanation: Elected body by whatever name called, means a body to which elections are, conducted by or under the orders and supervision or authority of Election Commission of India including State Election Commission or any governmental authority.

Deemed Automatic Sanction

493. Wherever limitation has been provided for completion or processing of any work, giving sanction or approval under any law, rules or procedure or scheme or bye laws etc, and the citizen or citizens have complied with the legal obligation and or formality, the sanction, approval, or permission shall be deemed to have been granted on the expiry of such period if no action whatsoever, has been taken by the authority concerned within the limitation so provided. If the work relates to condonation of delay or fine or any other penalty that will be, deemed to have been condoned, if the authority fails to own the same within the time laid down. Similarly, if it relates to waiver, grant, or sanction the same shall be deemed to have been waived, granted or sanctioned as provided under that law.

494. Any loss caused to the Govt. or authority or body referred to above, due to such negligence of the employee (s) concerned will be realised from him/ them, his/ her/ their assets, or property movable or immovable and he shall be liable to other actions including disciplinary action. Such negligence shall be determined and liability fixed prima facie by disciplinary authority after summary hearing.

495. Declaration of assets by Govt Employees: All government employees of State or Central Government whether of executive, legislature or judiciary, employees working under any authority, corporations or local and other bodies working

under the authority or control of any of the governments or under their supervision, judges and judicial officers, employees of public, co-operative and Joint Sector shall declare their assets including of parents, wife and children and if a joint family, of all those constituting the joint family and of wife's side, maternal side, and daughter's side if any, including:

(a) All assets, movable or immovable property, in cash or kind in India or foreign countries.

(b) Such declaration will be made at the time of joining service and every two yrs thereafter including the source there of.

(c) If the assets at any time are found more than what have been declared, all such assets shall stand seized and forfeited without assigning any reason and disciplinary action taken including termination of services and recovery thereof.

(d) An employee may if he so desires declare his assets at any time before the expiry of two years fixed for such declaration.

(f) This article shall apply to all those persons immediately on being, elected to any legislature or local body not less than a corporation or Zila Panchayat.

(f) If the assets - movable or immovable, in cash or kind, are disproportionate to the known sources of earning, or the sources of such income, and assets, or wealth, appear to be forged, dubious, or unknown or unaccounted for, the same shall be liable to be forfeited by the govt. after giving an opportunity of explanation to the person, and consideration of such explanation and subject to recording of reasons.

Claiming Immunity

496. Except to the extent provided, no act otherwise falling within the definition of crime or constituting an offence under any law, rules, regulations or this constitution will ever be deemed to have arisen out of legislative or judicial business, or in any way linked to or deemed to have been linked to or connected with Parliamentary, legislative, judicial or official affairs entitling any immunity on such ground and shall never

be immune from any such privilege or privileges and shall be proceeded with as such crime or offence unless it is proved prima facie, to have been committed in due discharge of duties, performance of official responsibilities of such office in good faith, or bonafide execution of official functions of that office.

497. No act constituting a crime or falling within an offence under any law or rules or instrument within the territory of India, committed by any person, anywhere at any time will absolve or immune such person of liability and punishment merely because he holds a particular position unless it is proved or established prima facie, that the crime was committed in bonafide discharge of duties and in good faith pertaining to that office and discharge of responsibilities arising out of such position.

FIR and Evidentiary Value

498. Any complaint, signed by three witnesses and filed immediately, or filed as FIR immediately, or such complaint posted under registered AD within 24 hours of incident, event, or occurrence, will be treated FIR and carry evidentiary value of same importance admissible in all the courts of law as a dying declaration, unless rebutted reasonably that the same was, signed under duress, coercion, threat to life or property or misrepresentation.

(1) If any police officer or Thana or police station having jurisdiction over, refuses to record an FIR, or complaint the aggrieved party or complainant may send the same by Registered AD or speed post at the address of such police station, keeping valid proof with, and if no investigation or enquiry is initiated within fifteen days send a reminder the same way, and if no enquiry or investigations start within next fifteen days, file prosecution before the competent court, and the court shall take up the complaint as FIR and the case as if filed by the state or police and conduct it as any other valid and legal case.

(2) The court may at any stage, direct the police officer concerned to investigate the case as or to the extent directed by the court treating it as an FIR.

499. A citizen of India could deposit money in foreign bank of a country he is serving in, or doing business transactions with, or with the national of a country or countries or business organisation, with the permission and sanction of centre government and;

(1) All business collaborations by individuals or private sector corporations or organisations or investment by them in foreign countries whether at individual or Governmental level shall be subject to Central Govt approval.

(2) Except as provided, no citizen shall open any bank account in any foreign bank, without the sanction of Central government, and no government other than Central government shall enter into any agreement, treaty or covenant with any foreign government except with private or public sector, for investment in business and industry or development of the state, but subject to the approval of the Central government.

(3) Any violation of any of the above provisions would be a crime inviting minimum imprisonment for five yrs but not exceeding 10 yrs with forfeiture of such money or fine extending up to Rs. fifty crores but not less than Rs. 1,00,00,000 as may be decided by the court objectively.

(4) Neither the Central, State government, nor any public, private person shall enter into any secret agreement or covenant or contract with any government or public or private sector or individual abroad against the provisions of this constitution, or any law, general public interest, interest of the country, her defence and security and all such agreements, covenants, contracts or assurances shall be open to scrutiny by courts and legislatures of the country and shall be void if found factual.

Calamities and Disaster Management

500. (1) All industrial disasters, calamities and accidents arising out of hazardous industrial operations, storages of chemicals, nuclear, atomic, gaseous substances, or arising out of electrical, electronic or other fires, resulting into any social, public disasters, calamities, general devastations, or any other human catastrophe, except caused by nature or act of God,

shall make the company or corporation, industrial organization by whatever name called accountable together with each director of the board, partners, proprietors, person or persons having the legal and factual management of day to day affairs of such industrial organization, and the occupier liable to criminal prosecution individually and collectively.

501. Any one or more of them prima facie held responsible shall reimburse the family or dependents of each person dead an amount of Rs. 10,00,000 and those fatally or grievously injured having least chances of survival, an amount of Rs. 5,00,000 each, and those seriously injured an amount of Rs. 2,00,000 each immediately, until final compensation is decided by the court fairly, objectively and legally.

502. Until such decision of the court, appropriate government shall, also asses the liability within three months and take appropriate action for recovering the compensation or damages from the industrial organisation within next three months depending upon the injuries and losses caused and also place the same before the court.

503. If the government fails to act in the manner, provided in foregoing articles; the victim (s) or any registered social organisation or society may take up the cause on the expiry of six months from the date of occurrence of such accident and file a petition before the Distt Judge for relief including compensation or damages and Distt judges shall constitute a special court for the purpose to decide all the matters within a year, including fixing of liability individually and collectively of all those responsible or liable for such happening or occurrence including criminal trial thereof.

504. The Distt Magistrate, Distt Police chief and Chief secretary/cabinet secretary of the appropriate government shall ensure an effective disaster management and contingency plan in each of such organizations for protecting the 50 km area, human and other lives and property of the Distt where such industrial organizations are situated or likely to have consequences. Any lapse on their part will make them also equally liable.

505. DM and police chief shall also ensure appropriate training for the purpose as provided in other provisions of the constitution. Chief or cabinet secretary as the case may be shall ensure compliance by DM and police chief concerned. For any failure, they shall be liable to punishment of imprisonment as may be decided by the court.

Traffic Management and Road Accidents

506. In all cases of road accidents or accidents arising out of traffic violations, a committee of three senior judges of the High Court appointed by CJ, shall appoint retired judicial officers not below the rank of chief metropolitan magistrates or CJM in the area of each police station / Thana or more than one Thana / station to decide instantly or at the spot or in any case within 24 hrs all such cases of accidents resulting in death or grievious injury likely to cause death or any injury resulting in loss of any limb or organ as provided herein below:

507. All such persons will be honorary magistrates with the power of and equivalent to CJM or CMM under Cr PC and shall be paid @ of each case decided by them being not less than Rs. 300 per case and Rs. 8,000 per month for stationary, paraphernalia and petrol. If however, the cases so decided exceed five on a particular day the maximum fee paid will not exceed Rs. 1,500 for the day.

508. Any person so appointed, if refuses to act as such shall loose his pension for any period and for the reasons to be recorded committee of Judges may decide to also withhold a particular lump sum of said pension or gratuity and appropriate government will act accordingly.

509. All such persons shall hold office for three years unless the committee for an act of corruption or immorality or dishonesty or gross negligence terminates the appointment earlier.

510. The station house officer or acting officer or any sub inspector or any member of the public may inform any of the Magistrate who is available immediately, giving the exact place or other details of the spot at which accident has taken place and nature of accident as far as possible.

511. The police officer concerned and the magistrate within reasonable time reach at the spot and investigate or enquire and record all the details of accident.

512. The police officer concerned will provide full security to the magistrate concerned who will examine the place of accident and instantly record the statements of witnesses if any and decide the matter subject to the conditions that:

(a) If death has resulted as a consequence of such accident and it is found that the driver was intoxicated or drunk or under influence of drug or was driving without licence or was a minor or the vehicle was not registered or licensed or was being driven rashly, the driver or the owner of the vehicle will pay Rs. 2,00,000 (one lac) as compensation immediately to the wife or the children or parents of the diseased which will be in addition to the insurance claims.

(b) The owner or driver will immediately deposit Rs. 10,000 (ten thousand) as cost and expenses with the magistrate and the magistrate after deducting his fee and one time monthly expenses as laid down herein above, ensure that the remaining amount is deposited in the treasury within next 24 hrs excepting holidays.

(c) In case the above amounts are not paid by the driver or owner or the driver, or owner of the vehicle is absconding the magistrate will have the power to get the vehicle disposed of by public auction immediately or at any time within three days and give a certificate to the purchaser to that effect and a clearance certificate as well and help ensure its registration if any with transport authority.

(d) Deserting of vehicle and absconding of driver or owner will prima facie be taken as the proof of premeditated or deliberate and revengeful murder or causing grievous injury to result in death.

(e) In case of loss of limb or organ same procedure will be followed except that the amount of immediate compensation will be reduced to Rs. 1,00,000 one lac but the cost of expenses will remain the same.

(f) Evidence as recorded together with the personal evidence of magistrate and the police officer concerned at the spot shall be final before any court of law including for insurance claims.

(g) The magistrate or police officer may immediately call any doctor, physician or surgeeon of nearest hospital, dispensary to treat and ascertain the chances of survival or treatment or refer the victim to a nearby Govt. or private hospital or dispensary and call for the relations of the victim if possible, and hand over the victim to him / them for immediate treatment.

(h) The magistrate may record the statement of the victim or visit the hospital for recording his evidence if already shifted, to ascertain the factual position and real cause of the accident including suspicion or identification of culprits.

(i) The magistrate, and police officer while recording the evidence or statement of the victim, shall apply their mind to the facts and circumstances of each case at the spot and decide depending upon the condition of the victim and need for first aid or treatment and for the reasons to be recorded may not record the statement of the victim immediately and record the same afterwards within three days. Such decision of the magistrate will not be, called in question in any court.

(ii) The magistrate may also record the evidence of relations, or any member of the public to ascertain the truth of correct happening including enmity if any.

(iii) The evidence so recorded by the magistrate and report prepared will be final, shall not be, called in question in any court of law, and shall supersede all other evidences.

513. Any death resulting, as a consequence of drunken or intoxicated driving or under the influence of drug or rash driving will be treated murder and deliberate accident with the intention of causing death out of enmity or revenge or ill will and the driver or any person accompanying him will be prosecuted accordingly.

514. Notwithstanding anything, to the contrary, if any number of parties voluntarily agree to compromise and settle the matters arising out of such accident or accidents and the Magistrate is satisfied of the reasonableness and fairness thereof,

he may settle the matter in writing and send a copy to the concerned Thana and Transport authority and the matter shall not be called in question in any court.

475. The number of such courts or officers shall be, decided by the committee of High Court Judges as above depending upon the need of area, number of accidents, frequency, convenience of the people and workload.

476. The magistrate may reasonably demand any place or accommodation including a hotel, restaurant, shop, hut, or hospital nearby for sitting temporarily and for recording evidence or deciding the matter amicably through negotiations and such purposes arising out of such accident.

477. No citizen or body will refuse the reasonable request or demand of the magistrate who may recommend action against such citizen or body.

Manually Driven Conveyances

478. All humanly or animally driven conveyances including rickshaws, carts and trolleys shall be licensed but charged only nominal uniform license fee throughout the country every year for which Parliament shall make the law and all income derived from such fee will go to the respective state government for reimbursing the same to local authorities except centrally administered territories the income wherefrom shall go to central government. Any such vehicle, transport or conveyance if not registered and licensed within one month of manufacture or use, shall be liable to be fined ten times such fee and confiscated in case of deliberate and habitual contravention and released only on payment of 30 times the fee prescribed in case of animal driven vehicles, trolleys or transportation by whatever name called and 20 times in case of human driven.

479. All vehicles used as transport whatsoever driven by mechanical, electrical or chemical, gaseous or atomic or electronic power, or any other motive force or automation shall be licensed and shall pay license fee as may be determined by law or notification by appropriate government keeping social

responsibility of such owners and maintenance of environment and pollution control in the background.

Action and Punishment

480. Any such vehicle, mentioned in above article 479 if not licensed and registered as provided, besides penalty shall also be liable to be forfeited, and auctioned within a month in the manner provided under the law and all compliances of law including registration and licensing if any, road taxes and insurance, etc., shall be made by the authority at the time of such auction or the vehicle may be released to the owner after completion of all none compliances such as licensing, insurance and pollution check within 30 days subject to payment of a fine of three times the license and registration fee of such category of vehicle and other compliances laid down under the law and rules.

481. All cinema / movie and TV serial heroes, heroines or director – producers shall give fifty per cent of their annual income over two crores to be spent on social – public welfare or rural upliftment that shall include the projects relating to education, hygiene, medicines, cleanliness, old age help and help to women and girls or undertake an industrial – business venture providing employment to minimum 50 persons per day. The expenses shall be all tax free if verified by AG or CAG as correct. Similar will be the obligations on TV / channel owners but instead of two crore the amount shall be read as five crores.

482. Other provisions of the present Constitution not inconsistent herewith will apply or apply *mutatis – mutandis*.

[illegible]

[illegible] shall be levied.

Action and Punishment

[illegible]

[illegible]

[illegible]

4

Conclusion

Need for so Detailed a Constitution for India

This is only a Draft Proposal for brain storming not only of intellectuals, experts and educated but of general masses through the length and breadth of the country, written in a language that could easily be understood by people from Kilar (HP) to Tangsi in (UK) to Kathua in (J&K) Una in (Gujarat) to Digha in (Bengal), Saiha and Banini in (NE) to Puttur in (AP), Kovalam in (Keral) to Nanguner in (TN). Better suggestions would always be welcomed and may collectively provide a treasure of knowledge for making it emotionally acceptable perfect Constitution. Every idea is an atom. It is idea that revolutionized the world since evolution. This Draft Proposal will be refined legally and codified juristically after national debate and discussions. It will then get compacted and concised as a 'Shastra' for governance of the country.

Many experts, legal luminaries, and intellectuals would question inclusion of so many provisions under the draft Constitution that would otherwise fall within or could be enforced besides Laws by Rules, Regulations or Notifications. The experience of last more than 60 years of erratic working rather inconsistent, unpredictable and contradictory functioning of legal - judicial system has taught us not to take any chance, not to leave anything uncovered on whimsical discretions as that would again derail the system and put it in the same square hole to demolish the facade. It matters not if Constitution becomes lengthy by a few pages rather than a problem for generations. As says a Shire;

फिर वहीं पे न आ जायें, जहां से चले थे हम

Many managers have the quality of managing by mismanagement; many others by confusion. There are also people who could manage only by chaos. Many believe that System binds rather handcuffs and acts as a chain limiting potentials, innovations and new experiments. Such people have the cynicism of creating confusion and disorderliness intending to make their selves indispensable. They live for their selves and their family alone least caring for the society or people in general. They can't live cosmically; they are divisionists having animalistic killing instinct and could never be metropolitans least the cosmopolitan integrators. Such people like Hitler, Mussolini, Saddam, Idi Amin, Marcos, Gaddafi, Assad either created war or degeneration of society and disintegration of nations for pelf and self. Thus, rather than working by systems and collective good governance and consensus they work by cults, egos, dint of power and individualism. This is what exactly happened in India, generally after 1971, particularly since 1990 but wholesale on and after 2001. We have made mess of state organs, the systems, governance, law, justice, and administration, one competing with the other for superiority and indispensability making ultimately the country dispensable and the people commodity in the market place for sale and purchase. For these and similar reasons no risk whatsoever was taken in the preparation of the present draft. Conversely all precautions have been taken not to leave any matter uncovered to whimsical discretionary interpretations making things impossible to be retrieved thereafter like present situation.

The youth of the country needs to understand the tenor, the essence, the substance and the core of the subject in the background of gravity of the situation, and prepare itself for desired transformation so that no government dares in future take 'Aam Aadami' for granted, a situation the urgency of which, has become a question of life and death for all countrymen, perhaps.

In the meanwhile, the relevant provisions of American and French Constitutions will also be studied for incorporation to the extent required with special reference to checks and balances and give the Draft final shape.

Right Time for Change

This is time to learn from our mistakes. The 'Sins' we committed until now have punished us to the maximum but no more now. Nature is also warning us continuously. She is showing trailers hoping we shall learn but if we continue to behave as America she will teach us without any more warning and sound. Unfortunately people besides their own sins also suffer for the sins, misdeeds and evil actions of rulers and governance but maximum for and because of injustice caused either by government, administration or judicial system. But at this stage we need also to be convinced that gone are the days of the proverb that says 'as is the king so are the subjects' 'जैसा राजा वैसी प्रजा'. We are no more in PrajaTantra but in Democracy and proposing to establish a Transformed system we call 'Lok Jan Tantra, resulting in reversal of the above proverb to 'as are the people so will be governance' meaning 'people of a country get the government they deserve' जैसा लोक वैसा सासन. With the old order has changed 'old adage' of by gone days. It is now democracy we are living in and are therefore no more Praja, or subjects of a King or Queen. People are now the King of Kings – neither Law nor Constitution – People are sovereign their own kings who can in peaceful democratic manner make or unmake Constitution, change the form of government, all of whom are for their service. People only have to realize that inherent sovereign power vested in them. If people only follow, ape, and become collaborators in the corrupt - sinful – evil acts of Netas, they will have to suffer equally for their 'Karmas' and pay the price of their sins. None else will come to pay for our sins or misdeeds or evil acts and suffer. This is the reason why people doubly suffer in addition to their own for the misdeeds of governance.

This is only to remind the people of their inherent

sovereign power, united strength and know their selves the same way as Jamvant of *Ramayana* reminded 'Hanuman ji' of his. It is time to ponder and pause or be prepared for the punishment of nature, unbearable. Nature will then hold 'Janata' equally liable for tolerating and not opposing the sinful, immoral, unethical acts of sinners, wicked and unrighteous power mongers. Nature will then ask for a price beyond our imaginations, as she will give us no time to bargain.

Therefore before patriotism becomes a joke, ethics and morality a mockery, Desh Bhakti or nationalism ludicrous, principles idiotic, humanity farcical, holism grotesque, justice and fairness scoffing jeer and virtues *'gali'* i.e. abuse and a heap of filth. Let people, therefore democratically take control for the change and change the form of government and the constitution to establish 'Bhartiya Lok Jan Tantric System' replacing the present rotten uncorrectable Parliamentary system. This will be real 'metamorphosis' for all times to come.

Vox Populi Vox Dei

The Model for System of Governance and form of Constitution presented in this book is like integrating 'Science with Dharm' and 'Marx with Gandhi' beyond which there could be no possibility of a perceptive module for India. With such paradigm transformational vision of the people would demise more than half of the existing laws with rare need for a law in future.

Big business scandalers, political scammers, bureaucratic swindlers, money launder realters, public wealth slashers, loose – black – cheap – easy - corrupt money minters, sexy looking, pleasure hunting, porn exhibiting, western oriented culturists have continuously been patting their heads and the back of all such governments who have looked after their interests well by more and more liberalisation and opening up of economy at the cost of survival of the society and life of general masses. But what of such reforms if they make people animal rather than man and the liberalisation that has made not only people but the countries of the world bankrupt. Today millions die of hunger in a spiritually divine country like India and millions sleep half stomach – half fed in a Jogi – Baba, Guru, Sanyasini - Sadhvi oriented society while lacs rot, wail and wait for justice in a legal system that calls law as the 'King of King' and where around 5 crore cases are pending decision in an all pervasive judicial system said to be based on the avowed philosophy of socialistic democratic welfare society.

What of that opening up of economy if millions rendered unemployed in an allegedly full employment economy, where landing on the moon is the only objective left with the government while millions on land die of thirst, without food, without medicine, without income, uncared for, un attended and un – insured. Where scientists find themselves busy discovering creation and experimenting with big bang but millions experiment with their 'Bhookh', experiment with their lives by committing suicide and killing their children out of sheer indigence. What of that delicensed progress where government and scientists waste millions on discovery of water on moon that would cost Rs. 2,00,000 a bottle that even Reliance Industries would not buy and man dies of thirst on land, kill each other for a drop of water. Where has gone the world-class rate of growth, if people still crave for clothing, shelter, education, roads, transport, security and safety though, hearing the slogans since 1952 and reading of human standard of living and fair wages in the Constitution of the country since 6th standard.

These champions, of open and liberalised economy, only want a democracy where people may have the satisfaction of freedom of voting and abusing as well as the power of electing their representatives so as to avoid any situation of the nature that arose in Arabic world. But retain to themselves the power of governing the governance of the country with money power and power of politics and authority. This is neither democracy nor communism. Merely casting votes and electing representatives is not democracy. With as high as 60 per cent mass illiteracy and consequent apathy towards governance coupled with casteism dominated community bondages, a country of over 120 crore population could not be run. Such a vastly diversified country needs governance, good governance not merely counting and spending time in promiscuity. We are neither America nor China in good governance. We have only aped bad of both. Our governments are doing not for people or the country but either to governing elites or a section of individuals or class of individuals or power centers but in the process pretend to show as if doing for the people and the country. But, now everything stands exposed. Our judicial system has failed having proved only a legal luxury, a waste of time and money and legal system a farcical catatonic. Both of them need revamping to automatically revamp other organs of governance which could not at all be done under present rotten system that itself needs complete overhauling.

While it is true that in this scientifically electronic age crimes and corruption have also become hi-tech, but in India both have by demolishing the democratic institutions have institutionalized themselves under the shield of injustice, no justice and flaggingly absurd legal system that is unethical, immoral and dishonest. And that's it.

To meet these hi-tech challenges the people of India also need hi-tech remedy once for all, even to overcome any and all devious future devices and designs which this draft Constitution does and has taken care of by building an inbuilt machenism of governance. However this is also a fact that as politics and corruption so have Cinema, visual, print-media and channels contributed no less in multiplication of sexual and economic - monetary offences and crimes in particular and ethical – moral degeneration in general. Entire politico-economic process and social system is working with business pelf mentality which has only one character and that is its duality like a tusker having different teeths.

People of India have already paid out of their pound of flesh for political coalitions resulting either in political instability or in scandalous scams. The stage is now set for a change. People of Arab world in particular the people of Egypt have proved their Gandhian mettle. They have opened the way for Gandhian peaceful non-violent revolution giving simultaneous message to the people of India that whatever the changes in world scenario, the Arabs, the Egyptians are nearer to Gandhi than the Indians. For the first time a revolution was, brought in an Arabian country on Gandhian principles of 'Ahimsa' and civil disobedience. Similarly, the people of Greece have also radiated the message of Civil Disobedience by saying 'we won't pay'. The people of France, Spain, Portugal, and Italy are following their footprints. In India we have been enduring the pains and carrying the evil burden of corrupt governments just by getting right to vote in elections not knowing what to do beyond though the medicines and remedies have been provided in the Constitution itself.

India like Italy of Europe has become a laundering country of Asia where as in Italy religion has failed to play its destined role, and will perhaps never play that role till these touts, and launderers, continue to trade in with the emotionality of the people, and play with superstitious ignorance of the masses, in the matters of and in the name of religion, despite pretending to be the cardinal centers of spirituality. They are as big slashers, money-mongering juggernauts as any other HR – management – economist THUG. These High-Tech Tantrics, Jyotishis, Mahants, Gurus, Gurains, Jogi – Joginis and Babas are the face of India's loose diabolic black money convertors, who would not hesitate loot chastity of women showing their Tantricised Black Magic and sorcery as do other big guns on the dint of money or authority.

We are the world-class apers as well, may, it be HR, Realty Shows, channel programmes, Laws, economics, or Constitution; but only of bad things as we did in the aping of Western Bhogavad, but refused to learn from Egypt. The country is suffering because of too many cats consequently the rats roaming free and fearlessly. It could, very well be said of economists that whenever, wherever 'there are two, they have either no opinion, or have three and a half opinion'. This adage is about Deshi economists, but when there are three Harvardians and a Deshi as in India at present, they could have no opinion except to doom the country and that is what is happening in India. This is analogically speaking a situation where a highly skilled worker on promotion becomes an incompetent supervisor and an efficient supervisor an incompetent manager.

Unfortunate as it is, Indian Politics has become a shelter to rascals and back door entry gate to insensitive heartless inhumans against all canons of morality, ethics, ideal traditions and basic tenets of democracy. The Prime Minister of biggest democracy of the world is not accountable to his own people but to western Bhogvad and indigenous capitalists and that is the cause of all problems and ailments of the country and sufferings of the people. In a country, where Ministers manning the prime portfolios of government i.e. Finance, Planning Commission, once Ministry of Home Affairs including the Head of the State and head of the government are said to be finance experts accountable only to such big businesses who mock rural India, hate the farmers, ridicule 'Aam – Aadami', insult agriculture sector as the sops and subsidy sector, call it a burden on the economy which otherwise is their very foundation and on which depends the existence of India and Indian people but who themselves loot the wealth of the nation putting her at ransom even at the time of need and emergency and siphon off the money in foreign accounts, nothing other than what is happening could happen. Late Lal Bahadur Shastri ji, a product of Kashi Vidya Peeth was far better economist and planner who saved the country at the time of severe crisis and taught economists a lesson and could have taught these Harvardians better, had he lived.

The quality of Indian politics and culture of governance has dipped down so low that not Gandhis, but Gandhi - Babas are now vying to run the governments which clearly show there is crisis of statesmanship. The famine of good people has reached a stage that we have to look to the Jogies, Babas and Gurus supposed to be ascetics, to take the reins of governance of the country probably because the country is religiously so spiritual. One of such Babas vying for Prime Ministership once blessed Lalu Yadav to be the PM, but subsequently getting annoyed with blessed Mulayam Singh Yadav the same way. The same Baba revealed the ninth wonder by describing Man Mohan Singh as the honest PM of a dishonest government and then asked not only for his resignation but reclusive seclusion. What does it mean? What more dishonesty could we expect from a political BABA?

A, poverty ridden country of the size and population of India needs an empathetic Prime Minister or President accountable to public, who has the feel of people's agony, their pains, sorrows, and difficulties. Who like Sharad Pawar, would not ask people to eat cake when they are asking for a loaf and salt. This country needs a man who is prepared to kick such corrupt coalitions rather than cling to position, bearing all humiliation and insults. The sufferings of coalition politics, and unfathomable loss caused to the country, has beyond all doubts proved that re-polls are better economically, morally ethical and the best overall. In the long run the interest of country's development is better served by re- polls than allowing a 'Bhanumati Ka Kunba' to run the country with politico-economic uncertainty, threats, duress and coercions of vested interests including scandals and scams asking people to pay the price out of their pound of flesh.

The proposed Constitutional changes will not be revolutionary as understood in communistic terminological parlance but transformational, meaning deliverance and conferring by people to themselves a governmental system that they could call their own. No deficit could ever be so big, so speaking, so glaring as ethical, moral and ideological and no depression as big as depletion of values, justice and humanity. More we are moving towards 'Bhogavad' or Epicureanism or 'Charvakism' cloaked as consumerism, more critical the deficit is becoming, analogically the same way as Sensex; higher it is more the possibility of investment of corrupt, loose, black, cheap, and easy money. The pall bearers of society could, call this change by whatever name - 'treasure or witch hunt, utopian or day dreaming, but it is really hunting the future of the people linked with the fate of nation'.

Over the period, it has become the dilemmatic irony of Indian politico-economic, social scenario that people have not only become poor economically but poorer morally, ethically. They have fallen to a serious social malaise because everyone knowingly, unknowingly, or ignorantly is in competition with the system for immoral pursuits for ill-gotten money and illegal gratifications even for mere bread and butter or sustenance as no one finds an alternative better than that even for meeting two ends.

As *netas* and the higher ups are, busy in amassing through illegal, unethical, and immoral means, therefore not only economic immorality and financial dishonesty but more ruinous has become ideological dishonesty and unprincipled bankruptcy of politicians for self and pelf. Their ideological bankruptcy has led to deception with electorates, defrauding even the party that gave them tickets to fight election, political instability and bargaining for self-aggrandisement without the approval of the people who elected them, besides suffering to the people in general and moral, ethical, ideological, cost to the society and financial-economic cost to the country.

Our governmental system has over the period developed in to accountability less Parliamentary democracy that outwardly appears accountable to Legislature but in practice to non, as the whole system has become self indulgent.

This challenge is now impossible to be, met by any means other than changing the form of government and the Constitution. The latest estimates of black money amounting to 450 billion dollars, is correct then definitely it is punishment to be honest. If another estimate of 1 to 1.5 trillion - dollar is believed it would be sufficient to make a saner, lunatic and lunatics to understand the reason of their lunacy. Even if, as is sure, the amount of Black Money is 70 - 70 lac crores, 'It would be Sufficient for Transforming and Changing the Politico – Economic face of the Country by changing the form of governance and the Constitution'.

Present system of governance and parliamentary form of Constitution coupled with globalised economic liberalisation has let loose de-licensed, limitless, unbounded scandals, corruption, scams, frauds, lust, passion, injustice, nude and naked Epicureanism, sexy hedonism and incest sex; the cause of all evils and ills of society. Not only economically but morally and ethically these parrots have mortgaged the image of country under the pretext of making it buyers market where as consumer is at the verge of selling his everything and his human pride is at the verge of extinction. The elite rich class is following Italian 'Bango – Bango' model of Berlusconi as if all sensibility has collapsed, awaiting the Gaddafi fate. Patriotism has sunk; country is at the brink of dissoluteness.

Accountability in this system of governance is lost, not only in form but also in substance. Proposed changes, which in effect are transformational, make the governance and the system together with all state organs and functionaries accountable to public in action and practice.

Enough is enough, empty speeches no more. Let these be stopped now as they have become irritating, polluting and frustrating to the conscience, defiling to mind and poisoning to the environment.

India, however, needs no jasmine revolution but Lotus Evolution. She has already democracy but needs 'yet another change' an emancipation to convert 'Swaraj' in to 'Suraj' i.e. freedom into good governance. Egyptian said 'Mubarak Ho', India shall say 'corruption go, bad governance, crimes, misrule, poverty, hunger, unemployment, diseases, unemployment, squalor, exploitation, injustice, casteism, communalism, scams, scandals Swaha meaning oblation in to fire for reducing it in to ashes and Swaha 'Prajatantra' i.e. the Rule of a King or Queen over his or her subjects and Welcome to 'Loka - Jana – Tantra i.e peoples own self governance. But this shall not be possible until we are prepared to say 'This rotten Parliamentary System SWAHA'. As early we say so, earliest shall we say 'We are proud Bhartiya, the Gandhians' as every Egyptians proudly said 'I am Egyptian'.

After sixty four years, at least people have now come to know that there was no system to run the system of governance of the biggest Democracy of the world, which was, run on adhocism. *Netas* and Administrators not only took the Constitution as a piece of paper but took the illiterate ignorant masses as *Bheed* (crowd) and people of the country in general as *Bhed* (sheep).

We are now one push away from the sea whether we throw the system or system throws us in the Ocean is the only question. Therefore, this is the last final choice for people with a fool proof proposal for their own governance in its true sense.

The youth of the country particularly needs to understand and awake now and take lead before it becomes too late in the day to retrieve the nation and the people from 'ISM' dominated governance, anarchic system and chaotic legal – judicial administration.

With these Provisions in the Constitution half of the existing laws in India would become redundant rather die instantly and there would be rare need for laws in future except Rules, procedures and schemes for giving effect to proposed constitutional provisions.

Hopefully, the vast majority of three-fourth (3/4th) population of India would not only agree to such constitutional changes rather heartily welcome them sooner the better.

"Long Live Bharatiya Lok Jan Tantra

Long Live Transformation of Prajatantra

Long Live Metamorphosis to Lok Jan Tantra"

Appendix

Chart shows the Investment – Utilization Pattern of Black / Corrupt Money recovered to the extent of 15 lac crores only.

(i) Modernization of Defence Forces 2.00 lac crores

(ii) Responsibility of families of those citizens dying for public -national cause including protection of property 0.25 lac cr

(iii) Responsibility of families of defence / Para military and police personnel dying for national / public cause 0.50 lac cr

(iv) Unemployment allowance / insurance coverage = 0.50 lac cr

(v) Conversion of Railway line into four track = 1.75 lac crs

(vi) Connecting and garlanding of Rivers throughout the country, flood control and providing water to each family within a radius of one Km = 2.00 lac crores

(vii) Controlling natural disasters protecting environment = 0.50 lac cr

(viii) Building 20 crore Ton capacity Mal godams (grain storage godowns) in the country = 1.00 lac cr

(ix) Semi – Atomic power or other power generation = 2.00 lac crs

(x) Agriculture prosperity, forest and land development = 1.00 lac cr

(xi) Improvement of hospitals – medical and health = 0.50 lac cr

(xii) Eliminating hunger - starvations and poverty = 0.50 lac cr

(xiii) Improvement and provision for free or easy 'Q' education in Govt owned / run Institutions = 0.50 cr

(xiv) Underground electric wiring conversion = 1.00 lac cr

(xv) Improving communications, transport and roads = 1. 00 lac cr

Note: Any amount recovered beyond 15 lac crs, which is sure to be recovered, would make India Golden Bird once again.

Index

G

H

I

J